WILLIAM WALKER'S
WARS

WILLIAM WALKER'S
WARS

HOW ONE MAN'S PRIVATE AMERICAN ARMY TRIED
TO CONQUER MEXICO, NICARAGUA, AND HONDURAS

SCOTT MARTELLE

CHICAGO
REVIEW
PRESS

Published by Chicago Review Press Incorporated
814 North Franklin Street
Chicago, Illinois 60610
ISBN 978-1-61373-729-3

Library of Congress Cataloging-in-Publication Data
Names: Martelle, Scott, 1958– author.
Title: William Walker's wars : how one man's private American army tried to
   conquer Mexico, Nicaragua, and Honduras / Scott Martelle.
Description: Chicago, Illinois : Chicago Review Press Incorporated, [2019] |
   Includes bibliographical references and index.
Identifiers: LCCN 2018009571 (print) | LCCN 2018033295 (ebook) | ISBN
   9781613737309 (adobe pdf) | ISBN 9781613737316 (kindle) | ISBN
   9781613737323 (epub) | ISBN 9781613737293 (cloth)
Subjects: LCSH: Walker, William, 1824–1860. | Nicaragua—History—Filibuster
   War, 1855–1860. | Filibusters—Nicaragua—Biography. | Filibusters—United
   States—Biography. | Americans—Nicaragua—History—19th century.
Classification: LCC F1526.27.W3 (ebook) | LCC F1526.27.W3 M37 2019 (print) |
   DDC 972.85/044092 [B] —dc23
LC record available at https://lccn.loc.gov/2018009571

Typesetting: Nord Compo
Map design: Chris Erichsen

Printed in the United States of America
5 4 3 2 1

For the lovely Margaret, as always,
and for Rochelle Lewis Lavin,
a dear friend and fighter of great courage

CONTENTS

PROLOGUE
TRUJILLO, HONDURAS,
AUGUST 21, 1860

WITHIN THE STONE WALLS of the three-hundred-year-old Fortaleza de Santa Bárbara, dozens of men, some wearing rags and blood-soaked bandages, worked quietly in soft lamplight, their faces glistening with sweat from stress, humidity, and fever. They struggled to bend the barrels on rifles, drive spikes into the touchholes of cannons, and drench surplus gunpowder with water. Anything to ensure that the weapons they'd leave behind would be worthless to whichever enemy took over—the Honduran soldiers just beyond rifle range, or British marines from the HMS *Icarus* at anchor nearby in the warm Caribbean waters.

Not all of the men were fit enough to flee, though. Bullet wounds immobilized three of them, and illness incapacitated three others, including a *New York Herald* journalist sent to write about the adventurers. A surgeon and an aide would likewise remain behind to oversee their care in a makeshift hospital ward created by stringing hammocks across a large room. Each of them was given a gun and a small reserve of ammunition in case they needed to defend themselves against an attack, but their plan was to beg mercy from whoever arrived first.[1]

As the weapon wreckers worked, William Walker—a short slip of a man with light blond hair and eerily expressionless gray eyes—moved among the hammocks to offer thanks and final words of encouragement to the sick and the wounded. Even though they were Walker's men—his soldiers, really—he barely knew most of them. But one, Colonel Thomas Henry, had been a close confidant and strategic adviser, and Walker spent a few extra minutes with

1

him, speaking softly into his ear above the gaping, maggoty wound where his jaw had been shot away. Walker asked whether Henry had uncovered any information that would help them track down José Trinidad Cabañas, the former Honduran president now waging an insurrection against the current government. Henry, numbed by morphine, scrawled an answer on a piece of paper: Cabañas would be found somewhere along the Río Negro (now the Río Seco), about forty miles east of Trujillo. Walker whispered a few more words, then rushed the visit to an end.[2]

The weapons sabotaged and a path forward determined, Walker ordered his remaining men—about seventy of them in various states of health and strength—to gather on the fort's parade grounds. Showing unusual discipline for such a ragtag squadron, the men quietly assembled a little after midnight then followed Walker through the ancient fort's main gate and over empty streets before disappearing into the jungle.[3]

William Walker. *Mathew Brady, courtesy of Library of Congress Prints and Photographs Division, LC-USZC4-10802*

Skulking off in the middle of the night had not been in Walker's plans. He'd left New Orleans nearly three months earlier expecting to take over the small Caribbean island of Ruatan, less than fifty miles off Trujillo, at the invitation of English residents who feared for their futures once Great Britain fulfilled a treaty promise and turned the island over to Honduras. But Walker's infamy preceded him. After learning he was in the area, the British delayed the handover, leaving the Union Jack fluttering high above the island's main settlement, Coxen Hole. Walker neither wanted nor could win a battle against British warships, so he decided instead to seize Trujillo and from there invade Nicaragua, his ultimate target all along. But that plan ran into trouble, too, with the arrival of the *Icarus* and a demand from its captain that Walker and his men surrender. Instead, they ran.

The force traveled lightly, each man bearing a rifle and 120 rounds of ammunition, and a few also carrying sidearms and knives. Paralleling the Caribbean coast, they made their way east through the moonless night and into the next day, a remarkable display of stamina against August's tropical heat and humidity. They passed through hamlets whose residents hid from view and along jungle paths as birds squawked and trilled and small monkeys howled and chattered. Walker stopped them at dusk to establish a camp along the bank of a creek, but shortly after sunrise the men forded the river and marched on. They raided small farms but found little to eat except beef. When night fell, they again camped, and at daybreak they resumed their flight. By midafternoon, Walker felt they had put enough distance between themselves and Trujillo for the men to take a lengthy rest, clean their weapons, and let some of the heat of the day dissipate before trying to walk any farther.

As the men relaxed at a spot along a wide creek, gunfire exploded from the underbrush, the lead balls shredding leaves and slamming into the earth, tree trunks, and human flesh. The Americans scattered and dove for protection. Some returned fire at the attacking Honduran soldiers as others hastily put their weapons back together. Amid the chaos, Walker ordered the men into two small companies, then sent them sprinting into the brush in a screaming wave of suicidal bravado and gunfire, panicking the Hondurans into flight. But the battle was costly. They'd spent valuable ammunition, and Walker counted one dead and seven or eight others wounded. The commander himself was among them: blood oozed from Walker's creased cheek.

The men quickly packed up and moved on, carrying the severely wounded and helping the sick. As they worked their way along the trail, occasional harassing gunshots came from behind, one of which struck a top aide, Major Huff, adding to the list of casualties. They reached a mahogany camp near the coastal town of Limón that Walker was surprised to find abandoned, and soon they were off again. Reaching the Río Negro, they found a canoe and ferried themselves across to a trading post run by an Englishman named Dickens. There they also discovered what was left of Cabañas's encampment: cold camp-fires and empty rifle pits. "We are lost," one soldier wrote.[4]

The Hondurans were stuck on the other side of the river, but escaping them had left Walker's men exhausted, bleeding, and even sicker and more dispirited. No good would come of pushing them further, so Walker ordered the men to bivouac in Cabañas's rifle pits, which offered a little protection from the occasional potshots their pursuers fired across the Río Negro. Walker himself, shivering and sweating with fever, commandeered Dickens's house as his headquarters. "Every once in a while," the same soldier wrote, "one of their bullets hits a man, and we have none to spare. . . . Walker calls the roll—thirty-one [healthy and unwounded] men are left."

Looking back, Captain Nowell Salmon of the HMS *Icarus* admitted that he had been too accommodating of Walker. The captain and his crew could see the fort at Trujillo from their ship, and they watched Walker's men as they moved around the walls at sunset. But in the dark of the moonless night, the British forces didn't see the men spike the fort's cannons or slip away into the jungle. At sunrise, the fort seemed from the ship to be as abandoned as the village itself. Salmon deployed men to investigate. They reported back that only the surgeon, his aide, five sick and wounded men, and the now-dead Colonel Henry remained, and that the rest of the Americans had followed Walker on an overland trek to Nicaragua. "I must confess," Salmon later wrote to his superior, "he fairly gave me the slip." Salmon advised two Honduran regiments stationed outside Tru-jillo to take possession of the fort but posted sentries to protect the Americans, whom he claimed as prisoners. Norberto Martinez, commanding the Honduran troops in Trujillo, also dispatched a squadron to go after Walker and his men.[5]

Salmon used couriers to keep abreast of Walker's movements and those of his pursuers. He anticipated that Walker would head for the mahogany works in search of a seaworthy boat, but he still asked Honduran general Mariano Alvarez, who had arrived with two hundred soldiers from Olanchito, an interior city about fifty miles southwest of Trujillo, to station men around the fort in case Walker doubled back. Salmon set sail on August 27 for a three-day trip to drop the seven captured Americans at Ruatan, and learned when he returned that Walker had indeed reached the mahogany works but, finding no boats, kept moving overland. Salmon speculated that Walker would continue on to the Río Negro, where he could use smaller boats to navigate inland and then move on foot through the mountains to Nicaragua. But he also found that Alvarez had decided on his own to pursue Walker by sea and was preparing a ship with his men. So the two ships sailed together to try to catch up with Walker.

As the *Icarus* reached the mouth of the Río Negro, it intercepted a schooner carrying reinforcements and supplies from Ruatan for Walker. One of the passengers, a man named Thompson, had already reached shore in a small dory. Salmon seized the schooner "and made prisoners of all on board," then anchored. Salmon led a small reconnaissance trip a short way up the river, where he found Thompson's dory beached and his footsteps trailing away into the brush. "This satisfied me that Walker had not crossed" the river—it's unclear why he drew this incorrect conclusion. He thought he still had a chance to get in front of the fleeing men and head them off. "I therefore contented myself as night was coming on, with removing all the dories I could find to the other side and thus effectually stopping his advance."[6]

The next morning Salmon returned to the river and encountered two of trader Dickens's employees, who told Salmon that Walker and his men had already crossed the river and taken over the trading post, driving off those who lived there. Illness and wounds had incapacitated most of the Americans, and Walker himself had a raging fever. Salmon summoned General Alvarez to the *Icarus* and laid out two possible approaches. Salmon and his men could move upriver without the Hondurans, find Walker, and persuade him to surrender, or Salmon could step back and let Alvarez and his men proceed alone. Salmon rejected the idea of mounting a joint operation; he told Alvarez that he doubted Walker would surrender to "any native force," and that he himself had no intention of "assisting . . . in the wholesale butchery" of the sick and wounded

Americans. And should Alvarez choose to proceed without the help of the British, Salmon warned, he should not consider his victory assured, as Walker had a history of winning impossible battles. The Honduran general agreed to let Salmon and the British make the approach—but demanded to go along.

By midafternoon the expedition was ready. Sailors rowed several small skiffs up the river toward the trading post, where Walker's sentry spotted them and alerted the camp. "Looking away down the river, we saw a flag," one of Walker's men later wrote. "It is the Union Jack." All but one of the boats steered for the bank about five hundred yards downriver from the outpost, the men ready if needed. Salmon continued on and alit with Alvarez, then walked to Dickens's house, and Walker. Salmon's ultimatum was direct and short. His ship was within easy cannon range. Alvarez's ship, with two hundred Honduran soldiers, was anchored nearby as well. Walker was in an untenable position: sick, in charge of a depleted squadron, and with insufficient ammunition to defeat the force arrayed against them.[7]

Walker asked if his surrender would be to Salmon as a British officer, and thus to the British government. Yes, Salmon said. Walker, wanting to make sure he would not become a prisoner of Honduras, repeated the question. "Yes, you surrender to me as a British officer," Salmon replied. "You may thank me, too, that you have a whole bone in your body."[8]

Walker agreed to surrender and sent an order to his men to fall in. They staggered out of their rifle holes and resting places and sentry postings to line up between the building and riverbank. Walker told them they were done. The soldiers handed over their weapons, down to their personal knives, and were placed under guard. The condition of the men, who only a week earlier were the defenders of the fort at Trujillo, stunned Salmon. The march, the lack of food, illness, and combat had taken a significant toll. "I found that the accounts I had received of their 'wretched condition' had not been at all exaggerated. That out of the whole number (73) ten were wounded, and 21 sick in hospital, and of the rest not more than 30 could have walked a mile."[9]

Salmon returned to the ship, leaving the Americans under the guard of a detachment led by one of his lieutenants. A few hours later, as the sun settled over the jungle, the lieutenant decided to separate Walker from his men to reduce the chances of an escape attempt. He ordered escorts to take the adventurer and his top surviving aide, Anthony F. Rudler, to the *Icarus* while the rest of the men spent one more night in the jungle.

The defeat wasn't the first for Walker. He had become accustomed to surrendering to ship's captains or military commanders, and then getting repatriated to the United States to plot his next move. If Walker harbored any suspicions that this intervention might end differently, he kept them to himself as he drifted along river currents through the dark Honduran jungle to the sea.

1 | NASHVILLE

LONG AFTER THE BRITISH NAVY captured William Walker in the wilds of Honduras, and longer still after he led private armies to invade Mexico and Nicaragua, people wondered what motivated such an unimposing man to undertake such audacious acts—what, indeed, had earned him a reputation as "the gray-eyed man of destiny." The answer likely lies in Nashville, where on May 8, 1824, Walker became the first of six children born to James S. Walker, a Scottish immigrant, and Mary Norvell Walker, a Kentucky native. There, amid a large and enterprising family in a community built around ambition, his dreams and his view of the world first took root.[1]

Nashville at the time was just a few years removed from its frontier-town roots, but if it had an upper crust, Walker was born to it. In 1820 his father had arrived from Glasgow at age twenty-two to join his uncle Robert T. Walker in a general merchandise business. Shortly thereafter, the two men partnered with three others to buy a riverfront warehouse and a small fleet of steamboats—placing them at the center of commerce in the region. Situated on the Cumberland River, Nashville served as a crucial nexus between north-central Tennessee farmers and markets in both the North and the South. Most of the region's farms and plantations produced tobacco, corn, and cotton, and relied heavily on slave labor, as did the townspeople of Nashville. The city relied on steamboats to transport their goods down the Cumberland to the Ohio River, then up the Ohio to Pittsburgh and down the Mississippi River to New Orleans. There was money to be made, and young James Walker and his partners found their success. James soon left, though, to cofound the Nashville Commercial

Insurance Company, which brought him into intimate contact with Nashville's expanding business community.[2]

It's unclear how and when James met his future wife, though it's easy to guess: Mary Norvell was the sister of two of his partners in the shipping business. Born in 1802, Mary had moved to Nashville to join three of her nine brothers, the first of whom had arrived around 1807. In 1820, when her future husband arrived, she was living with her brother Moses (eventually one of Walker's partners), along with seven other "free white" people and six slaves. A letter Mary wrote in October 1822 to another brother, William, then living in Lexington, Kentucky, doesn't mention Walker or the prospects of romance but evidences the Norvell family's closeness. "We shall in the course of two or three weeks begin to look for father," apparently coming for a visit from his Kentucky home, "and it is not impossible but that some of us may return with him, however as it is yet uncertain, I shall say little about it, but Moses talks of [his wife] Hannah's spending the winter in Lexington, and if she goes I shall accompany her, and shall do myself the happiness of spending the greater part of my time with you."[3]

While the details of James and Mary's courtship are lost, it must have been a bit of a whirlwind. They married on August 7, 1823, and nine months later almost to the day she gave birth to William, known in his youth as Billy. Another son, Lipscomb (who later went by his middle name, Norvell), followed in 1826; a third son named James, after his father, in 1828; a daughter, Alice, in 1831, who died nine months later; followed by another daughter, also named Alice, in 1833; and their last child, Joseph, who died seven months after his 1836 birth.

The year after Billy was born, the Walkers bought their first home, on High Street a few blocks from the public square, and then in 1840 moved two blocks south to a two-story redbrick house on Cherry Street, where their neighbors included some of Nashville's wealthier and more powerful citizens. Their new home was grand by Nashville standards, fronted by a narrow grass strip and a large stone block to help people alight from carriages. Three stone steps led to the door, where just inside was "a graceful staircase leading to the upper floor." A kitchen and porch stretched across the rear of the house, and at the far end of the backyard stood a small building for servants. Census records from 1830, when Nashville's population was just under fifty-six hundred people, had indicated that James Walker owned no slaves, unusual for the time and for his place in the community. But the 1840 Census recorded Walker owning four adult slaves, two men and two women.[4]

Religion played a significant role in the Walker family. Mary had been raised Baptist; some of her relatives were lay leaders in their congregations, and her brothers opened one of their warehouses for regular church meetings. Her husband, on the other hand, was a member of the Disciples of Christ—he donated $150 in 1842 for a church-supported college in Kentucky. John M. Bass, writing for the *American Historical Magazine* in 1938, said that William Walker's "parents are described as of strong and somewhat stern character." He didn't specify exactly who had described them that way, but that bearing would mesh with the expectations of their fellow churchgoers.[5]

The family followed political developments quite closely. Mary counted among her acquaintances Sarah Polk, wife of future US president James K. Polk, who was a member of Congress, was named Speaker of the House while Billy was growing up, and was elected governor of Tennessee in 1839. Polk was a Jacksonian Democrat; Mary's brothers owned the *Nashville Whig* newspaper and stridently opposed him. In a letter to her husband in June 1841, Sarah Polk detailed political maneuverings and the gossip from Nashville on who would be running in legislative races: "The Whigs are not in good spirits here; they I am told, think or fear that they will loose [*sic*] the Legislature." She admitted she had been too busy with unspecified distractions to keep up with the Nashville papers but that she had picked up some tidbits about the Whigs from "Mrs. Walker (from whom you know that I get a good deal of news)." For her part, Mary Walker felt deep embarrassment over her brother Caleb's editorial attacks and once told Sarah Polk, "I haven't opened my brother's paper to-day, for I dislike so much to read what he says against your husband."[6]

Mary's health weakened over time, and young Billy became her devoted companion. "He spent every morning with her in her room reading to her," a family friend recalled years later. "He was very intelligent and as refined in his feelings as a girl. I used to go often to see his mother, and always found him entertaining her in some way." Billy was precociously bright, but also quiet and aloof. "He is described by his contemporaries, many of whom yet live, as cold, quiet, studious, painfully modest; slight, effeminate, almost insignificant in appearance," Bass wrote. "One says of him that he was uncompanionable, and another speaks of him as a boy who remained long in apron strings."[7]

Billy attended the Nashville English and Commercial School, a small private establishment run by Irish immigrant Alexander Litton. There his physical appearance and demeanor stood out. "A freckled face, almost flaxen hair, and eyes that reminded one of blue only—for they are gray—make up the appearance of his head and face," classmate J. W. Bradford wrote years later. "He was always of a grave turn, never talkative, and when spoken to, answering in a drawling, nasal tone." He came across as preternaturally melancholy with a "voice that made me think of sadness without becoming so." Despite his reserved nature, Billy was friendly, "and none in school was more ready to oblige his fellow with" a little money or extra help with a difficult lesson. He prided himself on his own intelligence and his prowess with lessons, to the point of tearing up if he volunteered a wrong answer, as though mortified at fallibility. "I never saw him lively in my life," Bradford added, "that is, I never heard him laugh out loud, as boys do at play."[8]

————————

How much of young Billy's personality was the result of his parents' influence is unknown. Early biographers tried to link the trajectory of his later life to the stern character of his father, but other childhood role models were likely more influential—including his mother's family, about which more is known than the Walker side.

In 1827, Billy's seventy-year-old grandfather, Lipscomb Norvell, moved to Nashville from Kentucky following the death of his wife, and eventually moved in with Billy's family. Norvell was a veteran of the Revolutionary War who fought in the battles at Brandywine Creek and Trenton and Monmouth, New Jersey, and survived the infamously dreadful winter at Valley Forge. In February 1780, he arrived as part of a brigade of reinforcements for the port of Charleston just in time for a six-week siege that ended with the revolutionaries' surrender—the colonists' worst defeat of the war. As an officer, Norvell likely was imprisoned at Haddrell's Point at Mount Pleasant, just outside the city, where records suggest he stayed for a year before being paroled.[9]

With his late wife, Mary Hendrick, Lipscomb Norvell had a dozen children, four of whom forged careers in newspapers. Their son John founded the *Philadelphia Inquirer* in 1829 and later became a US senator, representing

Michigan when it was admitted to the union in 1837. All three of their sons in Nashville—Moses, Joseph, and Caleb—were involved with the *Nashville Whig*. Moses and Joseph founded it in 1812 at the outset of the war with Great Britain, then sold to the *Nashville Banner* in 1816. Caleb resurrected the paper in 1838 and continued to edit an array of local newspapers before eventually leaving for the East Coast. There, in 1851, he became the founding "commercial," or business, editor of the *New York Daily Times*, which dropped the *Daily* from its title in 1857. Moses and Joseph, who remained in Nashville, branched out from their newspaper and shipping businesses to serve in public positions, including city treasurer, justice of the peace, and trustee of the University of Nashville.[10]

Ultimately, seven of Billy's uncles became involved in politics or journalism, while five served in the military, most in the War of 1812. Scores of Nashvillians, including Billy's uncle Lipscomb Norvell Jr., joined expeditions to Texas, the first rumblings of what would become known as *filibustering*— private groups of armed Americans seeking to wrest control of non-US territory. Robert T. Walker, the uncle whose business Billy's father joined when he first arrived in Nashville, went as an agent for a land company, only to fall ill and die. (His three minor daughters then moved in with Billy's family.) The Texas Revolution broke out when Billy was eleven years old, sparking a fresh recruiting drive for American volunteers willing to fight for the region's independence from Mexico. A regiment formed in Nashville consisting of seventy-five men, including Billy's cousin William Norvell, and headed west, but it was captured within days of arriving in Texas. Most were summarily executed by Mexican troops, but Billy's cousin was among a handful who escaped death. James Robertson, a neighbor, died at the Alamo on March 6, 1836. All of this occurred during the last years of Andrew Jackson's presidency, and when that ended in March 1837, Jackson retired to his Hermitage plantation about ten miles outside Nashville—which means that Billy's neighbors included one former and one future president, the latter of whose wife was a close friend of Billy's mother.[11]

With these sorts of role models—presidents, war veterans, newspapermen, and Texas fighters and settlers—it's easy to imagine how Billy's childhood could have shaped the path the adult William Walker would ultimately follow.

Billy Walker ended his studies at Litton's school around the time of his thirteenth birthday in May 1837, and within days enrolled at the University of Nashville. While that may seem inordinately young, it was not uncommon at the time; his friend John Berrien Lindsley enrolled a year later at age fourteen. Nevertheless, the university's curriculum was rigorous and its admissions standards were high. Entering students were "expected to be accurately acquainted with the grammar, including prosody, of the Greek and Latin tongues" as well as with English grammar, math, and geography. Once admitted, students pursued trigonometry, principals of constitutional and international law, philosophy, natural history, and religious studies. Discipline was strict: Students attended chapel twice a day and stood for a communal prayer before each meal. "Quiet hours were enforced, and activities like horse racing, dancing, or going to the theater were strictly prohibited."[12]

Walker developed a handful of deep friendships there, including with fellow student Robert James Farquharson. He, Walker, and Lindsley shared a devotion to one of their instructors, Dr. Gerard Troost, a Dutch-born teacher of natural history, geology, and mineralogy. Walker also embraced religion much more firmly than before. According to his old acquaintance J. W. Bradford, "He became a Christian youth, and pursued this high calling with all of a 'zeal according to knowledge,' and soon became . . . proficient in the Christian law, and honest in its walk." There was talk of a career in the ministry. Yet even while focused on his studies, Walker maintained a keen interest in world politics. He became active in the Agatheridan Society, a literary debate organization for which he served as secretary and eventually president. One of his responsibilities was proposing debate topics, and he came up with several that were both political and military. "Was it politic for the French to assist the U.S. in the American Revolution?" "Was it preferable [sic] a monarchical or Republican form of government?" "Has the career of Napoleon Bonaparte been of benefit or injury to the world?" His team won seven of eleven debates during the sixteen months it took him to earn his degree. Walker graduated summa cum laude on October 3, 1838, just five months after his fourteenth birthday. His demeanor had not changed much. He could be open and loquacious with friends, and proved to be a persuasive public speaker during Agatheridan Society events, but otherwise maintained a mien of reserve.[13]

Somewhere in the course of his studies, Walker had turned from religion toward science, and he decided to become a doctor. To ready himself for medical school, Walker spent two years under apprenticeship with Nashville physicians, primarily Dr. William G. Dickinson. That gave him sufficient grounding to win admission to the medical department of the University of Pennsylvania, where Farquharson and Lindsley would eventually pursue medical degrees as well.

Walker saw himself as something of an advance guard for his Nashville friends looking at futures in medicine. In November 1841, he sent a report "according to promise" to Lindsley and three others with his first impressions of the personalities and calibers of various professors in Philadelphia. He found the "anatomical theater" to be "well-arrayed, being lighted from above; the professor standing in the center of a circle of benches rising one above the other, and immediately under the skylight." He described instructors in detail—one "is very precise and oratorical; speaks indistinctly (from syphilis, it is said)." He sought in return reports from his friends on the caliber of the programs in Louisville, where several of them were studying, and promised to send along his notes from the lectures he attended, asking his friends to reciprocate.[14]

Walker wrote his thesis on "The Structure and Function of the Iris" and graduated, along with Lindsley, in 1843, with Farquharson finishing a year later. Lindsley would soon return to Tennessee to pursue both medicine and the ministry. Farquharson decamped for New Orleans and set up a medical practice in 1845.

Walker, though, had more distant horizons: to study medicine in Europe. Shortly after receiving their medical degrees on March 31, Walker and Lindsley "proceeded to the foot of Walnut St., which is the point of departure for New York," and took a ferry across the Delaware River to "take the cars at Camden on the opposite side." They spent the better part of a week wandering New York and attending medical lectures while presumably continuing their regular discussions of religion, science, and the world. On April 7, Lindsley accompanied Walker to the docks—"he is comfortably fixed, and in good health and spirits"—and saw him aboard the *Emerald* packet ship, which set sail that morning for Le Havre, France, a gateway to Europe.[15]

Walker arrived in Paris in late April or early May 1843, just before his nineteenth birthday, eventually settling into rooms at 11 Quai Voltaire on the Left Bank near La Pitié hospital and the Jardin des Plantes park, up the Seine River "at some distance from fashionable Paris." While in Europe, as he had in Philadelphia, Walker wrote regularly to his parents (who were supporting him with a monthly $100 allowance), and they presumably wrote to him, but those letters are lost. He also stayed in regular contact with Lindsley, and those surviving letters show that life in Philadelphia did little to prepare him for the more libertine Paris, where he found much to offend a moral view framed by his small-town conservative Protestant upbringing.[16]

"For two and a half months I have been in the *centre* of France, from which radiate all the influences, social, moral, literary, political, scientific, and religious that move the whole nation," he wrote, then marveled that his fellow students would deprive themselves of meals during the day to save money for nights out "at the coffee-house or the theatre." He was stunned at how many couples kept lovers on the side:

> Most of them have mistresses, and nobody thinks them any the worse for it. Indeed, the relations of the two sexes among all classes of society are horrible. You find many married couples, between whom there exists a tacit agreement that the husband may have as many mistresses and the wife as many lovers as they choose. . . . The poison [of infidelity] is found in every vein; the effects of it may be seen on the whole body. What a striking lesson may the moralist learn here![17]

Walker attended lectures at the Institut de France, where he heard renowned organic chemist Jean-Baptiste Dumas, and attended another series of talks by Dumas at the École de Médicin. He studied German, listened to astronomer François Arago, and attended sessions at the Sorbonne, "but there is not enough room for me to tell you about them all." Under a private tutor, Walker studied anatomy and physiology; the tutor also opened Walker to the idea of spiritualism in anatomy, looking at how the body reflects the soul.[18]

Walker spent the summer and fall of 1843 immersed in both his studies and his written discourse with Lindsley. The letters were tightly crafted yet flowery, filled with enigmatic asides and intimate revelations, as though Walker were writing to a lover. He discussed matters of faith, quoted poems, and tossed in Greek and Latin references in a uniformly warm tone that contrasts sharply with later assessments of Walker as cold and diffident. The letters were newsy, as well. The two men talked about the whereabouts of mutual friends, and Walker apprised Lindsley of political events in France, which he described as "extremely interesting." Concerns about a possible war had prompted the

French government to build a fortified wall with cannons around the city, a project still underway while Walker lived there. Parisians viewed the fortifications with distrust, believing that "as soon as there might break out a revolution, the government would turn the cannons towards the city."

There also were tensions within the university, with Catholic priests objecting to the power secular scholars wielded over academic inquiry. Walker's take on the struggle revealed his own deeply anti-Catholic bias. "To hear a Catholic priest talking of liberty, is like a monster talking of beauty," he wrote. "I become more and more convinced each day that the spirit of freedom and Romanism are enemies. . . . It is to be feared that Catholicism will get a hold in our country, and that there will be some trouble dislodging it."

Walker's experiences abroad fueled his own nationalism. While acknowledging that some European nations had stronger and better-established scientific and literary cultures, he felt they lagged far behind in recognizing and protecting individual liberties. His travels had "made me more of an American than ever—more fond of my country's institutions, and prouder of her history and her resources. . . . When I see in two of the august states of Europe (England and France) the existence of powerful shackles on the tongue, if not on the thought (for who can fetter thoughts?), I rejoice that there is a 'land of the free.'"

Despite his continued studies, Walker also seemed to be having second thoughts about a career in medicine. He questioned the wisdom of trying to make a living as a doctor during what were uncertain economic times. He speculated that colleges churned out more doctors than the market could bear, and that what had once been a promisingly lucrative career now ran the risk of undercut prices.

Walker also admitted that he had recently revived a faded dream of his own:

> It is said that no idea which enters our mind is ever entirely removed; often, we see the spectre, as it were, of our departed notions or opinions. By experience, I know how firm is the hold of these early and long-cherished ideas. With me, whilst a child and a boy, I had determined on a political career; there have been times when I thought that the last vestige of such an idea had disappeared, but often it re-appears to me, in my waking dreams, leaving me uncertain whether it be an angel of light or [an] angel of darkness.

By late March 1844, Walker had moved on to London and then continued his travels "through Belgium, Rhenish Prussia, up the Rhine through Switzerland into Italy" until, by November 1844, he reached Venice. Along the way he took in what sights he could, including cathedrals in Cologne and Milan, which he viewed with "such a thrill of awe." He mused, too, about the vagaries of fate and the consequences of single decisions, suggesting he was still struggling with whether to practice medicine or sally forth in a different direction.

> Is not every moment fraught with consequences of the utmost importance? . . . Such is the nature of our reflections when arriving at one of the turns in life we cast a backward look at the road over which we have passed. We are too young, however, to have a long road behind us, and we look forward more than behind. At least it is so with me. The future! The future! Something always coming but never here. Some portions of the past too are very interesting; the present, however, is almost always tiresome. When I was in Paris and London, I didn't enjoy them half so much as before I saw them or after I left them. Anticipation and recollection are the great sources of happiness.[19]

Walker was tiring of the travel, too. He wrote from Venice that he was looking "forward, with pleasure, to the time when I shall be again in the active, stirring world of the West." He told Lindsley he probably would be back in Nashville the following spring. "On the 8th of May I will be twenty-one; I hope to pass that day at home."

2 | NEW ORLEANS, AND ELLEN

DURING THE TWO YEARS WALKER spent in Europe, the restive nation he left behind underwent rapid changes. About the time Walker reached Venice, his fellow Nashvillian James Polk won the 1844 presidential election, capping a race that hinged on competing visions of the young country's future. As the Democratic candidate, Polk favored expanding the national boundaries, including annexing the eight-year-old Republic of Texas and taking sole possession of the Oregon Territory, over which the United States and Great Britain made competing claims. Polk's opponent was Henry Clay, a driving force in the Whig Party, who opposed the expansion. Though Polk failed to carry Tennessee, he narrowly won the national popular vote and trounced Clay in the Electoral College.

The westward expansion that Polk embraced was not a new concept. Thomas Jefferson had laid the foundation with the 1803 Louisiana Purchase, paying $15 million to Napoléon Bonaparte for 825,000 square miles of land mostly west of the Mississippi River. It was a massive addition of territory that doubled the size of the area controlled by the United States and added New Orleans as a southern American port. The purchase reflected Jefferson's belief that the nation should expand until it reached the Pacific Ocean.

That concept picked up a name in the summer of 1845: Manifest Destiny. John L. O'Sullivan, the founder and editor of the *United States Democratic Review* in New York City, wrote an essay on the negotiations between the United States and Great Britain over the Pacific Northwest. O'Sullivan believed—as did many others—that God himself had guided the birth of the United States

19

and that it was "our manifest destiny to overspread and to possess the whole of the continent which Providence has given us for the development of the great experiment of liberty and federated self-government entrusted to us." It was a romanticized, and false, view of liberty in a country in which freedom and enfranchisement extended only to white males (and often only those who owned property). Many proponents of Manifest Destiny believed that they, white Anglo-Saxons, stood apart as a superior race, and that they were pre-ordained to spread civilization across the vast continent for the sake of its cultural and economic advancement.[1]

But differing views on racial issues—in particular, the tension between the free states of the North and the slaveholding South—weighed on the nation's expansion. In 1819, the twenty-two states had been evenly divided between slaveholding and free, which also meant an equal balance in the US Senate. Missouri's petition to be admitted to the union as a slave state threatened to upset that equilibrium, and it set off an argument over how new states would be admitted. The 1820 Missouri Compromise allowed Missouri to join the union as a slave state but maintained the balance by admitting Maine—calved from Massachusetts—as a free state. For subsequent admissions from the Louisiana Territory, it set a dividing line: any state north of 36 degrees 30 minutes latitude would be free, while any state south of it would be slaveholding. The compromise resolved the pressing political dispute of the moment but not the underlying tension, which resurfaced as the United States gained more territory.

Knowing they faced little chance of adding slave territory in the north, slavery advocates began looking south, with talk of annexing Cuba or carving states out of Central America, and to western regions such as Texas, which won its revolution and independence from Mexico in 1836. In April 1844, President John Tyler's secretary of state, the pro-slavery South Carolinian John C. Calhoun, reached an agreement with the Republic of Texas that would admit it to the union as a slave state. Mexico almost immediately severed diplomatic relations with the United States, but the treaty faltered in the Senate and was voted down by a large margin. Tyler, abandoned by his fellow Whigs, dropped out of the 1844 election, which Polk ultimately won. Days before he took the oath on March 4, 1845, Congress finally approved adding Texas to the nation, leaving it up to the new president to determine how the boundaries and other related issues would be resolved. And Mexico began preparing for war.

Walker arrived back in Nashville a couple of months after Polk took office, and informed his family that he was giving up medicine for law. Following the practice of the day, he began studying Tennessee legal codes, procedures, and precedents under the direction of a Nashville lawyer, James Whitworth, himself recently minted as an attorney in the offices of Andrew and Edwin Ewing, brothers who also happened to be graduates and trustees of Walker's alma mater the University of Nashville. Walker was sticking with the familiar.[2]

By autumn, however, Walker decided that his future was to be found far beyond Nashville. In early December he moved to New Orleans, the biggest and most cosmopolitan city in the South (it held at least fifteen foreign consulates in 1846) and a rival to New York as a center of commerce and shipping. It was a growing, rough-and-tumble, disease-prone port town, home to wealthy cotton and sugar cane planters and the businesses that catered to them, from fine restaurants, posh hotels, and banks to gambling dens and whorehouses. High society preened at ostentatious banquets and balls, and private clubs organized parades.[3]

But it was all built on the backs of slaves, and even among the free population, few shared in the wealth. Most residents were mired in urban misery and filth. Unpaved streets became quagmires during rains, and heavy downpours flooded slums and working-class quarters. The sewers were open ditches that spawned regular cholera and typhoid epidemics. Distrusting the Mississippi River, residents relied on rain cisterns for water, so each yard had a breeding place for mosquitoes, which contributed to outbreaks of yellow fever and malaria. Such persistent pestilence pushed New Orleans's death rate to twice that of other cities.[4]

Fortunately, Walker had a connection among the more privileged residents of the city: his old Nashville schoolmate Robert Farquharson. Walker moved into Farquharson's three-story townhouse at 125 Julia Street, in a cluster of townhomes that became known as the Thirteen Sisters. This was one of New Orleans's newer neighborhoods, and not the wealthiest area in the city, but it was home to merchants and other well-to-do members of New Orleans society.[5]

A week after arriving in New Orleans, Walker began studying under a lawyer named Robert Mott, familiarizing himself with the Louisiana civil codes. He then moved on to a twenty-volume commentary on French civil law—the foundation of the Louisiana legal system—by French jurist Charles Bonaventure Marie Toullier. "Luckily these volumes are not very large, and I hope to finish, on an average, one of them every five or six days," Walker wrote to Lindsley in late February 1846. It's unclear how Walker supported himself, or whether his parents continued to cover his modest living expenses. "I am living with Farquharson, and we get on very well together. He has taken a high stand among the medical men here and will no doubt succeed in his profession. [Farquharson] dines at a restaurant, but I take my meals at a boarding house in our neighborhood."[6]

Much as he found the licentiousness of Paris shocking, the foul language Walker heard across his new city burned his ears. "You have no idea of the profaneness of the people of New Orleans," he wrote, including his "preceptor" in law, Mott:

> Looking at him, I would suppose him almost incapable of using an oath, but yet I hadn't been in the office long before my ears were saluted with such words that I had deemed long before consigned to draymen and porters. . . . This common use of oaths appears to be procuded [sic] by an absurd affectation of energy. Not content with activity and simple power, they must have bustle and swelling words. A man wants to have the appearance of strength although he is conscious of weakness.

Yet the *bon temps* ethos of New Orleans didn't turn Walker into a recluse. He found plenty of fellow Nashvillians roaming about the city; some were transplants like him, while others swept through on business or for personal visits. "Tennessee is numerously represented here—commercially, professionally, and fashionably," Walker wrote to Lindsley in April. "Crowds of Nashville people have been down within the last two months; and balls, opera houses, and theaters have been filled with our Tennessee ladies."[7]

The reference to women was unusual for Walker, at least in his letters. There is little to suggest that he dated or had interest in romance, perhaps a result of his personal reserve. But in New Orleans, his fancy was tickled. Ellen Martin, a comely young woman with brown hair and gray-blue eyes, lived with her family across the street from Farquharson. Popular and well-known in New Orleans's society circles, Ellen also was a deaf mute, the legacy of a bout of scarlet fever when she was five years old.[8]

Her parents refused to let her disability define her life. They insisted that young Ellen receive an education, and they had the money to ensure she could. When Ellen was ten years old, she boarded at the Kentucky School for the Deaf and then, four months later, at the Pennsylvania Institute for the Deaf and Dumb, where she spent four years about a mile from where Walker would begin studying medicine just a few months after she left in 1840. Ellen was bright, achieving good grades without much effort, and became adept at sign language as well as written expression. According to a classmate, "her eyes were not large, but beautiful, soft, and brilliant. She conversed divinely, and with an exquisite mixture of vivacity and sweetness." She went on to the American School for the Deaf in West Hartford for a brief attempt at learning French but quit and returned to her parents' home in New Orleans in early 1841. There she became a voracious reader and steady letter-writer, particularly to a cousin, Elizabeth Martin, in South Carolina.[9]

Ellen's letters to her cousin are overstuffed with family news, much of it benign. As one of five children of a wealthy cotton broker, Ellen enjoyed a life of relative leisure. A regular attendee at balls and parties, she carried a pad of paper and a pen to converse with those who didn't know sign language. She traveled at least once or twice a year, usually to visit relatives or friends. In 1843, Ellen, her mother, and at least one brother traveled to Tennessee—including Nashville—and South Carolina, a trip marked by tragedy when a yellow fever outbreak claimed her ten-year-old brother, James. Three years later, Ellen and a school friend spent several weeks traveling by steamboat and stagecoach to Kentucky, Ohio, New York, and then Massachusetts, visiting friends and relatives along the way. But Ellen's ultimate destination was West Hartford, where she arrived in late summer to begin a new training regimen at the American School for the Deaf under Lewis Weld, the principal, who had recently returned from a tour of deaf schools in Europe with a technique to teach speech to the mute. The plan was to spend a year under Weld's care, but Ellen was back in New Orleans by early the next summer, and the lack of further mentions suggests the technique had failed.[10]

Beginning in 1847 Ellen began updating her cousin on her father's attacks of "apoplexy"—strokes—which led to lengthy stays in hospitals and discussions about convalescent care. New Orleans endured a vicious outbreak of yellow fever in the summer of 1847, with more than thirty-four hundred deaths, including another cousin, Henry Haywood, "after six days' illness in which he suffered a great deal." But there were warm moments, as well. Ellen's mother had given birth in 1845 to another son, Hugh Wilson, whom the family called by his middle name. "I wish you could see little Wilson trying to talk to me with his fat little fingers, he is a great beauty and I may say that he is a perfect Apollo in miniature. He knows several letters of the alphabet though he will be only three years old in the last part of July."[11]

The young men of New Orleans beat a steady path to the Martin family door, a parade of suitors that Ellen felt in June 1848 took up too much of her time. "Today I have a very welcome rain which keeps intruders at a distance therefore I have the disposal of my time entirely for writing at one quiet sitting. I have had a greater number of visitors than usual for gentlemen come in and see me almost every evening . . . until it is bedtime." One, a Mr. Wood, Ellen had apparently met at one of the boarding schools for the deaf. "He has paid his first visit to this city to see how 'his dearest Ellen' looked since she had been moulded into the state of woman. He has grown so horribly ugly that any one would be scared away when he sees him make signs, but he is as fine minded as he has ever been and I find myself much interested in him. He is an owner of a lordly mansion near Natchez and also has plenty of dimes in his possession." Ellen named another suitor, as well, a Mr. Apthorp.

Oddly, Ellen never listed Walker among her beaus. Nor did Walker's correspondence mention Ellen. The only allusion to women and marriage he made in the sparse records that survive is an oblique and somewhat immature comment to Lindsley, the person to whom he had often waxed eloquent about the strength and depth of their own friendship:

You have heard much of the trading character of the people here. Now I am going to tell you a secret—fingers on the lips, Mind!— confidential, sub rosa, and all that. No doubt that much speculation in cotton, corn, sugar, and negroes is carried on in New Orleans: but there is one speculation as thriving as any of these—that of marriage or the speculation in wives. The sales in this article have not been very numerous; for the market has been overstocked, glutted, filled to overflowing, and purchasers became nice in their choice and sellers were not disposed to lower their demands. Not a word of this to any one, or I am a ruined man; nay, prithee, if thou dost not burn this letter, put it under lock and key, hide it in thy most secret drawer and carefully keep it from other hands. I am almost afraid to [*illegible word*] it under the guardianship of a seal.[12]

Later, as Walker's infamy grew, the story of his romantic relationship with Ellen would become an intricate and seemingly inflated part of his legend, with newspapers reporting conflicting details attributed to unspecified friends of Walker. He supposedly learned sign language so they could converse. They were inseparable and became engaged. He left law for a career with better prospects so that he could better provide for his love. They had a falling out after Ellen misunderstood the acceptable displays of affection by a society woman (an odd assertion, given that she was an integral part of New Orleans society).

The letters written by the two putative lovers themselves, though, support none of these stories. Had there been such a deep relationship, it's hard to believe that neither would have mentioned it when writing to their closest confidants. Yet it's also unlikely that such a major part of the Walker legend would have been constructed out of whole cloth—particularly since the stories were repeated in newspapers that Walker must have read, yet he never refuted them even as he wrote to editors to correct the record on some of his later escapades. Clearly, he and Ellen shared some romantic connection, and a 1916 biography of Walker by William O. Scruggs, a professor at Louisiana State University, suggests the most likely scenarios. Perhaps Walker became smitten with the young woman but his interest was largely unrequited. Or perhaps their romance blossomed quickly near the end of Walker's stay in New Orleans, shortly before the time when any relationship with the lovely Ellen became impossible.

Walker had continued to study Louisiana law through 1846, and in the process struck up a friendship with Edmund Randolph, a lawyer from Virginia who served as the clerk of the federal district court for Louisiana. Randolph descended from a wealthy Virginia family; his namesake grandfather served as an aide-de-camp to George Washington during the Revolutionary War and later as attorney general and secretary of state during the Washington presidency. The younger Randolph became one of Walker's main sources of introductions to New Orleans upper classes and political circles—some accounts say he introduced Walker to Ellen Martin. Walker passed the bar exam in spring 1847 and hung his shingle outside an office on Canal Street. But he had trouble attracting clients.

Walker maintained his interest in politics and the larger world. He looked skeptically at the war with Mexico, which had begun in May 1846, and at those promulgating it. "Tennessee has, I suppose, the Texas or Mexico fever on her; the malady has abated considerably in this place," he wrote to Lindsley in June. "For a little time the patient was far gone in a delirium of joy and destruction. War was preached of as being the noblest and sublimest of all the states and conditions of men—a spectacle of delight for gods and demi-gods." Walker scoffed at the

> mere twaddle about the irresistible power and incorruptible virtue of the American people. A Methodist preacher volunteered as chaplain to one of the regiments; and on going to his [regimental office] in order to know how to equip himself, was quite surprised to hear that he was not to wear a sword and put on a coat with bright brass buttons. Some of the chaplains seem to think that the people in Mexico are Pagans; for they talk of planting the standard of the Cross amid the plains of the conquered country.[13]

Walker's sense that the war fever had abated conflicts with what was really happening in New Orleans. The war began in April, and on the day Walker wrote to Lindsley, the New Orleans newspapers were filled with details of the fighting and the marshaling of forces and supplies. New Orleans was the closest major US port to the war zone, and with the rail system still being developed, weapons, men, food, and other requisites of battle moved down the Ohio and Mississippi Rivers to the Crescent City's riverside quays, then to oceangoing ships for the trip across the Gulf of Mexico to the Texas and Mexico coastline.

Walker's fascination with current events, combined with his failure to gain traction in his legal career, led him to develop an interest—like his mother's brothers—in the newspaper business. His first published article appeared in the January 1847 issue of the *Commercial Review*, a year-old New Orleans–based monthly published by James Dunwoody Brownson DeBow, a pro-slavery writer and editor who advocated for the broader economic and industrial development of the South. In the same issue as Walker's first article were pieces on expanding cotton growing and cotton markets, the history of Louisiana, a proposal for a statewide public education system, and other subjects. Walker's topic? The history of Venice, which he had visited during his European sojourn and which was "a matter of interest to the merchant and the philosopher, as well as to the painter and the poet."[14]

Walker sent a copy to Lindsley in Nashville, describing DeBow as "a particular friend of mine." DeBow was also interested in publishing an article on the "history and statistics of Tennessee," and Walker recommended that Lindsley's father be commissioned to write it. He asked Lindsley to serve as a go-between, adding that if his father "has not sufficient leisure himself, he might furnish you with the material and let you prepare the article." Walker offered to "pay special attention to the proof sheets," suggesting that his role at the *Commercial Review* was more than that of a contributor. He also asked Lindsley to suggest names of other potential writers from Nashville. "If you would speak to them on the subject you would greatly oblige me as well as DeBow." Neither of the Lindsleys wound up writing for the *Commercial Review*, and Walker's own role faded away. Three months after his first article appeared, DeBow published Walker's second and last piece for the newspaper. The article, intended as a review, was an uncritical rehash of the second volume of Charles Étienne Arthur Gayarré's deeply detailed *Histoire de la Louisiane*.[15]

The 1847 yellow fever outbreak that claimed Ellen Martin's young cousin also affected Walker. He joined the exodus of the healthy from the city until the crushing heat and humidity of summer broke. Walker went to the "lake shore"—presumably along Lake Pontchartrain—for much of August and stayed into the fall. "The fever is uncommonly violent in its forms this year, so that everyone who can leave town—even those who thought themselves acclimated, is flying from the infected region," he wrote to Lindsley. "There are no particular reasons for my remaining in the city, and so I came over here. A Frenchman was saying the other day that he thought it a bad excuse for staying that a man couldn't leave his 'business'; for, said he, what will a man's business be good for when he is dead?"[16]

The death of Ellen's cousin Henry turned out to be only the first wave of grief for the family. On December 30, 1848, Ellen's father succumbed to his series of strokes. "It was a most dreadful blow to us for we had seen him survive his peculiar attacks for two years so that we had not the least apprehension that it might end in paralysis fatally," Ellen wrote her cousin Elizabeth in South Carolina. "He was fortunate enough to escape in November and therefore our hopes were greatly revived. The cholera was making such fearful ravages among the lower class of citizens that we felt very uneasy lest some of us might have it unexpectedly for we have a large family, but thanks be to the good and merciful above we were preserved."[17]

Elizabeth responded with condolences over her cousin's loss, but in early March 1849 Ellen came down with an unspecified gastrointestinal illness that kept her from quickly replying. She finally sat down with pen and paper on March 19:

> It was a great source of consolation to us to read a letter from you so full of kind sympathy which I felt sure came from the bottom of your heart and indeed would I have written to you merely to express my best thanks for the same were it not for the want of self-possession and also for severe indisposition which has kept me in bed for some time.

Ellen was feeling better, but not for long. Two weeks after she wrote to Elizabeth, Ellen's young brother Wilson died—likely from cholera, although he'd also had the measles in mid-March. On April 18, Ellen herself fell ill again, this time catastrophically so. After only a few hours of unspecified "congestion," most likely rooted in cholera, she died.

The next day her grieving mother and surviving siblings hosted a small late-afternoon funeral at the family's Julia Street home, with Ellen's head shrouded in white roses, after which she was entombed with her father and brother in the family vault at the Protestant Girod Street Cemetery. She had turned twenty-three a couple months earlier, and the death devastated her mother, who had now lost a husband and two children in less than four months.[18]

No reliable record contains William Walker's reaction to Ellen's death, but an obituary surfaced in the *Daily Delta* newspaper that, in tone and passion, could well have been written by Walker. At the very least, someone with a close emotional connection penned it:

> Poor Ellen Martin! Who, that had the happiness of knowing her, can forget that eye so bright with animation, those chiseled lips, which seemed the resting place of joyous smiles, those winning manners, and that cultivated intellect? . . . Life, and its joys and pleasures, she loved. Her affections were highly cultivated—her heart a well-fount of love and kindness to all.

Death, though, had stilled her, the memorialist wrote, and ended whatever she dreamed of the future.

> She sleeps in the cold, narrow house, appointed for all living. The hands of devoted friendship will deck her tomb with flowers as pure as her life, and fragrant as her memory. While her earthly part will crumble into dust, her bright spirit shall dwell in that better land, where sorrow never comes. There the lips, which since the prattling days of childhood, had ceased to speak, shall join in the songs of the angels; there her ear, dead below to sounds of mortal endeavor, shall drink in with rapture the harmony of the seraphs.[19]

Whether or not those were Walker's words, they encapsulated his grief. Friends said later that Ellen's death was a turning point in his life. Walker had always been quiet and contained, but after Ellen died, coldness settled in. Walker's fundamental view of the world, and his place in it, began to change.

3 | A JOURNALISM CAREER BEGINS

AT THE TIME OF ELLEN'S DEATH, Walker was still in the early stages of yet another professional transition. His work for the *Commercial Review* may have fizzled, but it had whetted his appetite for the newspaper business, which grew as his interest in the law diminished. A later profile of Walker would argue that this was a natural move for someone who was "a vigorous thinker and a ready writer, full of information upon all topics of current interest." He would find his outlet in the *Daily Crescent* newspaper, founded in March 1848 by Alexander H. Hayes and J. E. "Sam" McClure to offer "enlarged and liberal views on subjects connected with our commercial enterprises and agricultural industry." Rejecting a defined political outlook, Hayes and McClure said they intended to run a newspaper "which, divested of all party politics, would discuss the great questions of State and National Policy with impartiality and freedom, and which, adapting itself to the spirit of the age, should be furnished at a price . . . within the reach of all classes of society."[1]

The paper did well, quickly establishing a regular circulation and a reputation for independence and high-quality writing. (Walt Whitman was a staff writer for a few months in 1848.) At the beginning of March 1849, just six weeks before Ellen fell ill, McClure, bothered by his own chronic illness, sought to sell his stake. Up stepped Walker with a $1,040 promissory note, and the doctor turned lawyer now turned newspaperman.[2]

As he joined the field full-time, Walker set a low bar of expectations. "In entering on a new and untried career, I am liable to fall into errors and make mistakes," he wrote in a brief article announcing that he had joined the paper.

For these, I shall not ask the indulgence of the public; censure will be the fitting reward and surest remedy for them. As the discovery and dissemination of truth shall be the objects of my editorial experience, I will be as happy in receiving aid to investigation as in imparting the results of my labors. And though my contributions to the general welfare may be trifling and unimportant, they shall be, like the widow's mite [a Biblical reference to the generosity of the poor exceeding that of the wealthy], the gift of all I have.[3]

Walker's new paper operated out of offices at 93 St. Charles Street, just a few blocks north of the bend in the Mississippi that gave New Orleans its nickname of the Crescent City. It reprinted items from papers mailed from the Northeast and California (where the gold rush was underway); published stories of local interest, shipping and commodities news, and occasional short essays; and shared news from Mexico, the Caribbean basin, and Europe—places of particular interest to New Orleans traders. A large share of the original articles were based on interviews with the captains of arriving ships, who related what they had seen at ports along their route.

Because the vast majority of the articles went unsigned, it's impossible to determine with certainty Walker's output or his influence on the tone and tenor of the newspaper. But his work earned him the respect of his peers. One contemporary editor described Walker as "a young lawyer with a ready and pointed pen." Another said he "wrote calmly, correctly, and well. His style was not over brilliant; but on the score of good sense and good feeling, in almost every instance, it was entirely exceptionable." Yet another: "Very quiet, very silent, very kind, and looked exactly like a man who was after a hard course of study. He always had a big book under his arm."[4]

Walker's interests and voice resonated in places. *Daily Crescent* editor John C. Larue had been writing most of the paper's main pieces, but with Walker there to share the workload, the articles began to range more widely. They now included theater news and reviews, takes on international relations, stories on the delivery of local government services, and philosophical essays on governance.

Although the *Daily Crescent* operated in the heart of New Orleans's slaveholding industry—surrounding businesses dealt in cotton and other slave-produced goods, and slave auctions regularly took place at nearby lots—the paper was relatively moderate on the issue. The editors accepted ads for slave markets and tacitly supported the practice, but they generally avoided the kind of invective their colleagues in the South employed when discussing abolitionists. Most of the paper's attention on the issue was directed toward countering positions that at the time were considered extreme—and casting a prescient eye toward the future. The *Daily Crescent* found particular fault with the Wilmot Proviso, an 1846 amendment to a failed congressional spending bill that would have banned expansion of slavery into new western territories. The paper argued that Congress should have no voice in whether slavery would exist in the territories—that this was a decision for the territories themselves to make, as it was with individual states.[5]

The paper was often critical of individual politicians, including Missouri senator Thomas Hart Benton, a Democratic supporter of western expansion and longtime slaveholder who, in June 1849, announced he was now "against the institution of slavery, and against its introduction in places where it does not exist." Benton engaged in a public and nasty back-and-forth with fellow Democrat John C. Calhoun, who by this point had returned to the US Senate, where he was an ardent defender of slavery and states' rights. The tenor of the discussion drew a rebuke from the *Daily Crescent* as it explained why it wasn't reprinting some of the exchange directly:

> It would have been a tedious and most unprofitable undertaking, to open our paper to the mutual recriminations of these distinguished men, pursuing each other through a course of thirty years, and searching into the motives and consequences of every public act. . . . We have already expressed our opinion of the offensive tone of dictation and infallibility which pervade both [men's statements].[6]

Yet, in the summer of 1849, the *Daily Crescent* engaged in several sharp-toned feuds of its own with New Orleans residents and competing newspapers, at times shrouding insults in a facade of niceties, at other times turning openly derisive. In July, the *Crescent* attacked the *Daily Delta* for running a series of articles about Canal Bank's discovery that a cashier had used $122,000 in bank funds for personal stock speculation. It also condemned a story on a decision by the bank to loan its president, who had personal financial problems, $40,000 if he resigned. The *Daily Crescent* worried that publicly airing the bank's internal problems might shake confidence in its health, sparking a run by depositors.

"From the fertility of words which characterizes the *Delta*, there is no telling when these histories will be ended," the *Crescent* wrote in an unsigned article. "We suppose what little substance there is in them will go on putrifying until the whole is converted into gas. Then we may hope to be relieved from effusions as offensive to good taste as they are to good sense and good morals." The *Crescent* went on to attack the *Delta* for what it viewed as an intrusion into the two unidentified bank employees' personal affairs—an odd position for a newspaper to take, even in that era.

> The interference with private affairs and family matters was inexcusable and calls for the reprobation of every right-minded man in the community. . . . How can any man feel secure in the enjoyment of domestic privacy when a merciless editor may, at his will, drag all his family connections and household arrangements before the public, and attempt to throw ridicule on what even the most vulgar minds are accustomed to respect and venerate?[7]

The *Delta* responded in kind, calling the *Daily Crescent* "a sickly sheet, which it would be absurd to elevate to the dignity of a rival!" That drew another broadside from the *Crescent*: "The professional spite which dictated the paragraph is the open expression of a paltry malevolence, which could only do mischief when confined to underhanded tricks and misrepresentations." Boasting that the *Crescent* would long outlast the *Delta*, Walker's paper wrote, "It will doubtless be taken by the public, as a good sign of our satisfaction, that we do not run to and fro, peering into private affairs, and hunting up scandalous stories, inventing gossip and puffing ourselves daily, for the purpose of infusing an artificial stimulus into a failing system."[8]

While Walker was feuding with a rival in New Orleans, Narciso López, a Venezuelan native and former Spanish general, was plotting a more serious confrontation in New York City. López had served in Venezuela and Spain, where for a time he was governor of Madrid, then a senator representing Seville. He then followed a patron to Cuba, a Spanish colony since the sixteenth century, where he became governor of Trinidad, a city and region on the island's south-central coast. Near the end of 1843, his patron lost power and López was pushed out of government, though he retained his military rank. He began engaging in private businesses, including mines and plantations, but failed badly.

Despite his distinguished career in the Spanish military and government, López had long harbored a belief that Cuba should shake off Spanish rule and seek annexation to the United States. This, he believed, would allow it to maintain its slave economy, which he and other free Cubans feared might succumb to rising abolitionist sentiments in Europe. Spain had already ended slavery across the realm in 1811, except in Cuba, Puerto Rico, and Santo Domingo, and Great Britain had similarly banned the practice in its empire beginning in 1834. At the same time, Cuban slaveholders feared an uprising like the Haitian Revolution, which ended in 1804 with the French army vanquished and the slaves of Haiti freed and in charge of the country. Aligning Cuba with the United States, particularly the slaveholding South, would give landowners access to military support if it became necessary to quash a slave revolt. The clandestine Club de la Habana quietly raised money, sought out American sympathizers, and arranged private meetings in Washington to solicit a promise that the United States would help should a war for independence come. John O'Sullivan, the "Manifest Destiny" coiner, was a principal player, and he won an audience with President Polk to press the case. So did Jefferson Davis, the Mississippi politician and soldier whose heroism in the recent war with Mexico had helped the United States secure victory and garnered him a seat in the US Senate. Davis brought along three pro-independence Cubans in the hopes of persuading Polk.[9]

At this point López was still in Havana, and as an ally of the Club de la Habana he met privately with the American consul, Robert Campbell. The diplomat told López that Polk had no military designs on Cuba. What he didn't disclose is that the president was secretly negotiating with Spain to purchase Cuba, and he intended to scuttle the club's planned insurrection lest it interfere with his efforts. Polk had sent private letters to Campbell and to Major General William O. Butler, in charge of the American troops preparing to leave Mexico after the end of that war. The letters instructed them to ensure that no Americans, military or civilian, took part in the Cuban insurrection. And then, in a move that Polk hoped would benefit his negotiations, the president forwarded copies of the instructions to Madrid. So the Spanish government knew a revolution was brewing before it even reached a boil.[10]

But all Campbell told López was that the United States could offer no support for the club's plot given the country's treaties with Spain. López took his *no* for a *yes*, concluded that America would step in on the side of an uprising, and started making plans. López picked the small port town of Cienfuegos, about forty miles northwest of the city of Trinidad, as the place to begin, and set the date for June 24, 1848, but a delay in the arrival of smuggled weapons from the United States forced him to postpone. In the meantime, a young man among the revolutionaries told his mother of the plan, who in turn told her husband, who relayed the news to the Cuban government. Authorities arrested the boy on July 6 and ordered López to report to the governor of Cienfuegos regarding an unspecified business matter. López, having learned of the boy's arrest, saw through their ruse and slipped away to the seaport of Matanzas. There he found passage on an American ship, the *Neptune*, that was about to set sail for Rhode Island.

The Cubans eventually tried López in absentia and sentenced him to death, but he was unchastened by his failure. After arriving in Bristol, Rhode Island, on July 23, he headed to New York City, where he began recruiting volunteers and financial backers for an invasion of Cuba. He found welcoming ears and open wallets, particularly among the Cuban Council, affiliated with the Club de la Habana and run by John O'Sullivan's brother-in-law, Cristobal Madan. López was part of a small delegation that met with Jefferson Davis to offer the hero of the war with Mexico $100,000 to lead the invasion. Davis demurred and recommended Robert E. Lee, then a rising officer in the army, who also turned them down.

Eventually López decided to lead the invasion himself, and in early summer 1849 he very publicly began recruiting soldiers in New York City. In March, the Whigs' Zachary Taylor succeeded Polk in the White House. As word spread of López's intentions, the Cuban minister in Washington lodged a complaint with the administration, and Taylor, who opposed his predecessor's idea of buying Cuba from Spain, nonetheless felt it necessary to come out against López's plan. In "Proclamation 51—Warning to United States Citizens Against Participating in an Unlawful Invasion of Cuba," Taylor cautioned that such a project would violate the Neutrality Act of 1818, which forbade attacks launched from American soil against nations with which the United States was at peace. Not only would combatants face charges, he wrote, but the US government would not come to their aid if they got into trouble. He added:

> I exhort all good citizens, as they regard our national reputation, as they respect their own laws and the laws of nations, as they value the blessings of peace and the welfare of their country, to discountenance and prevent by all lawful means any such enterprise; and I call upon every officer of this Government, civil or military, to use all efforts in his power to arrest for trial and punishment every such offender against the laws providing for the performance of our sacred obligations to friendly powers.[11]

The pronouncement did nothing to dissuade twelve hundred volunteers from signing up. López placed them under the direction of Colonel George W. White, a veteran of the Mexican-American War now based in New Orleans. With the $80,000 or so that López managed to raise, he and his supporters chartered the steamship *New Orleans* and bought two more ships, the *Fanny* and the *Sea Gull*. They were scheduled to depart for Cuba from two different points, New York City and Round Island, off the coast of Mississippi. By September 1849, several hundred men—most recruited in New Orleans—had gathered at Round Island, ostensibly preparing to move en masse to California. To plan an invasion on American soil would have violated US law, but to plan a gold-mining expedition and then have a sudden change of heart once at sea, well, where was the crime in that?[12]

The lie fooled no one. US warships, acting under Taylor's "Proclamation 51" and the Neutrality Act, blockaded Round Island, declared the occupants vagrants and mercenaries, and said they could either starve or accept free passage to the mainland. The standoff lasted several weeks, but the would-be invaders slowly left the island—some of them signing on as crewmembers on the very ships blockading them. The expedition fizzled. López, undeterred, would soon shift his operations from New York City to New Orleans, rightly believing that he would find more support and encouragement, and perhaps less scrutiny, in a place that owed its wealth to the institution he so desperately wanted to preserve in Cuba.

Walker and his *Daily Crescent* followed these developments closely. The news-paper favored annexing Cuba for a variety of reasons. In June, it had reprinted reports that Cuba was still importing slaves from Africa despite an international movement to end what the *Crescent* called "the piratical traffic," which the United States had banned in 1807 while retaining slavery as an institution. The paper suggested the government might need to intercede to "force compliance not only with established treaties but with common principles of humanity and civilization."[13]

Yet the paper's interest in Cuban slavery was also rooted in geopolitics. The island's proximity meant any instability there could pose a threat to the American South. The paper specifically feared a contagious Haiti-style revolt:

> If, for example, the great number of negroes now being carried into Cuba should end in a second Haytien [*sic*] insurrection, and in the establishment of a negro-state in the Island, it would be very injurious and dangerous for our Southern planters to have such a neighbor. Of course we have the right—and ought to exercise it—of preventing any policy that would lead to such a disaster.

That the Spaniards were unable to work the land without slaves was "proof positive that they are themselves becoming every day weaker and weaker," the paper noted (oblivious to the fact that the same argument could be made about white southern plantation owners). Continued Cuban importation of slaves would soon leave the white population massively outnumbered and at risk.

The paper urged the US government to "remonstrate with the Spanish government" and concluded that "the interests of humanity, as well as our own, call on us loudly to interfere and put a stop to this iniquitous and dangerous slave trade." Two months later, the paper fully endorsed annexing Cuba by buying it from Spain, and expressed surprise that northern anti-slavery agitators opposed annexation. The *Crescent* posed the chauvinistic argument that if the United States took over the island it could end the importation of new slaves and "slavery on the island would take the mild and comparatively inoffensive form in which it exists in the Southern States."[14]

Walker and the paper specifically endorsed filibustering, also known as freebooting. Filibuster expeditions like López's, the paper argued, were expres-sions of individual freedom and adventurism—some of the very ingredients that had led to the establishment of the United States. On September 3, 1849, the *Daily Crescent* took issue with the order to blockade Round Island, claiming no one had established that Colonel White and his men were violating any laws. Particularly irked that the blockade was effected by military rather than civil authorities, the *Daily Crescent* blasted the decision to "coop up a body of unarmed Americans on an island, depriving them of provisions, menacing them with force, to compel them to disperse." The men, the paper argued, had been deprived of their right to free assembly and movement based on a supposition. "Nothing can be more arbitrary in character, or offensive in manner, than these extraordinary assumptions of power. . . . It is not likely that the rights of free Americans can be so summarily abridged by mere military powers, without rousing a most determined spirit of inquiry into responsibility, and the strongest feelings of resolute disapproval of the act."[15]

The paper went on to describe in grandiose terms the right of Americans to pursue their own lives unfettered by their own government and, if they so desired, to pursue their dreams outside of the United States. "There is no law of nations, recognized in this country at least, nor of morals, which deprives a man of the right of expatriating himself if he pleases, to take his share in a foreign quarrel, which appeals to his love of liberty, or detestation of tyranny, or even to his mere sordid estimate of glory or gain." And in an article responding to descriptions of López as a pirate, the *Crescent*—in what reads like Walker's language—pointed out that the Marquis de Lafayette and Casimir Pulaski, both heroes of the American Revolution, were foreign-born men who moved to another country to fight for its freedom. Was López any different?[16]

Such sentiments would prove to be a blueprint for Walker's own future.

The previous month, Walker had demonstrated that the evolution of his political opinions was personal as well as philosophical. In August 1849, the *Daily Crescent* was again quarreling with the rest of the New Orleans newspaper world. This time the dispute was about whether the Spanish consul had kidnapped a Cuban man while he was visiting the Crescent City. The man's name was Juan Garcia Rey, and he had worked as a jailer in Havana until the previous March, when he helped three prisoners escape, including two of

López's coconspirators, then fled with them to the United States. The Spanish authorities alerted their consul in New Orleans that Rey was in the city, and the consul had agents track Rey's movements.

The details are murky, which helped provoke the controversy, but on July 5 Rey boarded the *Mary Ellen*, a ship bound from New Orleans to Havana, with nothing but the clothes on his back. His landlord noticed him missing a couple of days later and posted a notice in *La Patria*, the most influential Spanish-language newspaper in the country at the time. The paper declared that Rey had been kidnapped and accused the Spanish consul of involvement. Other newspapers took up the cause, eventually leading the Taylor administration to make inquiries in Cuba. Campbell, the US consul in Havana, met with Rey in the presence of five Spanish officers, and Rey told Campbell that he had returned to Cuba of his own free will; the consul went away satisfied. But a short time later Campbell received a secretly passed letter from Rey in which he said, "I came here by force, the Spanish consul having seized me under a supposed order of the recorder of the Second Municipality and having had me carried by main force on board a ship at nine in the evening." He said he'd lied in the face-to-face meeting "because the Captain of the port was present," and now sought "the protection of the American flag" and wished to be returned to the United States.[17]

In New Orleans, arrests were made, and the papers filled their pages with details and speculation. Editor John Larue had recently left the *Daily Crescent* and, as a lawyer, now represented some of those charged. The *Crescent*, meanwhile, argued that Rey had likely been conned, not kidnapped. "The offence against our laws and our government was in the forcible removal of the man from our territory," the paper argued. "If he went voluntarily, however induced, there was no abduction." Then the paper ripped into its rivals, particularly the *Daily Delta* and the *Picayune*, both of which had taken up Rey's cause as a kidnapping victim.[18]

The controversy also led to some verbal rock-throwing between the *Daily Crescent* and Eusebio Juan Gomez, the New Orleans–born editor of *La Patria*. Gomez supported Cuban annexation but opposed filibustering, and he came to believe, wrongly, that the *Daily Crescent* opposed annexation. From his offices in Exchange Alley, just a few blocks from the *Daily Crescent* on St. Charles, Gomez condemned the paper's supposed position in an article that was later republished in the New York–based *La Verdad*, whose co-owner was the pro-annexation agitator O'Sullivan. The *Daily Crescent* claimed to never read *La*

Patria and to have learned of its neighbor's attack only weeks later, when it received a copy of *La Verdad* with the reprinted article.[19]

Walker went on the attack. He described *La Patria* as "the merest apology for a newspaper that could well be manufactured" and described its opinions as "the soughing of the wind—mere froth in the water agitated by the breath of a boy." He went on to restate the *Daily Crescent*'s position that the United States should buy Cuba from Spain. Why, he asked, would *La Patria* misstate the *Daily Crescent*'s position? The papers continued to gnaw at each other, with the *Crescent* publishing, ominously, a single paragraph on November 17 that referred to "insinuations" published in *La Patria*. "As to the only definite statement made in its article, we intend to investigate the matter, and if we can fix the responsibility, hold the parties to a strict account."[20]

Four days later, Walker and Larue, who despite having left the *Crescent* in August clearly maintained some connections with the publication, showed up at *La Patria*'s offices. They approached the editor, whom Larue knew but whom Walker had never met; "There is Mr. Gomez," Larue said, and Gomez offered a slight bow. Walker said he had written a letter to Gomez a few days prior, but Gomez, not yet knowing who was standing before him, said he didn't know what was being talked about. "My name is Walker, of the *Crescent*." Gomez replied that "the only answer we could give the *Crescent* appeared in our paper of Sunday."[21]

With that, Walker swung his cane, striking Gomez in the head. The editor stumbled backward, then reached for his sword cane on a table about five feet away. Larue moved in and grabbed Gomez as the editor pulled a pistol from his pocket, and others in the office joined in to restrain both men. "They were afraid I would shoot anyone, I was so enraged," Gomez said later. Criminal complaints were filed, but the available records don't indicate whether anyone was ever convicted.

For people who knew Walker, his resorting to violence was out of character. With his slight build, physical altercations weren't likely to end well for him. His best weapons were words. No written record hints at what might have set him off other than a bruised ego, and a sense that his dignity and integrity had been cast into doubt—the groundwork for a challenge to a duel in those days. Yet he didn't offer that challenge. Instead he marched to the offender's office and physically attacked him.

He was, in many ways, becoming a new William Walker.

4 | SAN FRANCISCO

READERS PICKED UP the *Daily Crescent* on February 4, 1850, to find in the middle of the front page a notice that its owners had sold the newspaper for a "large and satisfactory . . . consideration" to three men led by experienced editor John W. Crockett, a former Tennessee congressman and son of Davy Crockett. With that, Walker's career as a New Orleans editor-provocateur ended.[1]

Walker's *Crescent* partner Alexander Hayes soon took off for California, where he planned to invest in or open a newspaper in San Francisco, a small bay town rapidly turning into a thriving city as the main gateway to the Gold Country. Walker stuck around New Orleans for a few months, but by mid-summer he too pulled up stakes, intending to join Hayes in his San Francisco newspaper venture. The journey west was arduous: Booking passage through the Atlantic Mail Steamship Company, Walker left New Orleans aboard the steamer *Ohio* on June 15 bound for Havana. He spent a few days in Cuba before taking the *Georgia*, another steamer, for Chagres on Panama's Caribbean coast. From there he made his way across the Isthmus of Panama, taking small riverboats up the Chagres River where he could and hiking—at times through swamps and tropical forests—where he couldn't. He had plenty of company; thousands of Americans drawn by the gold rush were following the same path to the West Coast, rather than taking the slower routes around the tip of South America by sea or across the North American continent by horse and wagon.

Walker spent a couple of days in Panama City, then bought passage on the Pacific Mail Steamship Company's San Francisco–bound *Oregon* on July 2. He was one of 317 passengers, all but six of whom were men. The vast majority were Americans, who found themselves celebrating the July 4 holiday at sea. They sat for a celebratory banquet presided over by Dr. Peter W. Martin of Nashville, leader of a small expedition of mining hopefuls, during which a minor-level diplomat aboard read the Declaration of Independence aloud. Walker then followed with what a later newspaper report called an "eloquent impromptu address suitable to the occasion. The passengers then sat down to a sumptuous repast—joy and hilarity prevailed, appropriate toasts were drank, and the glorious Fourth was passed off in a delightful manner."[2]

The *Oregon* stopped in Acapulco for more coal, gathering reports about twelve thousand deaths from cholera in Mexico City, and then steamed on, two of its own passengers dying en route of unrecorded causes. On the evening of July 21, the *Oregon* arrived at the Golden Gate to a warm welcome from the local press; it entered "the bay in beautiful style, with great speed, her decks crowded with passengers—kept off beyond Rincon Point—sounded to and dropped anchor. As it was Sunday evening, and a leisure time, every boat which could be procured was called into requisition, and the water teemed with the fragile craft."[3]

Walker moved into the St. Francis Hotel at Clay and Dupont Streets in the heart of the city, and learned quickly that Hayes had caught gold fever, scrapped his newspaper plans, and headed east to the Sierra Nevada. Walker tracked down another New Orleans friend, Edmund Randolph, who had moved to San Francisco in 1849 to practice law. Randolph was well connected both in legal circles and among the city's Democrats. He also co-owned the recently founded *Herald* newspaper, and he introduced Walker to his partner there, John Nugent. In short order Walker was back at work as an editor and writer.[4]

If anything, Walker's writing was even more pugnacious in San Francisco than it had been in New Orleans. The city certainly gave him a lot of topics to work with. In the two years since gold was discovered at John Sutter's mill about 130 miles inland, San Francisco had exploded from around five hundred residents to upwards of twenty-five hundred. Many were jammed into tents or shacks at the edges of the more permanent houses and buildings—primarily wood-frame or adobe—between Telegraph Hill and Rincon Point, with the city's commercial heart clustered around Portsmouth Square, "a bare spot, relieved alone by the solitary liberty-pole, and the animals in and around it." The square was surrounded by grand "gambling-houses, flooded with brilliant light and music, and with flaring streamers which attracted idlers and men seeking relaxation" while the side streets were "filled with shabby dens and public houses of the lowest order, frequented by sinister-looking men and brazen-faced females, who day or night were always ready either for low revelry or black crime."[5]

It was a city of "gamblers and Adventurers. They swarmed the Streets and Trade Marts, disdaining to keep to the sidewalks, and were constantly hustling each other, reminding me of Dante's Restless Spirits in his *Inferno*," wrote one fresh arrival to the city.

> There were neither gas lights nor hydrant water; we paid fifty cents per barrel for Spring Water, and camphine [distilled turpentine] furnished our lights. The streets were in a wretched condition. Politicks were corrupt; the city was controlled by gamblers and their friends, and the courts were largely in the hands of the same power. . . . The use of deadly weapons was an everyday affair. Villainous women from China, Chile, Mexico, France, and New York, were imported by shiploads for merchandise.[6]

With all that congestion and turmoil, fires were inevitable, and the heart of the city had burned to the ground on Christmas Eve 1849. Five more fires of varying scale followed in 1850. Some of the blazes started accidentally, but not all. A loosely organized group of ruffians known as the Sydney Ducks—most were former British convicts by way of Australia—found robbing and stealing an easier way to get a piece of the gold rush action than panning or mining. The Ducks were suspected of setting several of the blazes so they could take advantage of the confusion to burglarize unattended stores and houses. The city police force of about seventy-five men, many of whom were confederates of the very criminals they were charged with policing, were ineffective defenders of the peace. Bribery and other forms of corruption reached so deeply that even judges often protected the crooks brought before them.[7]

Walker and the *Herald* routinely published their outrage at the government's inability to deal with crime. Following the robbery-murder of a man named Tay and an unsuccessful attempt to steal a safe by cutting through the floor of a wharf-top office, the *Herald* asked, "When citizens are murdered and robbed and their houses are feloniously entered in the most populous portions of the city, is it not time there were some action taken to vindicate the law?"

In essence, the paper was calling for organized lynch mobs. "We have urged the formation of a volunteer night patrol, and until such a body be organized we doubt if there can be any security. A summary example must be made of the first person detected in the commission of these crimes."[8]

The *Herald* lambasted the courts as inept, but an undercurrent to their coverage was the suggestion that judges were on the take. Walker took direct aim at Judge Roderick N. Morrison, sitting on the probate bench, who was trying to unscramble a thorny estate controversy and was subsequently accused by one of the parties of soliciting a bribe. In August 1850, Morrison was tried on bribery charges before Judge Levi Parsons, who found him innocent, citing lack of evidence.

Walker and the *Herald* were incensed, believing that Parsons had done a favor for his fellow judge—or perhaps had been bribed himself. Over the next few months, Walker mounted a campaign impugning Parsons's legal impartiality and character, while continuing to target Judge Morrison as well. In another case, Morrison reassigned oversight of the estate of a cholera victim named Coleman from the port collector to the public administrator, the practice when no heirs could be found. But the dead man had relatives in Boston. When they filed a claim via affidavits sent to a representative in San Francisco, Walker and the *Herald* offered a full-throated defense of the easterners' claim—and again denounced Morrison:

> There is now in this city a power of attorney from the representatives of Coleman, authorizing persons here to act for them. In a few days, therefore, the public may have an opportunity of judging how the public administrator preserves vacant estates. There is some fear that the Coleman estate, may be found "pickled" instead of "preserved," and if so, the public shall know the facts. We shall shortly understand why the Probate Judge and Public Administrator wanted to get Coleman's effects from Collector Collier. The agents of Coleman's heirs will see that the matter is thoroughly sifted.[9]

Morrison's defenders, a half dozen clerks and protégés, became increasingly offended and agitated by Walker's campaign. After the Coleman article appeared, one of them, Frank Morrison Pixley, sent a scathing letter to the *Herald* denouncing its coverage and describing the unidentified writer of the article as "a liar, a poltroon, coward, using all the string epithets of a bloody vocabulary." Walker responded with a challenge to a duel, which was accepted by another Morrison protégé, William Hicks Graham, who set the terms: revolvers fired at ten paces.[10]

The two men met in Hayes Valley at ten o'clock in the morning on Sunday, January 12, 1851. The pistols were five-shot Colts, and the agreement was that the duelers would fire simultaneously and, if both missed, take one step closer and fire again until the five shots were discharged or someone was wounded or killed. Each had an attendant, or "second," to support him, and a handful of witnesses were on hand, too.

The men took their positions, with the seconds and onlookers safely off to the side. At the signal, both men fired. Walker's shot missed; Graham's shot ripped through Walker's pant leg, "slightly breaking the skin." Each man stepped forward and again the command was given, and again Walker's shot missed. This time, though, Graham's bullet struck Walker in the thigh, blasting through skin and muscle but missing bone. Walker crumpled to the ground, and the duel was over.[11]

———————

Getting shot did nothing to lessen Walker's criticism of the courts or of the endless street crime and thuggery that afflicted the city. Two days after the face-off, without reporting the details of the earlier gunplay, the *Herald* chastised those who thought they could silence the newspaper through intimidation. The paper also shrugged at threats by Morrison's other supporters to continue to defend Morrison's honor—an implicit warning against any newspaper considering writing negative articles about the probate judge. "It is unnecessary to say that as far as this intimation is intended as a menace to deter us from the discharge of our duty, we regard it with scorn and defiance. . . . If they expect to control the sentiment of a whole community by force, we think they have misjudged both its spirit and its tolerance."[12]

To Walker and the *Herald*, San Francisco's feckless courts and the lawlessness they enabled were a threat not only to individual victims but to the stability of the city itself. Similar concerns were growing all over the city, and on the evening of February 19, a single crime ignited a furious backlash. Two men entered C. J. Jansen's general merchandise shop on Montgomery Street, cracked him over the head with a hunk of lead attached to the end of a stick, and made off with $1,586 in cash and gold. Jansen survived, but the city was united in its outrage at an attack on a popular and respected businessman.

In the next day's *Herald*, Walker raised the rhetorical question: "If a man is not safe in his own house, with hundreds [of people] a few yards off, where is he safe!" Crime had reached epidemic proportions, and "the audacity of criminals have [*sic*] become frightful. Something must be done to strike terror into the hearts of these miscreants." Yet the courts and the police had so far failed.[13]

This time, however, the crime did not go unaddressed. After Jansen tentatively identified one of his attackers, authorities arrested two suspected Sydney Ducks, James Stuart and Robert Windred. Walker was unimpressed. On February 22 the *Herald* reported on the arrests but in the same edition printed Walker's renewed call for a vigilante movement. The editor urged the formation of a

> band of two or three hundred "regulators" composed of such men as have a stake in the town, and who are interested in the welfare of this community. The very existence of such a band would terrify evildoers and drive the criminals from the city. If two or three of these robbers and burglars were caught and treated to "Lynch law" their fellows would be more careful about future depredations.[14]

Either Walker was prescient, or the city was listening. Hundreds of people descended on the four-story wood-frame city hall at the corner of Kearny Street and Pacific Avenue to attend Stuart and Windred's arraignment in a courtroom inside. When the hearing ended, part of the crowd surged forward amid shouts to grab the accused. City officials, fearing just such a mob, had arranged for a local militia, the Washington Guards, to secretly station itself inside city hall. When the mob moved to take over the courtroom, the militia rushed in, bayonets fixed, and slowly cleared the room before escorting the two defendants to safety.[15]

The next morning, a crowd of thousands convened outside city hall. Orators took to the second-floor balcony, their speeches alternating between demands for street justice and pleas, one by Judge Levi Parsons, to let the courts do their work. Amid shouted demands for a hanging, the mob voted to create an ad hoc "people's court," including a jury, to take instant testimony so there could be some sort of finding of guilt before the men were strung up. Over the ensuing hours, the crowd grew—at one point reaching six thousand people—and shrank as the ersatz judge and jury worked through questions about the reliability of Jansen's uncertain identification of one of the attackers and whether that was enough to convict. Patience wore thin as the deliberations continued late into the night. The jury finally appeared and announced that nine of them had voted for conviction, but three had favored acquittal. It was a hung jury. The mob responded with a violent roar and "broke in the windows, and rushed in at the doors, and broke up the railing round the bar, and were about to make an attack on the jurors." The jurors, pulling their revolvers, retreated into the building as the Washington Guards once again headed off the mob, which was now yelling for both the defendants and the jurors to be hanged. It wasn't until the wee hours of the next morning that the crowd, and the passions, had dissipated enough for the jurors to leave.

Walker and the *Herald* cheered the mob's actions:

> At last the people are aroused. At last the men of San Francisco have shown that they are determined on having justice administered in their midst—that though our courts may be weak and our officials corrupt, that though crime may be daring and law sickly and mealy mouthed, yet the immutable rules of right on which all true strength and prosperity depend must be maintained in this city. . . . Terrible is the retribution which our citizens will visit on the unworthy public servants who have thus reduced them to the necessity of defending themselves from the convict colony emigrants and their associates.[16]

The *Herald*'s editorials annoyed the San Francisco judiciary, particularly Judge Parsons, whom Walker excoriated yet again after he instructed a grand jury over which he presided to not return a criminal indictment unless there was sufficient evidence to secure a conviction, not merely sufficient evidence to send the defendant to trial. "Thus," Walker wrote, "the district court instructs the grand jury to aid the escape of criminals."[17]

When the March 1851 court session began, Parsons urged a grand jury to issue an indictment for libel against the *Herald* and its editors. Parsons acknowledged both the right to and the need for a free press but argued that when newspapers were filled with scurrilous comments about government institutions and people, then a grand jury should step in and hold the press accountable. The grand jury disagreed and declined to indict.

The *Herald* got wind of Parsons's efforts, and in an editorial the next morning, Walker issued his own indictment of Parsons under the headline THE PRESS A NUISANCE, reflecting Parsons's statement to the grand jury that "the papers of the town constitute a nuisance and should be prosecuted as such by the county authorities." The article framed Parsons's attempts to cow the press as part of the city's "judicial madness," and issued a veiled threat:

> If we were the guardian angel of the District Judge we would whisper in his ear, "Beware!" How can man be so blind or so weak, as some of our Judges appear to be? Do they think the patience of the people eternal, because judgment against an unfaithful servant is not executed speedily? Do they dream that the public will forever remain quiet, that the air will be forever mild, the breezes forever gentle, and that the hurricane will never rise to sweep them from the land, and bury them in the deep? Again we say to the judges, one and all, "Beware."[18]

The *Herald* had barely hit the streets when Parsons issued an order for Walker and Nugent to appear before him and explain why he shouldn't hold them in contempt of court. The men complied, with Randolph appearing as Walker's lawyer. They told the court that Walker had written the article at which Parsons had taken offense but argued that Parsons had no authority to pursue charges. Contempt citations were to enforce court rules and ensure that people followed court orders. A newspaper article critical of the court, if based on falsehoods, could be the subject of a libel complaint, which the grand jury had already rejected. So Parsons had no legal authority to issue a contempt of court citation. Parsons, unsurprisingly, disagreed. The judge found Walker guilty a few days later and fined him $500, then ordered him held until the fine was paid. Walker, as obstinate as ever, refused to pay the fine, and so was taken off to jail.[19]

Word of Walker's incarceration zipped around the city, drawing outrage from business leaders who had been pressing for a more vigilant police department and judiciary, as well as from most of the competing newspapers, who saw the imprisonment of any editor for what he wrote as a direct threat to themselves. (In fact, Judge Parsons later ordered the editor of a competing newspaper to explain why he should not be held in contempt as well, after he dared to compose an editorial backing the *Herald*'s right to publish.) Some of the main players in the mob at city hall convened a special meeting at the Portsmouth Square the day after Walker's conviction to discuss his incarceration. It was an informal group, but it quickly took on a formal character, voting to approve a series of resolutions. It began with a blanket endorsement of the need for a proper judicial system in San Francisco, one that the public would consider just and free of corruption. It averred that the public had a right to challenge judicial misconduct whenever it occurred. And it went on to castigate Parsons for his "unwarrantable exercise of power, as a violation of the law and of the constitution, and as an alarming attack upon the liberties of the people." The group demanded the judge's resignation, asked state representatives to begin impeachment proceedings if he did not, and designated a committee of ten to present the resolutions to Parsons in person. It also urged that its resolutions be published in the city's newspapers and posted publicly. (The leaders of the group would go on in a few years to be the principal organizers of the Committee of Vigilance, a notorious band that lynched four suspected criminals.)[20]

Walker's contempt citation was reversed by a split panel of the superior court, which ruled that Judge Parsons had misapplied his authority; it granted the editor his freedom on March 15. But Parsons refused to resign, and the pro-Walker group now looked to the legislature to intervene. Their appeal was assigned to a committee, which found Parsons had indeed overstepped and should face impeachment. The full assembly demurred and appointed another committee. It took testimony from Parsons, among others, and determined that Walker may well have been in contempt, and "that testimony given in support" of Walker's complaint "show no cause for impeachment." But it did recommend that the legislature look at clarifying libel laws and procedures governing contempt of court.[21]

The contempt case also brought new attention to Walker and the *Herald*'s anti-crime campaign. Walker decided to ride the wave of interest into politics. He won the nomination as the Democratic Party's candidate for a San Francisco alderman seat, representing the fourth district. Public awareness, though, can only do so much, and Walker lost badly in the April 28 election.

Yet a larger setback was looming. Late in the evening of May 3, 1851, less than a week after the election and five days before Walker's twenty-seventh birthday, a fire erupted in a paint shop overlooking Portsmouth Square. At first, it didn't seem like much—a small collection of carelessly treated materials began smoking then smoldering. The fire call was sounded, and volunteers came running, but the little fire grew quickly and whipped through the building, picking up strength from the flammable paints and resins before exploding into an adjoining building. And then another, and another, and the city was once again aflame, with the firefighters too overwhelmed to stop it. The flames swept southward and eastward through the core of the city, destroying everything in their path. The *Herald* building, a brick structure a block south of Portsmouth, was among the early casualties. The fire roared through the night and into the next day, finally burning itself out after consuming wharves jutting out over the bay. The fire claimed at least seven lives, and gutted or leveled more than a thousand buildings, including the offices and printing presses of every newspaper in town save the *Daily Alta*, which offered a grim report on its front page the next morning:

> It is sufficient to say that more than three-fourths of the business part of the city is nothing but smouldering cinders. It is impossible to give a list of the buildings burned or the names of the sufferers. . . . Here and there a brick building stands like a tomb among a nation of graves, yet even they in most cases have nothing but their walls standing. Scarce a fire-proof building in the whole burnt district has stood the test. . . . We have experienced several severe conflagrations in this doomed city, but none of them can compare in extent and destruction of property and life with this, which is still in progress.[22]

With the *Herald* building leveled, Walker once again found himself finished as an editor-provocateur. Within weeks, he took off for fresh pastures in Marysville, near Sacramento, where a friend, Henry P. Watkins, had established a law practice catering to those fighting for and over mining claims in the Gold Country. Walker remained involved in San Francisco Democratic politics from afar, serving on some committee posts, but his career was again shifting in a new and unforeseen direction.

After his failed effort to invade Cuba, Narciso López had directed his recruitment toward the American South, first moving from New York City to Washington, DC, and then, after cutting ties with the Club de la Habana, setting out for New Orleans. The cause of Cuban freedom was already popular in the Crescent City; residents hung Cuban flags in their windows and held regular public meetings to discuss the matter, which also propelled discussions in salons, saloons, and pulpits.[23]

López and his compatriot Ambrosio Gonzales traveled by stage from Washington to Pittsburgh, then down the Ohio and Mississippi Rivers by steamboat, arriving in New Orleans around April 1, 1850, just ten weeks before Walker left for San Francisco. Within weeks of López's arrival in New Orleans, they'd organized a second invasion force: three ships carrying a total of five hundred filibusters (a regiment each from Kentucky, Mississippi, and Louisiana) left New Orleans between April 25 and May 7 for the Yucatán, where they combined into one force aboard the steamship *Creole* and headed for Cuba. Accounts of the expedition filled the newspapers, though the organizers again maintained the lie that they were preparing for a mining expedition to California.[24]

The organizers planned to land at Cárdenas, about seventy miles east of Havana, but the *Creole* sailed too close to shore and the authorities in Havana spotted her. By the time the invaders landed—they were delayed for a few hours when the *Creole* grounded on a sandbar off the harbor—Spanish soldiers were on the move to meet them. Nevertheless, when they alit at about 2:30 AM on May 19, they swiftly seized control of the city's main plaza, and at sunrise managed to break into the fortified army garrison and rout the four hundred or so Spanish soldiers within. Casualties were relatively light—about twenty killed or wounded on each side—but López had hoped to take Cárdenas without a fight. From the beginning, he operated under the delusion that the Cuban people would join with him in an uprising against the Spanish crown, but after seizing the garrison, the invaders found an indifferent and fearful civilian population.[25]

They also found a very engaged Spanish military. The invaders seized a rail station, including three locomotives and several cars they could use for the next phase: the taking of Matanzas, midway between Cárdenas and Havana. But word of the invasion reached Matanzas after the *Creole* was first sighted, and troops cut the rail line to forestall the invaders advancing by rail. A Spanish force also moved into Cárdenas itself, some two hundred infantrymen and another hundred lancers taking cover in houses and gardens. Fearing a slaughter, López ordered the invaders back to the ship as Spanish fighters advanced; about thirty men were killed or wounded before they could reach the ship and escape the harbor. López wanted to steam westward and try again by landing at Mantua, in a section of Cuba populated mainly by Creoles, whom López thought could be more reliably expected to give them a warm welcome and join the insurrection. But López had lost control of his troops, and they redirected the *Creole* north to American soil.[26]

The filibusters landed at Key West and López traveled on to Savannah, Georgia, arriving on the evening of May 25. He was almost immediately arrested but then released for lack of evidence. Reports of the invasion filled the newspapers, and López became a hero to many. Yet President Taylor remained adamant that the filibuster movement be stanched, and when López and his top aides arrived back in New Orleans, federal authorities again arrested them. By now, though, López was widely popular and supported. After three trials ended in hung juries, the government dropped the prosecutions in March 1851.

Unsurprisingly, the hung juries emboldened López, who began arranging yet another invasion, this one a two-pronged mission leaving from New Orleans and from New York City. By this point there had been a change in the White House; Taylor died in office on July 9, 1850, and was succeeded by Millard Fillmore. The new president also opposed filibuster expeditions, and in April 1851 federal marshals seized several ships in New York and New Jersey and arrested several hundred filibusters, as well as prominent leaders like John O'Sullivan, and the effort fizzled.[27]

Three months later, overblown reports arrived in New Orleans about an uprising in Cuba. López hastily put together another force, and on August 4 the steamship *Pampero* headed down the Mississippi from New Orleans for the Gulf of Mexico, but mechanical problems idled the ship, delaying its departure for a couple of days. It finally hit open water with a force of about four hundred men on August 6, planning to head for the east coast of Florida, near Jacksonville, to pick up additional men and weapons. On the way they made a planned stop at Key West, where fresh reports of a growing revolution and the *Pampero*'s dwindling coal supplies led López to decide to sail directly for Cuba lest the moment be lost.

Unfortunately for López, the reports were radically overblown. By the time he set sail the Spanish forces had quelled what had actually been a minor flare-up. On August 12, the *Pampero* dropped the invaders at El Morrillo in northwest Cuba. López left 120 men at the port, under the command of William L. Crittenden, to guard supplies. He himself led a force of about 280 men—a mix of Americans and Europeans, including a large group of Hungarians—ten miles inland to the village of Las Pozas. Spanish forces attacked the next dawn, cutting López and his men off from Crittenden, who loaded his men into four boats and set off for safety. They were intercepted two days later by a Spanish warship and ferried to Havana. The next morning Crittenden and all his men, most of whom were Americans, were executed by firing squad.

Meanwhile, López and his men took to the mountains. He had managed to persuade only a handful of Creoles and other Cubans to join him, and what began as an invasion became a game of cat and mouse. López's force traveled at night, hoping to avoid capture as they sought a route to the sea and escape—a task made more difficult by a bounty the authorities had placed on López's head, which meant that even encountering civilians exposed them to the risk of exposure and capture.

López presumed that the Spaniards would execute him and feared that his continued presence among his men further endangered them. During the night of August 24, the commander slipped off on his own, accompanied by his young servant. But they were discovered five days later by a small band of countrymen chasing the bounty with bloodhounds, who turned him in. (They received $1,000 each.) The men López had abandoned learned of a three-day *libero*—a promise of clemency if they surrendered—and gave themselves up. Most of those men were sentenced to ten years of hard labor in Spanish mines but were freed by the queen after President Millard Fillmore intervened through diplomatic channels.

López, though, was doomed. Soldiers took him to Havana, where on September 2 he was escorted to a square outside the city jail. Despite the early hour, scores of soldiers and townspeople surrounded an elevated scaffold upon which sat a garrote—a wooden chair backed by a thick vertical post holding a metal collar with an iron screw to adjust its circumference. A small group of black-clad priests carrying a black flag entered the square, followed by López, "dressed in a long white garment resembling a shroud, with a hood which covered his head but did not conceal his features." López climbed the scaffold, accompanied by the priests and a couple of military officers, and at the top knelt with the clerics for a prayer, then kissed a crucifix several times as he regained his feet. One of the military officers barked out a command to the crowd for silence, and López delivered a brief statement: "My countrymen, pardon me for the evil, if any, I have caused you. I have not intended any evil, but good, rather. I die for my beloved Cuba. Farewell!"[28]

López then sat on the garrote's chair. The executioner fixed the metal collar around his throat and began tightening the screw at the back of the post, slowly choking the life out of the man who had hoped so desperately to lead the island to independence.

———————

López's adventures made the newspapers, so it's likely Walker followed the developments from Marysville. His opinion of them likely echoed that of the *Crescent* back when he was editor: skeptical of López's cause but drawn to the romantic notion of people like him seeking their fortunes in foreign lands.

Walker watched that adventurist impulse play out closer to home, as French émigrés in California turned their eyes toward the region along the recently redrawn border with Mexico. The 1848 Treaty of Guadalupe Hidalgo that ended the Mexican-American War had ceded 525,000 square miles to the United States. Part of the new border was drawn along the Gila River north of Tucson, following the waterway west to the Colorado River. The treaty committed the United States to securing the mostly empty border region, but in spite of such US outposts as Fort Yuma on the Gila River, the territory proved too vast to control. And the Mexican government had neither the men nor the resources to properly protect the villages on its side of the border, so the region had become a lawless no-man's-land.

Into the void moved a number of French adventurers, beginning with Hippolyte du Pasquier de Dommartin, who sought land grants from the Mexican government for European settlements south of the Gila River. He hoped these settlements would serve as a barrier to further American expansionism and imperialism—including the American rail promoters who were contemplating routing a transcontinental line through the region. Though the settlements were never established, a book Dommartin published in France about his travels in California and Mexico whetted the appetites of others. Parisian companies popped up selling shares in gold mines in the Sierra Nevada and farm co-ops in the Central Valley, and raffles for free passage to San Francisco. That drew an influx of would-be miners and farmers, and San Francisco became home to a community of some six thousand French expatriates.[29]

The Mexican government saw the French as a safer bet to help pacify the border region than Americans, fearing that too many settlers with US connections might cost Mexico more territory. In 1851, Charles de Pindray, a French-born San Francisco hunter with dreams of grandeur, received permission from the Mexican consulate to establish a colony in the north of the Mexican border state of Sonora. He put together an expedition of eighty-eight fellow French San Franciscans to head for Guaymas, the Sonoran port midway up the Gulf of California. By spring, they were developing an agricultural settlement near the abandoned Cocóspera mission, about thirty miles southeast of Nogales. But support from the Sonoran state government dried up and Apache raiders mounted several attacks, managing to get away with the settlers' horses.

Feeling as though they had been left twisting in the wind by the Sonoran government, Pindray traveled to Ures, the state capital, to demand more support. The meeting went poorly. Pindray lost his temper, and the governor ordered him to settle his affairs and leave the country. But Pindray never made it. On the way back to Cocóspera, he was found dead in his room at an inn with a single gunshot to the head. Whether it was suicide or murder was never determined, but without him, the settlement fizzled, and many of the original settlers filtered back to San Francisco.[30]

A second French expedition took off in March 1852, led by Lepine de Sigondis, who sought to revive abandoned mines of the Gila and Santa Cruz Valleys, but that also failed within months. The third effort was led by Count Gaston de Raousset-Boulbon, described by the *Daily Alta* as "affable and courteous," who won a settlement grant from the Mexican government to try to revive what were known as the Arizona mines in Sonora. He and two hundred men arrived in Guaymas in June 1852, but the regional military commander, Miguel Blanco, was tiring of the adventurers from the north and suspicious of their aims. He made life difficult for them, reneging on promised support and interfering with efforts by the French to obtain the Mexican citizenship they had been promised. When Raousset-Boulbon discovered that Blanco had aligned himself with a rival firm seeking to reopen the same Arizona mines, he and his men revolted, marched on the military fort at Hermosillo, and, despite being vastly outnumbered, seized the town and sent Blanco and his forces fleeing into the desert.

But Blanco didn't go far. Mexican ranchers and friendly native tribes who feared that Raousset-Boulbon planned to seize control of the entire territory joined Blanco's small army. As they prepared to retake the city, Raousset-Boulbon fell seriously ill, and the French settlers lost their nerve—seventeen men had died and another two dozen had been wounded in taking Hermosillo, and the men who remained didn't relish another battle, this time against an even larger force. Placing Raousset-Boulbon in a litter, they took off for Guaymas, hoping to escape by sea, but were cut off by a large contingent of Native Americans and some soldiers, and after a brief standoff they surrendered. Blanco allowed them all to return home, most arriving back in San Francisco by December 1852.

The ongoing French settlement efforts intrigued Walker, whose life as a Marysville lawyer was for the most part an exercise in the mundane. (His mother died in Nashville on January 6, 1852, but no records suggest Walker returned home for the funeral.) A fellow lawyer there, future US Supreme Court justice Stephen J. Field, described Walker as "a brilliant speaker [who] possessed a sharp but not a very profound intellect. He often perplexed both court and jury with his subtleties, but seldom convinced either." Walker took on a wide range of clients and handled at least fifty-seven cases, winning twenty-four and losing sixteen; the rest were settled out of court or passed off to other attorneys. He tried one death penalty case against an accused thief—Walker lost and the thief was hanged—but all things considered it couldn't have been very satisfying work for someone drawn to the role of instigator.[31]

So in early 1852, Walker, Henry Watkins, a man named Frederic Emory, and several other men met in Auburn, California, to discuss an audacious plan: they, too, would seek Mexico's permission to establish a settlement in a mining region in northern Sonora. In return, they would protect Mexican villagers and ranchers from Apache and Comanche raiding parties and from marauding bands of Mexican and American outlaws. Emory and another man were dispatched to Guaymas to seek an audience with the governor, arriving about the same time as Raousset-Boulbon and his men. After a brief stay the emissaries returned to San Francisco, their plans abandoned since it seemed unlikely the Mexican government would give them permission to undertake, in essence, what the French were already undertaking. But with Raousset-

Boulbon's failure and return to San Francisco, Emory suggested to Walker that they revive their own plans.

Walker agreed. In June 1853, he, Watkins and Watkins's son, and one James L. Springer obtained passes from the Mexican consulate in San Francisco and set out for Guaymas. Their ship, the *Arrow*, bearing forty passengers, sailed south along the Baja Peninsula, rounded the tip, and headed north into the Gulf of California, arriving at Guaymas near sunset on June 30. But the consul in San Francisco had sent quiet advance word to the Mexican government that there were rumors Walker's visit was no idle trip by a curious tourist, that the slightly built American reportedly planned to build border settlements.

When port officials checked the passengers' paperwork, the captain of the port became suspicious of Walker's small group and sent off a message to the commanding general, Blanco. "Your Excellency will perceive," he wrote, "that there is undoubtedly an intention to invade this portion of the Mexican territory, and that one of the principal promoters of this invasion, the American citizen William Walker, has come as passenger in the brig *Arrow*."[32]

The governor of Sonora, Manuel Maria Gándara, ordered that Walker be detained in Guaymas and barred from moving farther inland. Over the next month Walker, Watkins, and the US consul in Guaymas, Juan A. Robinson, tried to change the governor's mind. Walker's physical appearance invited underestimation. Despite the hot summer sun and temperatures reaching one hundred degrees, Walker walked around wearing "a huge white fur hat, whose long nap waved with the breeze," a poorly tailored short-waisted blue coat with gold-colored buttons, "and a pair of gray, strapless pantaloons." He was "as unprepossessing-looking a person as one would meet in a day's walk. . . . Indeed, half the dread which the Mexicans had of filibusters vanished when they saw this, their Grand Sachem, such an insignificant-looking specimen."[33]

The Mexican authorities weren't dissuaded. Their experiences with Raousset, and Gándara's mistrust of the Americans' intentions, led to a hard line. At the end of July, Walker gave up and boarded a ship bound for San Francisco. But Walker had learned much during his month ashore. Just before he left, word came that

> Apaches had visited a country-house, a few leagues from Guaymas, murdering all the men and children, and carrying the women into a captivity worse than death. The Indians sent word that they would

soon visit the town "where water is carried on asses' backs"—meaning Guaymas; and the people of that port, frightened by the message, seemed ready to receive any one who would give them safety.

Several women, Walker wrote later, urged him to "repair immediately to California, and bring down enough Americans to keep off the Apaches."[34]

Those conversations, and the ease with which Raousset had taken Hermosillo (even though his settlement ultimately failed), left a deep impression on Walker. He believed "that a comparatively small body of Americans might gain a position on the Sonora frontier, and protect the families on the border from the Indians; and such an act would be one of humanity, no less than of justice, whether sanctioned or not by the Mexican Government."

Once back in San Francisco, Walker began to make plans in earnest. He would return to Sonora not as a putative settler, but as a conqueror.

5 | THE REPUBLIC OF SONORA RISES

IT TAKES A LOT OF WORK, and time, to organize an invasion. Walker, who remained a well-known figure in San Francisco, began holding small meetings with friends and acquaintances, seeking both investors and men. His ultimate plan: "to establish at as early a time as possible a military colony—not necessarily hostile to Mexico—on the frontier of Sonora, with a view of protecting that State from the Apaches." He worked quietly but not in secret—whispers of the pending invasion swirled through San Francisco as men expressed interest in joining what was being euphemistically portrayed as a mining expedition. The rumors even reached the pages of the local newspapers, with some editors excited about the prospect and others condemning filibusterism in general, asking rhetorically how Californians would respond if a band of marauding Mexicans crossed the border and set up their own country on American land. If Walker read any of the criticisms, they didn't deter him.[1]

Walker initially intended to mount his expedition by land, traveling southeastward through California until the expedition reached the border at the Gila River and then continuing on southward into Sonora. But he slowly realized it would be easier, faster, and probably cheaper to sail south around the tip of Baja and march inland from Guaymas.

And so Walker and his intimate circle of schemers began laying plans and raising money. They sold $500 bonds at half the face value for the Independence Loan Fund of the Republic of Sonora, for which the investor would receive one square league (nearly seven square miles) of land in the new country. In a city filled with gamblers and high-risk investors, it was

not difficult to attract speculators eager to buy up the paper dreams of a new nation; pro-slavery backers of southern expansion likewise invested in the hopeful republic's bonds. But the project required manpower as well as money, so Walker and the others also began tapping friends and acquaintances to sign up as settlers and to offer leads to other men who might want to join.[2]

Some of the sales pitches arose from chance encounters. Henry Watkins was walking down a San Francisco street when he encountered Charles Pancoast, an old friend. As Pancoast later recalled, "Watkins told me I was the very man he wanted." Explaining that he was second in command under Walker of a fifteen-hundred-man expedition, Watkins offered his friend a position as a lieutenant, telling him that Mexico protected Sonora so poorly that it would be easy to seize and defend territory, and that as "an officer and a man of intelligence" Pancoast would be in line for "an ample share in the distribution of the spoils." Pancoast, broke and with no prospects, was tempted, but ultimately said that he had been raised a Quaker and that "my training did not predispose me to go to War."[3]

Others, though, readily signed on. A laborer named William Spillen introduced his friend James Hamilton to Walker at a house "on Vallejo Street, just above Stockton. There was no assemblage there, there were only three or four persons present." It was in Walker's lodgings that the meeting occurred, and according to Hamilton his host cagily said only that he was organizing a mining outfit for a project in Sonora, with no mention of a fighting force or of seizing territory. Walker also didn't issue invitations, Hamilton said, he merely sketched out his putative plans and waited for those who were interested to ask if they could join. It was a strategic dodge. Though the Neutrality Act made it a crime to organize an invasion on American soil, Walker apparently believed that he couldn't be held in violation if the invaders volunteered unprompted.[4]

But Hamilton provided this account months later, under oath in a courtroom, so he was likely being less than fully honest about what he knew of the nature of the expedition to avoid charges himself. While Walker had no experience in organizing an army, he must have known enough about human nature to realize that he couldn't organize a very disciplined fighting force if it consisted of men who signed up for a mining job only to discover later that they stood a good chance of getting killed as they invaded a foreign country. In fact, Walker's true intentions were so well known the Mexican government asked the US minister in Mexico City about it, who then wrote to officials in San Francisco "to keep a sharp lookout for any expedition, and to prevent it if it should be attempted. . . . Any expedition of the kind will inevitably lead to hostilities between the two Republics."[5]

General Ethan Allen Hitchcock, commander of the US Army's Pacific Division based in San Francisco, also heard rumors of an expedition intended "to set up a revolutionary government" in Sonora. The grandson and namesake of Ethan Allen, the Revolutionary War hero from Vermont, Hitchcock was under orders from newly elected Democratic president Franklin Pierce, himself a brigadier general during the recent war with Mexico, to intervene in any filibustering operations that might arise on the West Coast. (Beyond

Walker, other organizers had designs on the Sandwich Islands, and political exiles from Ecuador were trying to mount a challenge to the new regime there.)[6]

Learning of the Republic of Sonora plans in mid-September 1853—about a month after Walker arrived back in San Francisco—Hitchcock asked the port collector to monitor ships for signs that they might be preparing for an invasion. A week later, Hitchcock noted in his diary that he had received a message from the collector that identified "the brig *Arrow* as being fitted up for a large number of passengers and as having arms on board. His men had seen suspicious parcels and packages apparently stowed away as if to hide them under the after cabin."

Walker had, in fact, hired the British-flagged ship, owned by merchant Henry Dreschfeldt, to ferry him and his men to Guaymas. Walker provisioned the ship with some $1,500 worth of supplies, including more than sixteen dozen cups and pans, eighteen casks and barrels of hardtack, and sixty pounds of potatoes. And there were stacks of firearms and ammunition. Hitchcock weighed his options with the US attorney in San Francisco, who told the general he had the authority to seize the ship. So Hitchcock did so. At 10:00 PM Friday, September 30, a squadron moved from the Presidio down Clay Street through the heart of San Francisco to the bay, then swarmed the dock and the *Arrow*, ousting the captain and his wife and others aboard the ship. Hitchcock turned the ship over to the US marshal, leaving a handful of soldiers aboard.[7]

The next day, San Franciscans of all stripes made for the foot of Clay Street to watch the spectacle of armed US soldiers with fixed bayonets guarding the dock and the deck of the *Arrow*. According to one newspaper account, "She lay quietly fastened to the wharf, her decks covered with wood and barrels, apparently of bread and pork, with an occasional one whose contents bore the marks and brands seemed intended to supply, should it be necessary, that kind of courage which has been attributed to the Dutch." In other words, whiskey casks.[8]

The takeover outraged Walker. His legal team, led by his old friend Edmund Randolph, sued in state superior court for the release of the *Arrow*, arguing that the army lacked the legal authority to take possession of a ship in port without evidence of a criminal act—and that loading it with weapons and mining equipment hardly qualified. Walker denied that he was planning an invasion or any other action that might run afoul of the Neutrality Act, and demanded the ship be released. Judge John Satterlee issued a writ ordering the San Francisco sheriff to seize the brig from the US marshal while the case proceeded, which pitted local officials against Hitchcock and the federal government.

The sheriff sent a small band of deputies to the dock and insisted the marshal turn the ship over; the marshal said he didn't have the authority. He then walked off the ship, leaving it solely in the hands of Hitchcock's troops, who told the sheriff to go talk to the general. At Hitchcock's office, the two men matched their authorities, the sheriff carrying Judge Satterlee's writ and the general displaying President Pierce's order to halt any foreign expeditions sailing from the West Coast. Hitchcock advised the sheriff "to think well of the matter, assuring him that I would hold the vessel against the State's authority." The sheriff, whose appointment to the office was to expire the next day, blinked, and did nothing.[9]

A couple of days later, the army officer aboard the *Arrow* "was privately informed that an attempt to take her out of his hands would be made on Tuesday morning by the men whom Walker had engaged for his expedition, whereupon he hauled her from the wharf and anchored her" out in the bay, where a boarding party would be more readily spotted and more easily thwarted.

But with more and more San Franciscans backing Walker's plan, the tide was turning against Hitchcock. The port collector now urged the general to order his men, in the event of an attack, to surrender the ship without violence. Hitchcock came to realize that the same strategy was supported by one of California's two US senators, William M. Gwin, a Tennessee native like Walker and a supporter of slavery. Hitchcock then consulted with the US attorney again, only to find that he too now thought the *Arrow* should be released. Hitchcock "lost all confidence" in the federal civilian officials, "who, I believed, had been let into the secret of the expedition after the arrest of the vessel." Hitchcock fumed. "I know I am right," he noted in his diary, "and that is enough for me."

Unfortunately for Hitchcock, the *Arrow* was far from the only ship in the bay. While the drama over the *Arrow* played out, Walker quietly made arrangements for another vessel, the *Caroline*, which was owned by the US consul in Guaymas, Juan Robinson, to take his men and weapons to Guaymas during the ship's regular trade run. The *Caroline* lay at anchor at Rincon Point, a safe distance from the piers, and after sunset on October 16, small boats began ferrying Walker's supplies, guns, and ammunition. A little after midnight, a police official named O'Regan and two other officers marched down the pier and interrupted the supply runs, seizing "18 cases of powder, 4 kegs of bar lead, a lot of percussion caps, about 300 pounds of balls, and a lot of [bullet] moulds."[10]

Fearing the seizure of the ammunition would lead to even more meddling by Hitchcock and his soldiers, Walker sent out word to his ragtag battalion that the *Caroline* would leave shortly, and men scurried to get from shore to ship. By the time a steam tug began towing the sailing ship to the open bay, where it could unfurl its sails and get away on its own, only about forty-five of Walker's men, many of them drunk, had managed to get aboard. While the *Caroline* carried some weapons and ammunition—a couple of four- or six-pound cannons, muskets, and carbines, "arms enough for the use of all the men"—the supplies lost due to O'Regan's interference and the seizure of the *Arrow* meant the expedition would be undermanned and underarmed. But Walker was determined, and in the darkness the *Caroline* cleared the Golden Gate and headed south.

James Hamilton wasn't the only one of Walker's men who later tried to claim that he knew nothing of the military nature of the adventure before the *Caroline* set sail. Still others, however, made it clear that only a fool could not have known what they were getting into. Henry A. Crabb, a boyhood friend of Walker's, had bought a ticket for the voyage and had been aboard the *Caroline* the night of its departure. "I intended to go on her as a passenger to Guaymas," he recalled. "I did not go because I understood before she sailed that she was to take down a party of men who had hostile intentions towards Sonora. I took my baggage off the vessel" and turned in his ticket for a refund.[11]

And if any of the men aboard the *Caroline* harbored real delusions about what Walker was planning, they were lost once the ship cleared the Golden Gate. "After we got out to sea . . . the men were drilled while aboard, at small arms," Hamilton later testified. "The drilling was almost an everyday occurrence for the first two or three days after we left the port. I did not see any mining implements on board."

The *Caroline* arrived at Cabo San Lucas near the tip of the Baja Peninsula—a trip of some thirteen hundred miles—on October 28. There Walker resupplied the ship with water and food, and, in his words, "we gained some little information of importance." Walker also made a strategic decision arising from the size of his landing force. "The smallness of their numbers" meant they would have trouble clearing Guaymas and moving inland to northern Sonora. So Walker changed targets to La Paz, the regional capital of Baja California, Sonora's western neighbor across the Gulf of California. He hoped to establish the Baja Peninsula as "a field of operations until they might gather strength for entering Sonora." As he later described it rather innocuously, "The men who sailed for Sonora were obliged to sojourn, for a time, on the peninsula."[12]

The *Caroline*, having sailed around the tip of Baja then north into the Gulf of California, anchored November 3 about six miles off La Paz, a dreary town of some six thousand people in small adobes and huts on a protected cove. The ship's captain, Howard Snow, was known in La Paz, and he escorted Walker and two of his men to the office of Governor Rafael Espinosa ostensibly as a courtesy call—but also to do a little reconnaissance. Espinosa was gracious and welcoming, and Walker concluded that the Mexicans had no idea what his intentions were and that La Paz was effectively defenseless. The *Caroline* moved closer to shore and anchored with the ship broadside to La Paz's port, with its two small cannons primed for action.[13]

Walker had named his force the First Independent Battalion, and gave himself the rank of colonel and ordained his follower Charles H. Gilman a lieutenant. Confident that taking La Paz would be easy, Walker ordered a squadron of a dozen men under Lieutenant Gilman to seize the town and the regional governor. His orders were carried out with no drama; Gilman and the men landed and walked to the governor's office, where, guns drawn, they captured Espinosa, struck the flag of Mexico, and replaced it with one Walker designed for his new republic: two horizontal red bars at the top and bottom, with two stars floating in the white field between. As the men aboard the *Caroline* saw the new flag rise on shore, they responded with a celebratory fusillade.

Most of the rest of the men moved to shore to secure the government buildings, where Walker began issuing decrees. Since redirecting his forces from Sonora to Baja, Walker's ambitions had grown. He now considered the Baja Peninsula not just a staging ground but the first part of his new republic, which he renamed the Republic of Lower California. From the governor's office, Walker issued his declaration of independence: "The Republic of Lower California is hereby Declared Free, Sovereign, and Independent, and all Allegiance to the Republic of Mexico is forever renounced," he declared, and to the rank of colonel Walker now gave himself the additional title of president.[14]

President Walker's first order of business was to organize his government. He appointed his friend and early conspirator Frederic Emory as secretary of state. He named John M. Jarnigan secretary of war, and Howard Snow secretary of a navy that didn't exist beyond Snow's *Caroline*. Walker also elevated Lieutenant Gilman to captain of the army, with John McKibben, Timothy Crocker, and Samuel Ruland as lieutenants. Ruland, though, was more than an army lieutenant—he took on the role of propagandist for the expedition, sending reports to the *San Diego Herald* and other US newspapers with updates on the early days of the new republic.

Walker also fortified the city. He took the governor's palace—"a fine though unprepossessing adobe situated on a beautiful plateau in the rear of the city"—as his own headquarters, and ordered field guns be positioned to cover the two main roads connecting the palace to the harbor. He ordered a general meeting of the residents, during which he demanded they turn over their firearms and ammunition. Americans living in the area brought in horses, though it's unclear whether they sought to join Walker or had been ordered to provide the animals. Many residents of La Paz, "apprehensive of some indefinite danger," simply left for their remote ranches.[15]

But Walker soon realized that remaining at La Paz left him vulnerable should the Mexican authorities decide to attack, and though he wasn't planning on losing, it would be a difficult place from which to flee. On November 6, he decided to move to Cabo San Lucas, where he would await reinforcements from San Francisco before proceeding with the invasion. Walker ordered his men and weapons back onto the *Caroline*, but as they prepared to leave, a Mexican-flagged passenger ship entered the harbor. Not realizing that his vessel was now in putatively foreign waters, the captain welcomed a boarding party of the Americans, who quickly learned that the passengers included Juan Clímaco Rebolledo, who was coming to La Paz to relieve Espinosa as governor. Rebolledo was summarily arrested and taken to join Espinosa as a prisoner aboard the *Caroline*.

There had been virtually no resistance from the people of La Paz to the city's sudden change in government, but that didn't mean they were content to allow their city to remain in the hands of armed interlopers, especially now that the invaders had decamped to their ship. When Walker sent a detachment ashore under Emory's command to gather firewood, an armed contingent of soldiers and townsmen mounted an ambush. It was led by Lieutenant Manuel Pineda Muñoz, who had been key in keeping Baja out of American hands during the Mexican-American War, and it sparked the first meaningful combat in Walker's so-far-bloodless invasion.[16]

Exchanging fire and burning village huts as they retreated, the American wood-gatherers made it back to the ship without injury, where they briefed Walker, Ruland reported to the *San Diego Herald*. Walker ordered the small cannons onboard the ship to be fired at the town, "which was kept up until Col. Walker landed with thirty men, when the fighting became general." They exchanged gunfire for about ninety minutes before the Mexicans retreated.

> The enemy's loss was six or seven killed, and several wounded. Our men did not so much as receive a wound, except from cacti, while pursuing the enemy through the chaparral, in the rear of the town. Thus ended the battle of La Paz, crowning our efforts with victory, releasing Lower California from the tyrannous yoke of declining Mexico, and establishing a new Republic.

Within hours of the skirmish, Walker and his men, with their two hostages, sailed for Cabo San Lucas.[17]

The new president continued to issue decrees. On November 7, apparently while still at sea, he abolished all tariffs within the Republic of Lower California, covering the Baja Peninsula and Sonora. And rather than create a body of laws and regulations, Walker announced that "the Civil Code of Practice of the State of Louisiana shall be the rule of decision and the Law of the Land in all the Courts of the Republic to be hereafter organized." Walker could have adopted the laws and constitution of California, with which he was as well versed as the Louisiana codes. But there was a crucial difference between the two that made the Louisiana codes more appealing: they allowed slavery, and the California codes did not.

Some observers later argued that this was an incidental distinction—that Walker was in fact opposed to slavery and that expanding its reach into Mexico could not have been part of his original plan. But an editorial in the *Daily Alta* offered a compelling argument to the contrary:

> Mr. Walker has lived in Louisiana, and is a man of intelligence and a lawyer, and, of course, knows that that code recognizes and protects and legislates for slavery. . . . By Walker's decree, slavery is made quite as lawful in Lower California as in Louisiana. It is entirely useless to say, in the face of this fact, that Walker is opposed to slavery. He expressly sanctions it by adopting unchanged the law of Louisiana, though four lines in his "decree" would have sufficed to have abrogated so much of the code as provides for or permits slavery.

The editors granted that not all of Walker's men may have known that they were engaged to establish a slave state but insisted that "persons acquainted with Walker and the expedition say that the purpose was adopted long before sailing from this port, to proclaim the code of Louisiana, and the legalization of slavery in such a vast territory could be no secondary purpose."[18]

No surviving documents detail whether Walker had an evolution of thought about slavery. Though he was a southerner by birth and his parents had apparently owned several slaves, he himself had no practical interest in slaveholding; no records indicate that Walker himself had ever owned a slave, or a farm or plantation built on slavery. As the editor of the *Daily Crescent*, Walker had defended the institution in the states where it existed, but that seemed rooted in his view of democracy and the right of the people of individual states to determine their slaveholding status. He didn't consider that this right of self-determination ought to extend to the slaves themselves, and his writings on slavery never engaged with the basic injustice and inhumanity of the practice. It appears most likely that he simply took it as a given, a function of presumptive white supremacy, and saw no problem with incorporating slavery into his plans to gain the backing of southern investors. He was more interested in the adventure, it seems, than in the issue itself.

It was disingenuous, then, that Walker characterized his advance on Mexican territory as a humanitarian effort intended to protect those already dwelling there. He described living conditions in the region—conditions he had not witnessed prior to his invasion—as "a disgrace to the civilization of the continent" and "more under the dominion of the Apaches than under the laws of Mexico; and the contributions of the Indians were collected with greater regularity and certainty than the dues to the tax-gatherer." That lawlessness, Walker argued, "furnished the best defense for any American aiming to settle there without the formal consent of Mexico . . . and justified by the plea that any social organization, no matter how secured, is preferable to that in which individuals and families are altogether at the mercy of savages."[19]

Walker may well have been propelled by a romantic notion that his invasion and new government would be the savior of the oppressed. San Francisco historian Frank Soule wrote that Walker was considered to

> be personally a brave, highly educated, and able man, whatever may be thought of his discretion and true motives of conduct in the expedition. He seems to have taken a high moral and political position in the affair, though his professions were peculiar and their propriety not readily admitted by downright sticklers for equity and natural justice. A few of his coadjutors were perhaps also men of a keen sense of honor, who forgot, or heeded not, in the excitement of the adventure, the opinions of mere honest men upon the subject. But the vast majority of Walker's followers can only be viewed as desperate actors in a true filibustering or robbing speculation. The good of the wretched and Apache-oppressed Sonorians was not in their thoughts. If they succeeded, they might lay the sure foundations of fortunes; if they failed, it was only time and perhaps life lost. In either event, there was a grand excitement in the game.[20]

It's notable that a decade earlier, Walker had routinely touched on political philosophy in his letters from Europe to his friend John Lindsley. But now, in establishing a new nation, the amateur political philosopher didn't craft a founding document of principles upon which his nation would stand. He simply borrowed Louisiana's legal system, and offered no political structure for governance or elections. He, in effect, was the state—such as it existed, and for as long as it might last.

The *Caroline* arrived in Cabo San Lucas the day after Walker issued his proclamations. The men set up camp at the edge of the town and maintained a steady guard, fearing an attack from the villagers. Word also reached the president that another veteran of the Mexican-American War, a Baja native named Manuel Márquez de León, was organizing a militia of ranchers and farmhands to oust the invaders. What Walker didn't know, but probably presumed, was that the Mexican government was on alert, and regional commanders and governors, upon hearing what transpired at La Paz, began fortifying their villages. Authorities in Guaymas expelled several Americans, erected a mud wall around the town, and augmented the defense force with several hundred armed men, including members of the Yaqui tribe from Hermosillo and other outlying communities. The authorities forced Juan Robinson, US consul and owner of the *Caroline*, to pay $10,000 toward the arming of the city, and directed all foreigners to join a special militia to fight the filibusters should they land—an order the foreigners rejected, fearing they would be used as nothing more than human shields.[21]

Another threat to the Americans loomed with the arrival offshore of an armed Mexican revenue cutter, the *Garrea*. Walker's expected reinforcements from San Francisco still had not caught up with him, so he ordered his new flag raised over their camp, and had men hoist flags over two unmanned ships anchored nearby to give the illusion of a larger, and seagoing, fighting force. The Mexican ship sailed off, and Walker decided to move his capital once more, this time to Ensenada, a coastal town on the Pacific side of the Baja Peninsula. Located about fifty miles south of the US border, it was the northernmost village of any real size on the peninsula, which meant it was the closest point to receive reinforcements, weapons, and supplies from San Francisco. It also provided an exit route if Walker needed it, as well as a spot from which he could begin to secure control of Baja and push into northern Sonora, with the Pacific at his back and the US border at his side.[22]

The *Caroline* reached Ensenada around November 30, 1853, and Walker and his men went ashore to explore the village. There wasn't much to it—a bunch of huts clustered around a protected cove and only one adobe house, the home of wealthy rancher Francisco Gastelum. Walker seized Gastelum's home for his own residence and headquarters, the foot-thick adobe walls and internal storeroom offering protection from gunfire, if not cannons. Situated on a rise about thirty feet above the sea at the start of foothills leading inland, the site was vulnerable to attack—the foothills gave attackers the advantage of elevation, and low sand hillocks near the adobe provided cover for the final approach.[23]

Walker, ever conscious of his need to keep whetting the appetites of fellow adventurers, had written a missive during the voyage to Ensenada explaining what he was up to and why, and he posted it upon arriving in the village. A copy also appeared in the *San Diego Herald*. Walker blamed Mexico for creating the conditions under which he felt he had no other option than to invade. The Treaty of Guadalupe Hidalgo had, Walker argued, effectively "cut off . . . the territory . . . from all direct communication with the rest of Mexico." Since the signing, "the central authorities have manifested little or no interest in the affairs of the California peninsula." Beyond the geographical separation caused by the Gulf of California, "the moral and social ties which bound it to Mexico have been even weaker and more dissolute than the physical. Hence, to develop the resources of California, and to effect a proper social organization therein, it was necessary to make it independent." There were resources to exploit, too, he added, but that required "good government and sure protection to labor and property," a role political leaders in Mexico City had either been unable to provide or chose not to.

> The Territory, under Mexican rule, would forever remain wild, half savage and uncultivated, covered with an indolent and half civilized people, desirous of keeping all foreigners from entering the limits of the State. When the people of a Territory fail almost entirely to develop the resources nature has placed at their command, the interests of civilization require others to go in and possess the land. They cannot, nor should they be allowed to play the dog in the manger, and keep others from possessing what they have failed to occupy and appropriate.

And because the Mexican government "has not performed any of the ordinary duties of a government towards the people of Lower California," the government could be seen to have abandoned the region and its people. "Leaving it as it were, a waif on the waters, Mexico cannot complain if others take it and make it valuable."[24]

While Walker's supporters boasted that the filibusters received a warm and thankful reception from the residents of La Paz and Ensenada, the opposite was actually, and not surprisingly, the case. The locals had lived difficult and tenuous lives before the invaders arrived, contending with freely roaming gangs of bandits and raids by indigenous tribes. That wasn't much different from the strong-arm tactics of Walker's men, who likewise pillaged as they desired, angering the people Walker considered his new subjects.

The *Caroline* remained at anchor with a handful of men aboard, along with the two Guaymas governors, still held prisoner. After setting up his command post in Gastelum's adobe, Walker interviewed ranch workers and others in the village to get a sense of where he might find supplies—including horses—for his men. The best source, he learned, was the ranchero of Don Juan Bandini, one of the wealthiest landowners in Baja. He lived part time in San Diego, where he had been justice of the peace when the area was under Mexican control. Within hours, Frederic Emory led a detachment of more than a dozen men on the fifteen-mile march northeast to Bandini's complex at Guadalupe, arriving in the middle of the night. A few of the men, including Emory, pounded on the door of the main house, forcing Bandini's son, Don José María, and other inhabitants from their beds, while the rest of the marauders swarmed the outbuildings, rousting the ranch hands and forcing their way into the stable, where they collected fifteen of Bandini's horses. According to Bandini himself, "The soldiers in the command betook themselves to the place where the saddles, ropes, and other articles used by the vaqueros were kept, and took whatever they wanted, preventing the ranch hands from mounting their horses and employing such force that the vaqueros had to yield." Bizarrely, Emory filled out a receipt for the stolen items, which included several sides of beef, and left it with Bandini's son. Emory and his men rode the stolen horses back to Ensenada.[25]

Next Walker sent Emory and four other men to San Diego; from there Emory would travel to San Francisco to rally more recruits. Acting on additional tips from locals, Walker sent a second detachment to La Grulla, a dozen miles southeast of Ensenada near the abandoned mission of Santo Tomas, to raid the ranch of the Melendrez family. As with the raid at Guadalupe, Walker's men used surprise to their advantage and quickly routed the few inhabitants. They took two prisoners, twenty horses, more fresh beef, and other stolen provisions with them—but they failed to discover Antonio Maria Melendrez, who hid inside one of the ranch buildings when he heard the marauders arrive. Melendrez, though only twenty-three, had been a persistent thorn in the side of Mexico's central government as it struggled to maintain control over Baja. Just the year before, he had been part of an unsuccessful mini revolt against government troops, and, despite his young age, he commanded both fear and respect among his fellow landowners.[26]

Walker's men had barely left La Grulla when Melendrez emerged from hiding, hopped on a horse, and sped to Santo Tomas, about five miles away, to alert Luis del Castillo Negrete, the governor of Baja, who was headquartered there. Negrete quickly put together a small force of men, who took off in pursuit of the horse thieves. None of the Mexicans understood at this point exactly whom they were chasing beyond some American bandits. They caught up with Walker's men, who apparently were taking their time and, according to some accounts, adding to their pillage at houses they encountered on the way. It's unclear how the ambush unfolded, but it ended with one of Walker's men—Bernard McCormick, assigned the rank of private—killed, two captured, and the rest running for Ensenada without the stolen horses and provisions.[27]

The captured men, under interrogation, provided Melendrez and Negrete with the first inkling that they weren't just running down some American horse thieves. Learning that they were now living in Walker's Republic of Lower California, Melendrez and Negrete assembled a resistance force of sixty or so soldiers, ranchers, and local Native Americans—most likely from the Kumeyaay tribe. Two days after ambushing Walker's men, they attacked Ensenada in broad daylight. After a brief exchange of gunfire that did little to slow the advance, Walker's sentries retreated and joined the rest of the expedition inside the adobe. Melendrez's men surrounded the complex, seized the horses stolen from Bandini's ranchero, and scuttled the small boat the Americans used to get back and forth to *Caroline*. Then the Mexican force attacked from the front, some of the men advancing on foot, others on horseback, but they were quickly cut down with blasts of grapeshot from Walker's cannons. Repelled, Melendrez and his men slipped back behind cover as the gunfire ebbed. Melendrez had suffered a dozen or more fatalities; Walker lost one man—Lieutenant John McKibben, shot through the chest—and eight others were wounded, including Captain Charles Gilman, who was shot in the leg, a "wound from which he suffered long and cruelly before the amputation of the limb." As night fell, Melendrez established an encampment in a nearby grove of willows and kept his men in position around the adobe.[28]

The attack became a siege, with occasional potshots by each side. Melendrez's plan was patience. Supplies inside the adobe, including water, quickly ran low, and the well was outside the walls, unreachable without drawing a fusillade from Melendrez's men. One day passed, then another, and another, with gunfire exchanged intermittently. No clear count exists of casualties among the Mexican fighters. Melendrez and Negrete tried two or three times to move men closer to the adobe under a flag of truce, to try to persuade Walker to surrender and to get a better view of how his men were arrayed, but none of the efforts led to much.

Captain Howard Snow had watched from the deck of the *Caroline* as the initial attack unfolded and through the first couple of days of the siege. His captives—the two Mexican governors—quietly worked on Walker's navy secretary, explaining that Snow himself was in grave danger. Walker was pinned down and done. Surely, the Mexican government had troops and ships moving toward Ensenada. The *Caroline* would be no match for an attack by trained, experienced soldiers ashore and sailors on warships. Convinced, Snow abruptly weighed anchor and sailed the *Caroline* out of Ensenada toward Cabo San Lucas, where he would free the two governors. In the process, he stranded Walker and his men.[29]

On the third day of the siege, Baja native José Matías Moreno arrived. Moreno had been politically connected in California before the United States took it over, and he still lived in San Diego. He told Negrete that the American military command in his city would be willing to send soldiers to help roust the filibusters. The United States had no intention of sending a military force into Mexico without a formal request from the Mexican government, so Moreno was either engaging in wishful thinking or had been misinformed. Negrete, though, took the suggestion at face value, gathered together some of his men, and left for the border, reducing the forces that held Walker at bay—though Walker had no way of knowing this. And even if he had, a coordinated rush from the adobe into the open to break the siege would have been foolhardy, especially since the *Caroline* was gone, meaning they'd have to fight their way to the border by land. So Walker sat and hoped the long-awaited reinforcements from San Francisco would arrive while Walker still had his ostensible country to defend.

Weather in Baja is generally predictable—warm and dry, except for the rainy season that begins in November or early December. It was right on time in 1853: on December 14, a week into the siege, clouds moved in and the skies opened up. Walker and his men were snug and dry inside the adobe. Melendrez's men, though, had only thin tents to protect them, and open fires that smoked and hissed in the rain. They were wet, and cold, and bored.

Walker felt the advantage. He put together a unit of twenty men—more than half of his remaining fighting force—under Lieutenant Crocker and sent them quietly out of the adobe in the dark of night to surround Melendrez's camp "in the bullrushes and willows." The unit found their enemies "in a torpid state from the cold, and somewhat sleepy from the effects of long watching and much unaccustomed exercise." Crocker gave the signal to attack, and the Americans opened fire as they ran into the camp, sending the Mexicans scurrying, many without their weapons. It was over in minutes. Several bodies of the Mexican fighters lay on the ground; two of Walker's men were wounded. They seized what usable items had been left behind, including food, a field cannon, forty rifles, two dozen horses and tack, and "articles of camp furniture and cooking utensils, and a number of bows and arrows of Indians who had been induced to join the ranks of the peninsulars, through fear, favor, or hope of reward."[30]

Negrete, meanwhile, finally figured out that the US military was not going to send troops, and he returned to Guadalupe, where Melendrez found him. Negrete turned the surviving fighting force over to Melendrez and left for San Diego and eventually San Francisco to try to verify that Walker's actions were not being carried out with the US government's support. Negrete's men quickly deserted Melendrez, leaving the freshly minted commander without troops to command. Over the next couple of weeks, though, he traveled through the interior of the peninsula, rallying more of his countrymen to help him drive the Americans from Baja.[31]

Slowly, a new resistance force came together.

6 | THE REPUBLIC OF SONORA FALLS

FREDERIC EMORY HAD RIDDEN to San Diego and there boarded the steamship *Goliah*, arriving in San Francisco on December 7 with two other Walker men. Emory's mission, as secretary of state, was to spread the word of the new country, raise money, and seek more recruits. Henry Watkins arrived a few days later, having been dispatched from Baja as well at some unknown point.

Newspapers noted Emory's arrival and the drumming up of adventurers. "Squads of persons might be seen at all hours of the day and night, collected in the streets and bar rooms, discussing the prospects of the expedition and various persons connected with it," the *Daily Alta* noted. A recruiting office, marked by the flapping two-star, two-stripe flag of the new country, opened at the corner of Kearny and California Streets.

> All kinds of extravagant predictions were made of the unexampled prowess and great exploits of the outlaws; recruits were to be found in any number; it was reported that a number of men of capital had engaged in the enterprise, and there was a fine prospect that the city would be to a considerable extent cleansed of her idlers, disappointed politicians, gamblers, and shoulder-strikers.[1]

Walker's old foe General Hitchcock heard the rumors that another ship was being prepared to join Walker but "had no certain intelligence of the fact." And even if he had details down to the hour of departure, he doubted he would be able to stop it as he had the *Arrow*, given the mood around the city. Even the state court had proven filibuster friendly, ordering Hitchcock to release the *Arrow* after the US attorney who confirmed the general's authority to seize it changed his position and testified that the federal government had no reason to do so. If Walker's people readied a new ship, Hitchcock realized, "I could not have seized the vessel without having a force sufficient to hold her against the more than probable decision of a state court" that he must again release it. The general decided it made no sense to intervene. In fact, he had already submitted a request to be relieved of his command, planning to travel to the Far East, and would soon be replaced.[2]

Thus, with no opposition before them and much of the city behind them, the second expedition came together quickly. Five days after Emory's arrival, the bark *Anita* was ready to sail. Although Hitchcock seemed to have stood down, Watkins had no idea whether US troops would try to keep them from leaving port. So he finalized the timing and other details surreptitiously, and planned to leave as one might organize a jailbreak.

Late on the evening of December 12, a heavy squall passed over the city. The clouds then separated to bathe San Francisco in the glow of a near-full moon. According to a later account by one of Walker's supporters, William V. Wells:

> About half way down from Front Street a door was thrown open, and, as if by magic, drays and carts made their appearance. Files of men sprung out and passed quantities of powder from the store, besides ammunition of all kinds. A detachment stood guard the while in utter silence, and the movements were made with such celerity, that the observer could scarcely perceive where and how the articles made their appearance.

It looked like "some smuggling scene in a drama," but one that quickly attracted a crowd of both the curious and the committed.[3]

Relative quiet gave way, under the influence of beer and whiskey, to a lively scene. "As the moment of sailing approached, the confusion and noise increased, and all the efforts of officers to keep silence were unavailing. Several of the men were drunk, and gave vent to the exuberant spirits by songs, and denunciations upon the 'Greasers' who had made the reported attack upon the party then in the Southern country." The "reported attack" was the pursuit and ambush of Walker's men after they robbed the Melendrez family's ranchero at La Grulla, a response that somehow, by the time the story finished ricocheting around San Francisco, had become an affront to Americans and to white men.

Around one o'clock in the morning, the steam tug *Thomas Hunt* approached the pier and affixed itself to the *Anita*, then slowly towed the adventurer-laden ship away from the pier. "Nothing could now restrain the men, and loud and repeated cheers rose from the vessel, which were heartily responded to from the wharf. The little fleet went up the bay to get clear of the shipping, and then turning, glided past the silent city with the strength of the ebb tide." As they steamed through the ship-choked bay, two small cannons and several other weapons were transferred from the *Thomas Hunt* to the *Anita*. When they reached the point where the *Anita* could unfurl its sails and navigate freely, the *Thomas Hunt* cast off clumsily, tearing away the *Anita's* port-side bulwarks, the wooden planking above the gunwales that helps protect the deck from waves and the sailors from going overboard. There was little to be done about it now, so the *Anita* pressed on toward the open ocean.

The *Anita* had bigger problems than a busted bulwark. Emory and Watkins had put together a body of about two hundred men ready to fight, but few of them knew how to sail. Only two men aboard the ship—the captain and the first mate—had significant experience. If that weren't enough, one recruit recalled that "almost all on board were more or less drunk," and the seas were running high. Once the filibusters cleared the Golden Gate, they encountered rough waters and a brewing storm. The missing bulwarks let the waves wash over the deck "and the greater part of the stores being on deck, and but poorly secured, with every roll casks, barrels, and boxes would slide about." The men were housed in steerage, along with "several thousand pounds of gunpowder, and yet the men were going about in the most careless manner with lighted segars [*sic*], pipes, and candles." The storm intensified, and the winds shredded a couple of the sails "as there were not sober hands enough to furl them." The discovery of water sloshing in the hold sent a panic through the men (it proved to be minor, just some deck wash making its way below), and when the ship "gave an awful lurch," two or three men and about twenty barrels of supplies disappeared into the sea, the waters too rough to try a rescue.[4]

Fear ran through the ship like a virus. Some of the men threatened the captain to force him to head for shore, but others pulled revolvers to insist the *Anita* continue on to Ensenada as planned. "The tumult gradually subsided, liquor or seasickness soon overcame most of them, and the decks were nearly deserted." By morning, the storm had passed and the sea had settled. Some of the men repaired what damage they could. The ship's galley was too small to prepare food for more than a third of the men at a time, so cooking and eating occurred in disgruntled shifts, keeping the galley busy nearly around the clock.

The *Anita* finally arrived at Ensenada on December 20, less than a week after Walker's men broke Antonio Melendrez's siege on the adobe, which Walker had renamed Fort McKibben after the first of his officers to be killed in battle. The new recruits had brought fresh weapons and ammunition but few basic provisions. So Fort McKibben suddenly had scores more mouths to feed. The only solution was more pillaging, and occupation.

Walker sent sixty-five men under Captain George R. Davidson to Governor Negrete's command center at Santo Tomas. They found it undefended and seized it without a fight. In his brag-filled reports north, Samuel Ruland reported that the wealthy ranchero owners, frustrated with lack of protection by the Mexican government, had fully embraced the new republic. He claimed that the locals offered Walker and his men free food and other supplies but that the self-proclaimed president had turned them down, his "forces now having abundant supplies from the confiscated property of the outlaw Melendrez." Ruland wrote that Walker intended to pay for "all supplies received from friendly inhabitants," and Walker issued a decree "condemning to death all persons guilty of plundering the property of the friendly inhabitants." In other words, ranch owners who opposed Walker would find their property pillaged, while those who acquiesced would be protected.[5]

But it was a weak protection. Walker issued edicts and talked about shielding the locals against marauding Indians and bandits, but he had limited control over his own men, many of whom robbed at will. Pillaged landowner Don Juan Bandini accused them of

> taking what they required or wanted, and neither Walker's own
> promises, which were made in his proclamation, nor the papers of
> safe-conduct given to several persons, were sufficient to insure safety
> or prevent abuses of power. Houses were broken into, families were
> forced to do the bidding of the invaders, and horses and saddles
> were taken from passing civilians. In short, the marauders were

behaving as though they were the absolute masters of the country. Heaven help anyone who resisted or in any way refused to do what they commanded, for then the fury of the entire company was vented on him.

In fact, Davidson's squadron stole seven hundred head of cattle, sheep, and horses and $2,000 from a church and a ranchero they ransacked.[6]

By early January 1854, Walker had some three hundred men under his command. He issued fresh decrees on January 18, changing the name of his dominion from the Republic of Lower California to the Republic of Sonora and dividing it into two states: Sonora and Lower California (the Baja Peninsula). While his headquarters remained at Ensenada, he established two outposts, at La Grulla and San Domingo. He tried to organize the men into a better-trained and better-disciplined fighting force, though none of the leaders had much in the way of military experience themselves. Walker himself had a habit of addressing the men with his arms folded across his chest, his eyes cast downward. Still, the men were willing to follow his orders.

Work crews repaired damage to the adobe from the siege and erected structures to accommodate the new troops. Others maintained the stolen livestock and replenished basic provisions during regular forays into the countryside. The Republic announced that communications could be sent to them in care of the *San Diego Herald* newspaper office, where their "special messenger"—a man named James Allen—would make a weekly stop to collect incoming mail and to dispatch documents, proclamations, and Ruland's glowing reports of life in the new republic for the consumption of American newspaper readers. Thus news of Walker's campaign traveled far, reaching the New York City papers.[7]

Despite the shining veneer Ruland tried to put on the expedition's efforts, it was crumbling badly from within, a function of the sorts of men Walker had accepted as recruits and the challenges of occupying a place with scant resources. While they could steal cattle and thus have beef, it was insufficient to fully feed the men, who wearied of eating "fried beef for breakfast, stewed beef for dinner, boiled beef for supper, burnt corn for coffee, parched corn for bread." Echoing the problems with the *Anita*'s galley, Fort McKibben lacked enough pots and kettles to cook for scores of men simultaneously, so "the principal occupation of the camp, from sunrise to sunset, was cooking the beef and corn and corn and beef." And despite a promise that all would be provisioned equally, Walker's recruits discovered that their commander and his officers had freshly made soft bread and other more palatable items on their tables. The camp awoke one morning to find that persons unknown had dismantled the oven in which the officers' bread was baked.[8]

Pay, from four to twelve dollars a day depending on rank, came in the form of scrip issued by the Republic of Sonora, which for the time being was worthless. Even so, the men harbored visions of riches, not just by cashing in once the new nation was firmly established but also by plundering the countryside. But that wasn't enough to cement loyalty within an army of opportunists. Desertions increased. Some men fell sick, and some died. Tensions came to a head later in January when a detachment of men under Captain Davidson returned from a pillaging run with fifty to sixty horses and mules, which Walker promptly confiscated and dispersed among the whole force—angering the thieves, who thought they should have been allowed to keep the horses for themselves.

Mutiny was in the air. Several men approached Walker and announced that they intended to leave. The president tried to talk them out of it, at first cajoling and then threatening by reminding them that desertion was a capital offense. Some of Davidson's men commandeered horses they had stolen from the rancheros and planned to ride them back to the United States. Fearing the imminent collapse of his expedition, Walker, who had no experience organizing a group of men, let alone running an army, ordered an all-hands muster to try to mute the discontent.

Standing in the afternoon sun, Walker reminded the men of why they had come from San Francisco in the first place and of the noble pursuit in which they were engaged. He concluded by saying any man who wished to leave could do so, and that those who wished to stay must swear "before Almighty God, to stand by" Walker "through weal or woe" as they worked together for the moment "when the two stars" of the Republic flag "should float in triumph on the walls of Guaymas." If Walker thought his speech and ultimatum would persuade the men to stick by him, he misjudged. While many took the oath immediately, forty-three men—about a quarter of the entire remaining force—decided they'd rather go home.[9]

Walker gave the men two hours to pack their belongings and leave, and ordered them to turn over their rifles, even though the men had brought the weapons with them from San Francisco. Recalled one such deserter, "I objected to this in vain, and at last surrendered it, first, however, clandestinely taking out the sight and removing the screw which held on the lock; so that I do not expect they are much richer for the robbery." Most of the deserters, though, refused to surrender their rifles, setting out on foot as a group, with their weapons but no other provisions. They got only about a hundred feet from the fort when a contingent of Walker loyalists on horseback, under the command of a man named Douglas, cut them off and demanded once more that they turn over the guns. The men refused; Douglas pulled his sidearm and threatened to shoot anyone who didn't comply. The deserters replied by pulling their own sidearms or leveling rifles at Douglas and the loyalists. Back at the fort, the men assigned to guard duty were ordered to open fire on the deserters, but they refused. "Corporal [Carroll] Mullone was the first to declare that he would not shoot down men with whom he had just shaken hands. Sergeant Barstow also refused. Thereupon the guard dispersed and returned in confusion to their quarters, where Mullone announced his intention of" joining the deserters.

The men strode off. A few minutes later, Walker went after them, accompanied by some of his officers. The president overtook the group and asked the men to stop and listen to him. Walker pointed out that with their departure, his army was now reduced to 140 men, and "that he did not want their arms as a gift, but as a means of defense for those who really needed them, and who, without them, would be exposed to the savage vengeance of the Mexicans." Walker also urged the men to return to the fort to gather some rations before their long overland journey. The men refused to return, but several gave up their rifles. Then the party moved on, walking for four days to San Diego, where one of the men "sold my revolver, which put me in funds again" sufficient to buy sea passage back to San Francisco. He arrived there four days later, broke but alive.

———————

After the mass defection, and a less-noticed slow dribble of individual departures, Ruland sought to undermine the credibility of the deserters. He spoke positively of the fighters who remained, telling the *San Diego Herald* that "our men are in good health" and engaged in regular training and breaking of wild horses, while "topographical parties" were busy surveying roads and mapping out future military outposts to secure Walker's new domain. And for the men who had departed, Ruland offered only scorn:

> We have all heard here, with much regret, that a few trifling and worthless men, whom we have been compelled to get rid of, have, by their acts between this place and San Diego, endeavored to injure us. Such fellows cannot injure us worse than pretending to belong to us. No man other than a deserter, or one expelled, goes from here without some written evidence of his connection and position with us.[10]

This disinformation campaign was vital to Walker's success—he needed to recruit more men, and if deserters spread the word about the sorry state of the expedition, it would undermine those efforts. Recruitment meetings were still generating excitement in places such as Stockton, California, and the familiarly named Sonora, a small village in the gold rush country of the Sierra Nevada foothills. Walker's pitch proved especially appealing to failed miners—a rough-edged bunch looking around for another chance at adventure and riches.

In reality, however, things in the Republic of Sonora were not going smoothly. A squad sent out to loot provisions from ranches confronted a farmer named Don José Sáez and demanded he turn over corn to feed the troops. Sáez, who had been robbed by Walker's men before, refused, arguing that after the earlier confiscations he barely had enough corn left to feed his own large family. Walker's men began seizing the corn by force. Sáez pulled out a pistol and fired a single inconsequential shot, and in response the raiders shot him in the forehead. Remarkably, the bullet glanced off his skull, stunning Sáez but otherwise leaving him unharmed. Walker's men then tied him up, loaded the corn, all of Sáez's liquor, and other items from his house into a cart, and headed back to Ensenada, taking Sáez with them.

At Fort McKibben, Walker pardoned Sáez for the crime of defending himself and his family from the marauding soldiers of the Republic of Sonora. Bizarrely, two of Walker's top officers, Major Timothy Crocker and Lieutenant Joseph Ruddach, squabbled over Walker's decision, and argument turned to affront. One demanded satisfaction from the other, leading to a duel with six-shooters at ten paces. Both men emptied their chambers; Crocker suffered wounds to the side, an arm, and a leg, while Ruddach took a single bullet to the right foot. Miraculously, both survived, but they wound up in the makeshift base hospital together.[11]

In late January, Walker began making plans to shift the camp about forty miles south to San Vicente, a small town in a river valley "where the country was more favorable to the subsistence of the troops." But before he could move, two American ships anchored off Ensenada. One was the *Columbus*, a mail steamer. The second was the US sloop of war *Portsmouth*, under Captain Thomas A. Dornin. The latter vessel, manned by more than two hundred sailors and marines and outfitted with twenty cannons, had been dispatched to watch for Walker and interrupt the arrival of fresh recruits. For three days Dornin spotted someone at the adobe waving a white flag, which he ignored until he wondered whether the signal meant Walker and his men "might be desirous to quit the country and give up their lawless undertaking." He sent a boat ashore under command of Lieutenant James H. Spotts, who fought through rough waves to the beach. A sentry escorted Spotts and a couple of his men to Walker's office—a tile-roofed shed attached to the adobe and fronted by a canvas screen. The president of the Republic of Sonora did not cut an imposing figure. According to one of the *Portsmouth*'s men, "His uniform consisted of something like the cap worn by navy officers; a drab peacoat, such as those which were formerly worn by the New York firemen; and blue pants, stuck in the legs of his boots." Walker greeted the Americans coolly, "neither inquisitive, nor communicative, nor discourteous in reply." No, Walker told him, he had no intention of quitting Ensenada—the waving flag must have been the doing of some of his men, without his knowledge or permission.[12]

The detachment returned to the *Portsmouth*, and Walker, perhaps fearing a more insistent second visit from the ship, ordered his men to prepare to decamp. They spiked the fort's two heavy iron cannons so they couldn't later be turned on his force. Planning to travel light, Walker left behind four soldiers to protect the camp doctor, David Hoge, his assistant, and four badly wounded men recovering in the damp and dark dirt-floored sick ward, anticipating that the *Portsmouth* would come to their aid. Walker had barely left when locals began appearing on the hills, assessing their chances of attacking the fort. To Hoge's surprise, the detail Walker had left to protect them took off. Hoge quickly signaled the *Portsmouth*, and Captain Dornin again sent a detachment ashore. Within hours, the sick and wounded were safely aboard the *Columbus* for the trip to San Diego.[13]

Walker and his men spent several days roaming the countryside, pillaging as they went, before they arrived at San Vicente. Once Walker established his new encampment, he summoned ranchers and leaders of the indigenous Cocopah tribe to a conference, intending to demand their loyalty. Groups of men were dispatched with orders "to apprehend anyone who refused to attend," and decreeing that those who didn't would have their property seized. Some, such as Don Juan Bandini's son José María, fled rather than attend, but on February 20 more than sixty landowners gathered under the watchful eyes of Walker's armed men and agreed to accept the new government. Walker summoned them again nine days later, this time for an oath-taking ceremony.[14]

Ruland, in his typical fashion, reported to the *San Diego Herald* that the landowners came to the conference out of their support for the new nation. "The delegates from the convention visited our camp, and were received with all the honors, the Battalion being paraded, amid all of our paraphernalia of flags, big guns, etc., being exhibited." But the landowners saw the presence of the battalion, the flags, and the big guns for what it was: an act of intimidation.

Walker set up a table beneath two large, crossed flagpoles holding his republic's flag. He sat behind it flanked by his top officers and surrounded by eighty of his armed men. About fifteen Cocopahs and two of the landowners agreed to take the oath; the rest refused. Walker told them that if they didn't swear fealty they would be "treated as enemies and rebels, and that their punishment would be death and confiscation of their property." Most of the Mexicans capitulated.[15]

Soldiers led the landowners one by one to stand before Walker, where they recited an oath promising fealty to Walker and whatever actions his government would take. Then each man was passed through the arched flags to a plaza where, after all had sworn allegiance, "the troops gave three cheers, the artillery boomed forth a National Salute," followed by military songs performed by a brass band drawn from Walker's force. But five men, including Don José Sáez, refused to take the oath. Walker ordered them imprisoned, which ended Sáez's resistance. The president then wrote out a six-paragraph statement that he compelled Sáez and eight other leading ranchers to sign "on behalf of 62 members of the convention." The statement reasserted the ranchers' support for Walker and exonerated his men of responsibility for their looting. Walker, in turn, promised to pay for any future provisions he needed, an empty pledge.[16]

Walker might have been able to extort a meaningless promise of loyalty from the ranchers, but he held less sway over his own men. Desertions picked up; he left Ensenada with 140 men but was now down to about 100, many of them unruly. Even as the ranchers were swearing oaths, a group of Walker's men were laying plans to desert, but they were caught after they "sacked stores and dwellings." Walker placed the five leaders under arrest on February 28 and convened a military court-martial to try the men on "charges and allegations involving an attempt to desert, to take each a horse from the camp, to blow up the magazine, and to commit murder." Walker placed Secretary of State Emory in charge of the panel of seven adjudicators, and appointed Ruland, the propagandist, to handle the prosecution. The hearing lasted three days, and ended March 3 in the acquittal of one "on the ground that he was a good cattle driver" and the conviction of the rest. Two were put under the lash—one fifty strokes, the other twenty-five—and kicked out of the expedition. The other two—T. F. Nelson and Arthur Morrison—were considered the ringleaders and so were sentenced to death, a penalty that was carried out almost immediately.[17]

Walker viewed the executions as "a good test of military discipline; for no duty is so repulsive to the soldier as that of taking life from the comrade who has shared the perils and privations of his arduous service," he wrote later. "On this occasion, too, the duty was more difficult, because the number of Americans was small, and was daily diminishing. But painful as was the duty, the men charged with the execution did not shrink from the performance of it."[18]

To bolster his diminishing numbers, Walker ordered Emory to return to San Francisco and keep working with Henry Watkins to find more fighting men. But General Hitchcock's replacement overseeing the US forces on the Pacific coast, General John E. Wool, had received fresh instructions from Washington to bottle up the San Francisco port to preclude more filibusters from leaving. With the *Portsmouth* and the *Columbus* effectively blockading Ensenada, and the republic's headquarters now forty miles away at San Vicente, Walker didn't know that the captain of the *Portsmouth* had arrested Emory and sent him to San Francisco to face Neutrality Act charges.

General John Wool. *Courtesy of Library of Congress Prints and Photographs Division, LC-USZ62-110101*

Watkins, meanwhile, continued to recruit in San Francisco. He managed to slip out about forty men by renaming the *Anita* the *Petrita* and reflagging it as a Chilean ship. But the captain of the new *Petrita* saw the *Portsmouth* anchored off Ensenada and kept going, eventually putting in at Guaymas, where Mexican authorities arrested the new recruits, then shipped them in chains to Mazatlán in Sinaloa, the state just south of Sonora, where they were to be shot. The American consul managed to intervene and persuade Mexico to spare their lives in favor of deportation. Watkins was not one of those arrested, having remained behind in San Francisco. But General Wool was tightening his grip in the city, and after the *Petrita* set sail, he arrested Watkins and sent him to join Emory in jail.

Wool also broke up another scheme purportedly under the direction of Mexican president Santa Anna, who was fighting for his political life against reformists in Mexico, to recruit one thousand French and German men living in California to embark for Guaymas and then settle in Sonora. Santa Anna's supposed agent was Count Gaston de Raousset-Boulbon, the architect of the earlier failed filibuster to Sonora. Wool believed Raousset-Boulbon's expedition was actually an effort to either send reinforcements to Walker or supplant his expedition. So Wool arrested the French and Mexican consuls, sparking an international and legal uproar; Raousset-Boulbon slipped away to Santa Barbara. The interdiction of ships, though, meant Walker's pipeline of fresh soldiers went dry.[19]

Walker didn't stay long in San Vicente. A week or so after the executions, he announced that the army would march east to secure the Sonora portion of his new republic. Nothing in Walker's background suggests he had any conception of how hostile the journey would be—from Baja around the northern end of the Gulf of Mexico, across the Colorado River, and into the Sonoran desert.[20]

Leaving about thirty men behind to hold San Vicente, they left on March 20 with one hundred head of the stolen cows and many of the men on stolen horses, looking more like a down-on-its-luck cattle drive than a fearsome military expedition. As they crossed the mountains to the gulf side of the peninsula, two more men deserted and twenty head of cattle wandered off (or were purloined by the deserters). A band of about thirty Cocopah Indians followed them out of the mountains, and in an unguarded moment made off with thirty head of cattle. Walker's men managed to capture five of the natives and tried to trade their freedom for the return of the cattle. But the natives bolted, and three were shot dead as they fled.

Food again ran short. The men were reduced to eating mostly beef, and they grumbled about Walker's decision to reserve most of the scant corn supply for himself. The terrain was difficult, and too desertlike to sustain the cattle. The expedition moved slowly, and their clothes, particularly their boots, were no match for the conditions. Rocks shredded soles, and clothes snagged and tore on the desert brush. The group angled to the northeast, and after eight days and ninety miles reached the Colorado River about six miles from its mouth. At four hundred yards wide, the river ran deep and powerful, making it difficult for the men to swim the cattle across or to paddle makeshift rafts. After the currents swept away several of the weakened cows, Walker gave up on trying to take the cattle with them.

It took many trips back and forth to ferry all the men, and those on the east bank rested while the others caught up. With everyone tired and increasingly desperate, tempers frayed. Captain Douglas accused the soldier running the commissary of stealing corn. The soldier denied the theft. Douglas began swearing at him, the soldier argued back, and Douglas pulled out his revolver and fired a single shot into the soldier's chest, killing him instantly.[21]

The men camped on the riverbank for three days. It was cool at night but temperatures reached into the eighties during the day, the desert sun relentlessly beating down on them. Morale, and faith in Walker, plummeted as the president's incompetence wore through. "His vanity makes him tyrannical—his weakness renders him cruel, his unbounded and senseless ambition has led him to believe himself born to command." He was easily affronted, and "standing upon his dignity" he issued "vexatious orders upon etiquette." The men began drifting off, one by one or in small groups, most making their way to Fort Yuma, the US outpost about seventy miles up the Colorado River. They arrived in sorry condition—half naked, sunburned, starving, and in some cases shoeless—and described an expedition in full collapse, the desertions "a stampede." The commander at Fort Yuma gave the deserters a few days to recover and then provided each man with a week's worth of rations and directions west to San Diego and Los Angeles.[22]

Walker was in dire straits. His plan relied on slaughtering the stolen cattle as basic sustenance for the march into Sonora, but he now had no access to the herd. His force of a hundred men had dissipated, his army reduced to a few dozen ill-fed, ill-shod, bedraggled, and increasingly desperate followers who would have to head deeper into the desert as the days grew longer and the temperatures higher. Walker himself was down to one boot, his uniform of a peacoat and blue trousers in shreds. Recognizing the reality of his situation, Walker decided to return to San Vicente with his remaining force—mostly officers and loyal friends. They took the rafts back across the Colorado, gathered up their remaining stolen cattle—now down to about twenty-five animals—and began the slow westward trudge.

After getting routed by Walker at Ensenada, Antonio Maria Melendrez had busied himself putting together a force of ranchers, ranch hands, small-plot farmers, and Cocopahs all united against a common foe: the American invaders. Shortly after Walker began his eastward march to Sonora, Melendrez and his men surrounded San Vicente and laid siege to about twenty of the men Walker had left behind, who soon surrendered. Melendrez encountered another band of more than a dozen of Walker's men who had left San Vicente, apparently to forage for supplies. They were in a small village when Melendrez attacked. They scattered through the village, some trying to hide in reeds and shrubs along a riverbank. Melendrez's men quickly captured half a dozen of them, tied them up, then shot them. The rest apparently slipped away, bringing the story of the executions to the California newspapers. Meanwhile, Don Juan Bandini, in response to his own ranch being raided by Walker's men, had traveled from San Diego to Baja and put together another contingent of fighters, who would soon be working in concert with Melendrez.[23]

With Ensenada evacuated and San Vicente fallen, Walker didn't know that he had no sanctuary to return to. Upon finding San Vicente empty, he moved on to the nearby ranchero La Calentura, presumably seeking supplies. Melendrez watched from a distance, uncertain he had enough men to defeat Walker's core contingent of loyalists. The filibusters confiscated about sixty head of cattle and a large number of sheep and marched out for La Grulla and Melendrez's now-vacant ranch.[24]

Bandini put his force of thirty men in the charge of a man named Don Juan Mendoza, who led them to try to find Melendrez. They encountered Walker as the invaders rested at Rancho Guadalupe of the Osios, and from a hidden viewing spot "observed how carelessly the cattle were being allowed to graze." In a lightning attack, Mendoza's men drove off the cattle and sheep while engaging in a gunfight with Walker's men, who holed up in the ranch buildings. But Mendoza didn't have enough men to fully engage Walker, so he moved on, finally encountering Melendrez near San Vicente. With a combined force of sixty men, they were ready to take on the Americans, and they headed back to Rancho Guadalupe.

The main ranch buildings sat in the midst of an open space cleared of cactus and scrub brush, which meant Walker's men, barricaded inside the buildings, had the advantage over the makeshift Mexican cavalry. Mendoza and Melendrez arrayed their infantrymen, such as they were—few had rifles, most were armed with sidearms—around the clearing. They held their mounted fighters, which included Melendrez, at a slight distance. The two commanders sent a messenger under a flag of truce to the ranch house with an offer for Walker: if he and his men would lay down their arms, the Mexicans would guarantee them safe passage to the border. "Walker read the message and threw it beneath his feet, then, by a series of well applied kicks, ejected the courier from his presence."[25]

A short time later, Melendrez and Mendoza ordered their men to open fire from behind desert brush and low knolls beyond the clearing. Walker's men, protected inside the buildings, returned fire. After two hours of the mostly ineffective fighting, Walker, in a bold move, sent nine of his surviving men in a sweeping rush from the buildings and into the clearing, laying down a barrage of bullets into brush where the Mexicans had hidden themselves. The Mexicans held firm. Melendrez, seeing an advantage, galloped in a rush into the clearing with a half dozen other mounted men, fired at the exposed Americans, and separated them from the protection of the ranch house. Walker's men scattered and, as the mounted fighters left the clearing and turned for another pass, ran back to the protection of the buildings. The Mexican fighters pulled back. Each side lost two or three men.

Walker didn't have men to spare. Nor did he have food for the thirty-three fighters who were still with him. Since the start of the expedition, at least twenty-two of his men had been killed in action or died in the desert (one apparently drowned in the Colorado River), and eight others had suffered significant wounds. Most had simply walked away. Recognizing that his Republic of Sonora was lost, Walker decided to head for the US border.[26]

On the morning of April 30, the remnants of his little army emerged from the rancho as a group, expecting to have to fight their way out. But Melendrez and Mendoza had pulled back, anticipating Walker would eventually try to leave. They set up an ambush along the road to La Grulla, the Americans' most likely path, and Walker strode right into it, sparking a daylong battle as both sides huddled behind rocks, hillocks, and scant trees. At dusk, the Mexicans ignited the brush in a wide circle around the Americans, but in the darkness, Walker and his men managed to slip through the flames. As Walker continued on toward the border, the Mexicans "adopted the plan of remaining always on the defensive, depriving the invaders of all means of sustenance, maintaining a strict watch on their movements, leaving them always an unobstructed outlet to [the border], and preventing them from taking any road that would lead them to an easily fortified position."[27]

The Americans neared the United States on the afternoon of May 8, 1854—coincidentally, Walker's thirtieth birthday. The Mexicans still partially surrounded them, as though herding cattle. Word of their approach had reached San Diego, and spectators perched on a hill overlooking the border crossing. A small detachment of US soldiers under the command of Major Justus McKinstry idled on the American side of the border as Melendrez and his men moved to a spot on the road between Walker and the border, blocking the escape. McKinstry sent a messenger to seek permission from Melendrez to pass through to talk with Walker, which Melendrez granted while asking McKinstry to give Walker an ultimatum: unless the Americans surrendered their weapons, Melendrez would not let him continue down the road to the border.

McKinstry crossed the Mexicans' cordon, approached the filibusters, and conveyed Melendrez's demand. Walker responded tersely: "If Melendrez wants our arms, he can come and take them. We will not run, but it will be at his peril." The president of Sonora and the American major also discussed what would happen once the filibusters crossed back into the United States. They would, McKinstry said, be arrested, their firearms seized, and be taken to San Diego and then on to San Francisco to face whatever charges the government decided to file. Walker, whose other option was to remain in Mexico at the mercy of Melendrez, agreed.

McKinstry passed back through Melendrez's cordon, where he was asked whether the US troops were protecting Walker and his men. No, McKinstry said, if there was a battle on the Mexican side of the border, they had no authority to intervene.

Walker, while defeated, was not done. He gathered his men into formation and began moving northward along the road, led by nine soldiers on horseback. As they neared Melendrez's blockade, Walker gave the order to charge. The nine horsemen, guns drawn, spurred their horses directly at the human barricade, which quickly fell apart, clearing the road without a shot fired. Walker and the rest of the men followed to the border and surrendered to McKinstry, who, as promised, confiscated the men's weapons and arrested them all.

Seven months after Walker and his fellow filibusters slipped out of San Francisco in the middle of the night, the venture was over. Walker's Republic of Sonora, if it had ever really existed beyond his dreams, was no more.

7 | WHY NICARAGUA MATTERED

THE DISCOVERY OF GOLD in the Sierra Nevada and the subsequent admission of California to the United States had sharpened a geographic reality. Traveling to and from the newest state meant months of dangerous, arduous trekking across the Great Plains, through the Rocky Mountains, and over deserts. Or it meant weeks if not months aboard ships traveling around the tip of South America, a distance of thirteen thousand miles from New York City to San Francisco. Even those who took the same route as William Walker, sailing to the Caribbean coast of Central America, trekking across the Isthmus of Panama, then sailing on to California, risked scarlet fever and other diseases during the overland portion of their journey. There was a fourth possibility, too, but someone would have to create it.

When Spanish explorer Vasco Núñez de Balboa viewed both the Atlantic and Pacific Oceans from a mountaintop in Panama in 1513, he recognized that a canal could connect the two bodies of water, which were only thirty miles apart at the narrowest point of the isthmus. The Chagres River, which emptied into the Caribbean, gave a canal a good head start, but there were formidable challenges: mountainous terrain, tropical diseases, and regular periods of heavy rains and mudslides. Other locations had potential, also. At the narrowest part of Mexico, Tehuantepec, two hundred miles of relatively flat land—about half of it covered by the navigable Coatzacoalcos River—separated the Pacific Ocean and the Gulf of Mexico.[1]

Then there was Nicaragua, much wider than Panama but with fewer natural obstacles. Like Panama, Nicaragua had inland waterways to help the crossing.

The San Juan River emptied into the Caribbean at San Juan del Norte after coursing 110 miles southeast from its source, Lake Nicaragua, the largest fresh-water body in Central America. The river was navigable except for three sets of rapids, while the southwestern shore of the lake lay just twelve miles from the Pacific coast. Consequently, a canal to allow passage of large ships could be gouged out of the riverbed between the Caribbean and the lake, then dug overland for the remaining short distance to the Pacific.

Nicaraguans saw the construction of a canal as their national destiny—but lacked the wherewithal to build it themselves. After seceding from the disintegrating Federal Republic of Central America in 1838, the country was eager to find a partner for the project. It approached Belgium and France without gaining much traction, but Louis-Napoléon Bonaparte (nephew of the former emperor), recognizing the wealth to be had by making the world a little smaller, formed an investment company and circulated a pamphlet advocating a Nicaragua transit route. That, too, failed to yield results, but it kept the idea alive.[2]

By the following decade, the United States and Great Britain remained as the major promoters of such schemes, each for different reasons. Even before annexing California and the rest of the Mexican Cession, the United States wanted easier access to the West Coast; the British, who stepped into the Caribbean power void as Spain's dominance crumbled, hoped to shorten the trip from the Pacific to Europe. Fearing an expanding United States would dominate the region, the British decided to plant a flag. In 1847, Great Britain announced that it was reaffirming its protection of the Mosquito Kingdom, the lands of the Miskito tribe that stretched along the coastline of Honduras and Nicaragua, from Cape Honduras, near Trujillo, to south of the mouth of the San Juan River and San Juan del Norte, which the British called Greytown. The Central American nations—particularly Nicaragua, which claimed most of that territory—objected, but they had little ability to force the issue given the vast superiority of the British navy.

As promised, British troops landed at Greytown on January 1, 1848, ousted the Nicaraguan officials tending to the port, and put the weight of the empire behind the Miskito king, George Augustus Frederic II. He wasn't much of a king. The *New York Herald* dismissed Frederic as a monarch "whose throne is a rum barrel, and whose palace is a tent, built of boughs and old slabs, and scarcely fit for the shelter of a donkey." But by asserting the protectorate, the

British forestalled nascent efforts by the US government to negotiate a canal with the Nicaraguans, since the Caribbean end of the logical route was now controlled by Britain.[3]

The move deeply alarmed President Zachary Taylor, who recalled his thinking in a message to the US Senate a few years later:

> I considered the interference of the British Government on this continent in seizing the port of San Juan, which commanded the route believed to be the most eligible for the canal across the Isthmus, and occupying it at the very moment when it was known, as I believe, to Great Britain that we were engaged in the negotiation for the purchase of California, as an unfortunate coincidence, and one calculated to lead to the inference that she entertained designs by no means in harmony with the interests of the United States.[4]

The president's concerns were rooted in the Monroe Doctrine, the US policy that asserted, among other things, that the United States would not allow any European power to extend its colonies in the Western Hemisphere. Fearing the British efforts would lead to a military showdown, Taylor directed his secretary of state, John Clayton, to negotiate with the British envoy in Washington, Sir Henry Bulwer. Clayton and Bulwer hammered out an agreement under which neither country would control territory in Central America, but both countries agreed to build and control a canal through Nicaragua that would be open to the ships of the world.

Imprecise wording led immediately to disputes. Great Britain said that the treaty did not apply to existing possessions; the United States insisted that it did, and that Great Britain must withdraw from the Mosquito Coast, British Honduras, and the nearby Bay Islands. The diplomats squabbled, but the desires of empires would have less influence on transit across the isthmus than the wiliness of capitalism's kings.

The first regular and successful commercial transit link across the isthmus followed the Panama route, though it didn't involve a canal. Since the population of the Oregon Territory was growing after an 1846 treaty with England set the US northern border at the forty-ninth parallel (where it remains today), the federal government was eager to establish fast, reliable mail routes to connect the East with the West. Oceangoing vessels were the most attractive option, and eventually the government gave exclusive mail contracts to the Pacific Mail Steamship Company, run by William Henry Aspinwall, whose Manhattan-based family business, Howland & Aspinwall, had for years built and operated clipper ships to Europe, the Far East, the Caribbean, and South America.

The pact allotted the firm an exclusive $199,000 subsidy from Congress to ferry US mail to the West Coast from Panama; the unrelated United States Mail Steamship Company, under the control of George Law, a powerful steamship operator along the East Coast, had the contract for the US-to-Panama leg. Aspinwall used the Pacific contract as seed money to attract other investors and quickly built a small fleet of steamships to carry not only mail but passengers as well. The company even negotiated a monopoly to eventually build a short railroad to shuttle passengers on the overland route between the Chagres River steamers and the Pacific coast. And while the mail contracts were exclusive, there was no monopoly on carrying passengers, so Aspinwall soon had Atlantic passenger ships sailing as well, competing with Law's subsidized line.[5]

Aspinwall's timing was fortuitous. As he was establishing his Pacific service, the discovery of gold in California set off the mad rush of dreamers and schemers from east to west. Pacific Mail Steamship Company placed ads in eastern newspapers offering passage and up to three hundred pounds of baggage from Panama to San Francisco at $100 for steerage and up to $250 for a stateroom, with ships leaving Panama on the first of the month. Demand would soon push the schedule to semimonthly departures, with tickets available at the steamship company's New York office at 54 South Street, facing the wharfs of the East River. (At the peak of the gold rush, four or five ships a month would make the trip.) For the first year or so there were fewer ships to handle the Pacific run than the Atlantic run, which led to thousands of fortune-seeking migrants backed up along the land route across the isthmus. In 1848, a minimum of 335 people traveled across Panama from New York en route to San Francisco; the number rose to 6,489 migrants in 1849 and to a peak of 24,263 in 1852. By then, Aspinwall's Pacific line had absorbed the Atlantic line as well, though other competitors continued to operate.[6]

As the sea routes to and from the isthmus became better developed and more popular, the overland crossing only became more of a grueling ordeal. Frank Marryat, a British sailor and artist, made the journey from England in April 1850 with a servant, their baggage, and three dogs. They arrived at the mouth of the Chagres River just as an Aspinwall steamer anchored "and immediately disgorged five hundred American citizens in red and blue shirts." Ashore, Marryat found a ramshackle settlement "of about fifty huts, each of which raises its head from the midst of its own private malaria, occasioned by the heaps of filth and offal, which putrefying under the rays of a vertical sun, choke up the very doorway." After negotiating for his own passage up the river by canoe, Marryat set off for the Pacific amid the bedlam of the Americans' mad rush in their mismatched flotilla of small boats, the largest carrying up to a dozen people, nearly all men.

All was noise and excitement, cries for lost baggage, adieus, cheers, a parting strain on a [trumpetlike] cornet-a-piston, a round dozen at least of different tongues, each in its owner's own peculiar fashion murdering Spanish, a few discharges from rifles and revolvers, rendered the scene ludicrous, and had the good effect of sending us on the first step of a toilsome journey in a good humour.[7]

The good humor didn't last. As Marryat's boat moved up the river, it entered the jungle. Lush trees and vines filled with birds and monkeys edged the riverbanks, and crocodiles and caimans lurked in the murky water. "Ahead, astern, on every side are canoes; here, surmounting a pyramid of luggage, is a party of western men in red shirts and jack boots, questioning everybody with the curiosity peculiar to their race." Marryat spent two nights sleeping in the beached boat, his boatman finding lodging—and gambling—in river villages. After two and a half days, they arrived at Gorgona, where Marryat rented mules to cover the remaining twenty miles to Panama City and the Pacific coast:

We plunged at once into a narrow rocky path in the forest, where palm trees and creepers shut the light out overhead; splashing through gurgling muddy streams, that concealed loose and treacherous stones—stumbling over fallen trees that lay across our road—burying ourselves to the mules' girths in filthy swamps, where on either side dead and putrid mules were lying—amidst lightning, thunder, and incessant rain.

At nightfall they reached the Washington Hotel, advertised as having room for forty and fresh hot food for purchase "but a glance at the interior was sufficient to destroy all appetite. Round it, and stretching for yards, there were mules, drivers, and passengers, clustered and clamorous as bees without a hive." Most, it turned out, were returning from California, some rich with gold but far more "poorer than when first they started to realize their golden dreams. And these latter were as drunken and as reckless a set of villains as one could see anywhere. Stamped with vice and intemperance, without baggage or money, they were fit for robbery and murder to any extent." The forty beds were stained and rickety canvas cots; Marryat joined the throngs outside and slept among saddles.

It took a couple of days of slow-paced mule travel to clear the mountains, the travel impeded by the roughness of the trail itself, drenching rains, and the traffic jam of migrants moving in both directions. Fevers and other illnesses dogged them. Marryat encountered one man traveling in the opposite direction, to Chagres, but who sat by the roadside "attacked with fever, shivering with ague, and helpless." Marryat hoisted the sick man atop one of the mules. "He was very ill, wandered in his speech, and shook like a leaf; and before we got into Panama, he died from exhaustion. As I did not know what to do with him, I planted him by the road-side, and on my arrival at the town, I informed the authorities, and I presume they buried him." When Marryat finally arrived at the edge of Panama City, he found a massive migrant camp of people who could not find rooms among the city's hotels. Marryat, too, had to pitch a tent, and a few days later finally boarded a Pacific Mail Steamship Company vessel for the last, overcrowded connection to San Francisco. Hardly the travel of luxury.

Cornelius Vanderbilt, who had become wealthy running ferries and trade steamers in the Northeast, recognized that there was money to be made from that migrating mass of humanity. Looking at maps of Central America, he figured he could undercut Aspinwall and others vested in the Panama route by creating a competing route across Nicaragua. Since that route would cut some seven hundred miles off the journey from New York to San Francisco, Vanderbilt could market it as a faster and cheaper passage. And he had the wealth and connections to put it together.

Vanderbilt was born in 1794 on Staten Island, a son of a Dutch farmer who also operated boats ferrying farm products and other merchandise between that island and Manhattan. Vanderbilt began operating his own small two-masted flat-bottom boat, called a periauger, in 1810. With the end of the United States' second war with Great Britain in 1815, his fleet grew rapidly. In 1817, while still managing his own business, he began operating a steamship owned by Thomas Gibbons, a wealthy plantation owner from Georgia who had resettled in New Jersey. The two men teamed up to break a monopoly on operating steamboats in New York, and Vanderbilt—who already had a reputation for shrewdness—learned from the elder Gibbons how closely business, law, and politics were intertwined.[8]

Cornelius Vanderbilt. *Courtesy of Library of Congress Prints and Photographs Division, LC-DIG-ggbain-50402*

So when Vanderbilt, a long-standing business rival to George Law, turned his attention to Nicaragua, people took note. He hired a "fixer," Joseph White, a lawyer and former Congressman from Indiana who had connections within the Taylor administration. White met with Clayton, Taylor's secretary of state, and quietly informed him that Vanderbilt and a handful of other prominent New York backers had created the American Atlantic and Pacific Ship Canal Company to build a canal across Nicaragua, and they wanted the government's help with the Nicaraguan officials. Clayton had his own sense of the importance of such a project. In 1835, as a US senator from Delaware, he had joined in a failed effort to force the administration of President Andrew Jackson to negotiate a treaty protecting anyone who might try to build such a canal. The benefit for the United States, he believed, would be a tremendous boost in trade for American ports in the South and on the East Coast.[9]

Clayton dispatched Ephraim G. Squier, who was chargé d'affaires to Guatemala and whose portfolio also included El Salvador and Nicaragua. At Clayton's direction, Squier promised the Nicaraguans that in return for permission to build a canal, the United States would pressure Great Britain to give up its Mosquito Coast protectorate, would work with Nicaragua to protect the interests of the canal builders, and would ensure that any canal would be open for passage to all as long as the Americans ran it. With these guarantees in place, Vanderbilt's agent Colonel David White, brother of his newly hired fixer, completed negotiations in August 1849 for a monopoly contract to build a canal, promising to pay Nicaragua $10,000 at the ratification of the contract and then annually until the canal was completed. Nicaragua also would receive $200,000 in American Atlantic and Pacific Ship Canal Company stock and 20 percent of profits for the first 20 years of operation, then 25 percent until the deal expired eighty-five years after the canal was completed. The pact also gave Vanderbilt authority to build an alternative transit route across the isthmus while the canal was being built, which was expected to take twelve years; Nicaragua would get 10 percent of those profits.[10]

Anticipating the construction costs would be formidable, Vanderbilt traveled to London seeking investments from some of the largest banks in the world, offering them half of the project. The London financiers were interested but needed details before they decided to invest, including a specific route, estimated costs, anticipated revenues, and the other mundane elements that go into deciding whether to gamble millions of dollars. Vanderbilt hired Orville W. Childs, who as chief engineer for New York State had overseen approval of railroad routes and an expansion of the Erie Canal, to report on options and cost estimates for building the canal.

Childs arrived in Nicaragua in August 1850, a year after the contract was signed, and got to work. Two general options made the most sense, and each involved using the San Juan River and Lake Nicaragua. From there, the shortest distance to the Pacific was about twelve miles through low hills to the small town of Brito, which lacked a natural harbor and would require extensive jetty work. A longer path that required less excavation of hills followed the Río Tipitapa connecting Lake Nicaragua to Lake Managua to the north, and then cut through lower elevations than the Brito route to another river and on to the coast. The northern route involved about forty-six miles of excavations; the Brito route was twelve miles, but it required more locks to lift ships up and down the higher elevations. Nevertheless, Childs settled on the shorter route. The cost: about $31.5 million for a canal that would be 17 feet deep and 118 feet wide at the top, tapering to 50 feet wide at the bottom.[11]

Armed with this report, Childs and Joseph White traveled to London to seal the financing Vanderbilt needed. But the British bankers balked over the design, which would have left the canal too shallow to handle large warships and two-thirds of the ships engaged in trade with the Far East; they required a depth of at least thirty feet. And that would also require dredging shallow areas of Lake Nicaragua. It's unclear why Childs specified a shallower depth, as this violated a stipulation in the contract with Nicaragua that "the dimensions of the canal must be such as may be necessary for the passage of vessels of all sizes." To expand the canal's capacity would raise the construction cost from $31.5 million to around $100 million. The British bankers had other issues with the proposal, too. The necessary toll charged to shippers to defray the costs would be too high—at the proposed $3 a ton, a thousand-ton ship would owe about $3,000, about equal to the whole profit from a single voyage. And little of the India-England trade would use the canal, because the trip around the Cape of Good Hope, at the southern tip of Africa, was fifteen hundred miles shorter. It was a project of more interest and use to American investors than British. But Vanderbilt had turned to the British because the banks of London had the deeper pockets, and because Vanderbilt, despite his wealth and fame in the United States, did not have the trust of Wall Street bankers, who thought him crude and reckless and perceived his canal as speculative and "a vaporous fraud." Unlikely to raise the necessary investments in New York and unwilling to finance the project on their own, Vanderbilt and his partners abandoned it.[12]

By then, however, Vanderbilt had already put together the river and overland transit network that the agreement with Nicaragua authorized until the canal could be built. The company assembled small, short-draft open-air steamboats to ply the San Juan River, winch-and-pulley systems to pull them over the smaller rapids, a portage system to get around the Castillo Rapids (closer to a cataract than rapids), and steamers for Lake Nicaragua. And it pushed a road through the jungle—first dirt, later macadam—over which horse-drawn coaches could move the fortune-seekers and other travelers across the dozen miles of tropical forests and hills to the small port town of San Juan del Sur.

When the route opened for business on July 14, 1851, one hundred people had reserved passage from New York aboard Vanderbilt's nine-month-old and superfast steamer, the *Prometheus*. It anchored ten days later at Greytown. A smaller steamer then ferried passengers in groups to Punta Arenas—across the small and shallow harbor from Greytown—where Vanderbilt had built a wharf and offices, a coaling station, and a few warehouses and shelters for workers. From there, the passengers took riverboats up the river; Vanderbilt himself, in Nicaragua for the route's opening, accompanied his customers as far as the lake, then returned to Greytown. The passengers continued across the lake to Virgin Bay and the last leg of the overland journey, on the still-under-construction roadway to the Pacific. But there was no ship for them in the San Juan del Sur harbor. The *Pacific* stopped on July 29 and disgorged passengers headed to New York, but it was bound for Panama, farther down the coast. So the San Francisco–bound migrants had to wait several days for the *Pacific* to make its return trip, and finally they were on their way on the evening of August 16. Two weeks later, they arrived in San Francisco, forty-five days after the *Prometheus* left New York. Vanderbilt got better at it, and quickly. Soon the passage from New York to San Francisco was routinely completed about four days faster than the Panama route.

The transit route was meant to be a short-term endeavor for the twelve years the contract allowed for constructing the canal. But even before Childs traveled to London it was clear the canal would take a lot longer to complete. That didn't sit well with the Nicaraguan government, which began mulling whether it find someone else to build the canal and revoke the American Atlantic and Pacific Ship Canal Company's charter. As a precaution, Vanderbilt separated the canal project from the transit project, and through Joseph White successfully negotiated a separate charter in 1851, under which he created the Accessory Transit Company with exclusive rights to operate steamships (which Vanderbilt owned separately) on Lake Nicaragua and ferry passengers along the San Juan River, as well as permission to maintain the road from the southern edge of the lake to the Pacific.

But the contract carried within it the seeds of self-destruction. For years Nicaragua had been racked with internal conflict, which had been escalating since its independence from the Federal Republic of Central America in 1838. The clashing factions were the Democratic Party (a.k.a. the Liberals), centered in León, about ten miles from the Pacific Coast in western Nicaragua, and the Legitimist Party (a.k.a. the Conservatives), which operated from Granada, about eighty miles to the southeast, on the western shore of Lake Nicaragua. The parties' differences were philosophical but also entwined with family histories, class distinctions (the Legitimists included Nicaragua's landed aristocracy), and regional rivalries.

In the spring of 1849, the two rivals had come together in the face of local insurrections, forming a unity government that signed the initial canal contract with Vanderbilt. By 1853, though, the rivals were back at each other's throats, the Conservatives running the central government from Granada and the Liberals maintaining their Provisional Supreme Government from León. Joseph White negotiated the Accessory Transit Company contract with the Legitimists, an agreement with which the Liberals took issue, arguing that the Legitimists could not speak for the Nicaraguan government. "Under no title can you conclude the negotiations interesting this whole State with functionaries whose authority is in question," the Liberals wrote to White and Vanderbilt.[13]

In other words, Vanderbilt, through White, chose a side in a civil war, a dangerous roll of the dice in which the fate of the Accessory Transit Company would hinge on whichever faction ultimately won.

———

Frictions in Nicaragua were not just between the Legitimists and the Liberals. Under the Clayton-Bulwer Treaty, the United States expected Great Britain to relinquish the protectorate over the Mosquito Kingdom; the British believed the protectorate was grandfathered in. At stake was control of Greytown, where Americans accounted for half the population and the rest of the villagers were mainly British citizens and Miskitos, who often had competing interests and loyalties. Greytown was a duty-free port for goods, but it levied port fees on arriving ships to underwrite the cost of operating the harbor. Nicaragua had granted the American Atlantic and Pacific Ship Canal Company an exemption, but Greytown's British authorities refused to recognize it. When the *Prometheus* arrived in November 1851, Greytown demanded payment, but Vanderbilt, who was again in the country, refused. After the mogul returned from accompanying his passengers to Lake Nicaragua, port officials boarded the *Prometheus* and insisted again that it pay the fee. Vanderbilt again refused, hustling the port officials off his ship and back to shore.[14]

As the *Prometheus*, carrying five hundred outgoing passengers, prepared to leave its moorage for Panama and then New York, the British brig-of-war *Express* fired a cannon shot from a quarter mile away that passed about ten feet above the *Prometheus*'s wheelhouse. "In a few minutes, another shot was fired, which passed over the stern so near that the force of the ball was distinctly felt by several passengers," the ship's captain, Henry Churchill, reported later. Churchill dispatched a boat to the *Express* asking why the British were firing on an unarmed American passenger vessel. "The captain stated it was to protect the authorities of Greytown in their demand, and if we did not immediately anchor he would fire a bombshell into us, and ordered his guns to be loaded with grape and canister shot." Churchill paid the $123 port fee under protest.[15]

Once details of the incident reached the mainland United States, a massive and angry public outcry ensued, complete with murmurs of war. Senator Lewis Cass of Michigan said "a wanton outrage was committed by a British vessel of war upon the flag of the United States, which calls for speedy explanation and redress" and which, if repeated, "will be considered as an act of war, to be met by the whole power of the country, with an energy and unanimity as great as would an invading force crossing our boundary." President Millard Fillmore dispatched two navy ships "for the purpose of affording protection to American commerce and interests on that coast against any such interference in the future." The British, though, soon apologized, said the local commander and port officials acted outside of policy, and recalled the consul at Greytown who had asked the *Express* to intervene. The furor died away, but the tensions remained.[16]

In February 1852, business leaders in Greytown convened a meeting and effectively declared their independence from the Mosquito Kingdom—and the British protectorate—to create a new local government that would seek a charter from Nicaragua. Most of the men involved were Americans. The British government complained to the United States, with which it was working to try to stave off a war between Nicaragua and its southern neighbor Costa Rica over their shared border. So a flare-up over Greytown would only make negotiations trickier. In the end Nicaragua, still riven internally by its warring factions, rejected a deal that would have settled the border issue while ending the Mosquito Kingdom's claim over Greytown and the northern reaches of the San Juan River—and thus the British protection thereof. Instead, Nicaraguan authorities sent the matters to arbitration, and Greytown, much to the consternation of its non-Miskito inhabitants, remained under the control of the kingdom and the British.[17]

There were more localized frictions as well. The business owners of Greytown had presumed they would reap a windfall with the establishment of the trans-isthmus travel route. But since Vanderbilt's agents built their separate wharf complex at Punta Arenas, across the harbor from Greytown, most of their passengers never set foot in Greytown proper unless they were stranded for a few days before heading upriver. The Greytown business owners were greatly annoyed, which occasionally gave rise to physical threats against and altercations with Vanderbilt's employees.

On January 1, 1853, a man named George W. McCerran bought a small warehouse on Punta Arenas. McCerran was a trader in goods between the American South and Nicaragua, and he planned to convert the warehouse into a rooming house catering to Accessory Transit Company workers. The building sat on the ocean side of the spit of land, where it was "too much exposed to the washing of the sea," so McCerran moved it to a more protected spot across the river at Greytown, where he already owned some other buildings. Once the move was finished, McCerran left on a planned business trip to New Orleans. While he was gone, the city council notified the Accessory Transit Company that it lacked permission to erect the building and had five days to remove it. The company replied that the building didn't belong to them and requested a delay until McCerran returned.[18]

The city refused, and at noon on the fifth day, a group of about thirty men protected by armed guards arrived at McCerran's complex. According to McCerran, they swarmed the building, "which destruction they commenced by tearing down the American flags which were waving above the house and other buildings, and then wantonly destroyed the whole of the property. . . . In tearing down the buildings, these persons looked more like tigers falling upon their prey than human beings." When the owner returned to find his property destroyed, he blamed his losses on the US government, which for more than a year had not dispatched a warship to make it clear that the Americans of Greytown were under its protection. "If one does not come very soon, it is likely that but very few Americans will be left here able to tell their story. Being apparently abandoned by their Government, the authorities of San Juan del Norte, or Greytown, think and believe that they can with impunity rob them of their property, and murder them if necessary."

The incident sparked another public uproar, which drew the US government's attention. In March, a three-masted sloop of war, the USS *Cyane*, arrived in port. The ship was outfitted with eighteen thirty-two-pound cannons and four twenty-four-pounders, and commanded by Captain John P. Hollins, under standing orders to defend the property of Americans as he saw necessary. And there was much to protect. The city was moving toward dismantling the entire Accessory Transit Company settlement to restore Greytown's dominance of the harbor. Hollins dispatched marines to guard the Accessory Transit facility and met with the village leaders, the US and British consuls, and Captain Thomas Wilson of the six-gun British sloop HMS *Geyser*, which was posted to the harbor. Hollins followed the meetings with letters in which he made clear he would obey his standing orders while awaiting fresh instructions from Washington. "All property belonging to either English or American citizens lying in or out of said city limits, is to be protected from any injury attempted on the same by the inhabitants of that town, peaceably if we can, forcibly if we must."[19]

It's unclear why Hollins was offering to protect British interests as well, since England had a ship at hand. Perhaps he wanted to signal that his focus was entirely on the villagers and their attacks, while sidestepping the fact that the British still considered the area under their protection. Wilson, though, said that the city council had acted within its rights in ordering the building torn down, and thus he had no authority to interfere. But, he wrote, until both captains received fresh instructions from their governments, "I will cooperate with you heartily in endeavouring to preserve the peace of the town, and affording protection to life and property."

The dispute moved fully into diplomatic circles, with letters and missives flowing from London to Washington and within the respective governments. Not only were there broader issues to discuss regarding the United States' and Great Britain's interests in Central America, but Great Britain was also facing great challenges elsewhere, getting drawn into the disastrous Crimean War with Russia. Locally, Accessory Transit replaced its top agent at Punta Arenas, and the new one began directing passengers to shops and other facilities in Greytown, which facilitated a rapprochement between company and town. But the fundamental challenge remained: Accessory Transit had permission to be at Punta Arenas from the Nicaraguan government; civic leaders in Greytown saw themselves as autonomous and under British protection, and they had not given the company permission to be there; the United States thought the British had no right to be there at all.

The situation festered for months before erupting again, but this time with a different flashpoint. Franklin Pierce was now president, and he had recently dispatched Solon Borland, a former Arkansas newspaper publisher and US senator, to be his minister to Central America. Borland believed that Manifest Destiny meant that the United States would eventually include portions of the Caribbean and Central America. "A 'fire-eating' expansionist of a rather ruffianly type," Borland was wholly unsuited for a job that demanded tact, patience, and sound judgment. Borland was given to speaking without thinking, and he had once broken the nose of a fellow senator during a brawl over slavery. But as a fellow military commander during the Mexican-American War, Pierce saw in him values others did not. It was a decision Pierce would soon come to regret.

Once in Nicaragua, Borland set himself on a collision course with his boss, Secretary of State William Marcy, who believed quiet and steady diplomacy with Great Britain would eventually lead the British to abandon Central America. Marcy also believed that the United States, in recognition of international laws and mores, should not interfere uninvited in the internal affairs of another country. Borland struck off on a more confrontational path, telling Nicaraguans in a public speech in Managua that it was his "greatest ambition to see the State of Nicaragua forming a bright star in the flag of the United States" and promising US support if Nicaragua sought to challenge the British protectorate of the Mosquito Kingdom—both of which conflicted with US policy. Marcy rebuked Borland in a letter, and Borland resigned.[20]

Borland's route back to the United States took him down the San Juan River on one of Accessory Transit's steamers. As they neared Greytown, the captain of the ship, a man named Smith, argued with a black Nicaraguan in a canoe, then shot him dead. At Greytown, villagers sought to arrest Smith for the killing, but Borland interceded, claiming that Smith was in his custody and that Greytown officials had no jurisdiction. Borland and Smith sought refuge in the home of the US consul, Joseph W. Fabens, where a mob of the dead man's friends quickly arrived to demand that not just Smith but Borland be turned over to them. Someone threw a broken bottle that struck Borland, gashing his cheek. He and Smith eventually escaped from Greytown, but as word of the assault on Borland reached the United States, a minor local disturbance became an international incident.[21]

And it was exacerbated by another confrontation between Greytown residents and workers of the Accessory Transit Company. Several villagers sneaked across the harbor and made off with a company yawl, which led to a chase, a scuffle, and the retrieval of the yawl amid a cascade of gunfire, though no one was struck. Other raids were more successful: The Accessory Transit Company reported regular losses of goods to burglars. After consulting with company officials, Fabens, the US consul, sent a letter to the city demanding $24,000 in compensation to Accessory Transit Company for damages to its buildings and the stolen goods—and an apology to Borland for his rough treatment. When the villagers ignored the demand, Navy Secretary James C. Dobbin ordered the *Cyane* back to Greytown, outlining for Captain Hollins what had occurred but directing him to consult with Fabens on conditions once he arrived.

"It is very desirable that these people should be taught that the United States will not tolerate these outrages, and that they have the power and the determination to check them," Dobbin wrote. "It is, however, very much to be hoped that you can effect the purposes of your visit without a resort to violence and destruction of property and loss of life. The presence of your vessel will, no doubt, work much good. The Department reposes much in your prudence and good sense."[22]

The *Cyane* arrived on July 11, 1854, and after a quick consultation with Fabens, Hollins wrote to the city officials that if they didn't pay up and apologize to Borland, he'd level the town. Hollins then visited the HMS *Bermuda*, a three-gun British schooner that had replaced the *Geyser* in watching over the town, and informed the commander of his ultimatum. While the British captain objected, his ship was no match for the *Cyane*, and it's unclear whether his orders would have allowed him to engage militarily with the US warship unless it was fired upon directly. Greytown refused to respond to Hollins's letter—it had disbanded its formal city council as a ruse—and upon a second warning from Hollins with a deadline, the villagers began moving possessions out of buildings and into the edge of the jungle.

At nine o'clock on the morning of July 13—just two months after the end of William Walker's disastrous expedition to Mexico—Hollins made good on his threat. The *Cyane*'s cannons fired methodically on the town for forty-five minutes, then paused for forty-five minutes as Hollins awaited word that the city leaders had come to their senses. When they still hadn't capitulated, a half hour later Hollins ordered a second barrage, this one lasting a half hour. Then three hours later he ordered a final twenty-minute barrage and dispatched a squadron to burn the remains to the ground.

"The execution done by our shot and shells amounted to the almost total destruction of the buildings," Hollins wrote in his report to Dobbin.

> But it was thought best to make the punishment of such a character as to inculcate a lesson never to be forgotten by those who have for so long a time set at defiance all warnings, and satisfy the whole world that the United States have the power and determination to enforce that reparation and respect due to them as a Government in whatever quarter the outrages may be committed.

The British objected, but to little avail. The more bellicose segments of the American public applauded the raw display of US power and resolve. And in San Francisco, William Walker—embraced by most in the city as a hero despite his abject failure in Mexico—prepared to go on trial for what he believed was a similar action: a military excursion to protect the unprotected.

8 | WALKER RETURNS TO SAN FRANCISCO

AFTER ARRESTING WILLIAM WALKER and his bedraggled group of insurrectionists on May 8, 1854, Major Justus McKinstry and his soldiers had escorted them to San Diego. Each man signed a "parole," a pledge that he would travel to San Francisco and surrender to General John E. Wool. Walker, though, signed a separate parole in which McKinstry inexplicably acceded to Walker's fantasy by describing him as "President of the Republic of Sonora" and elsewhere referred to the agreement between representatives of "the Government of the United States and the (so-called) Republic of Sonora." The designation drew derisive condemnation in some quarters, including the *Sacramento Daily Union* under the headline THE LAST ACT IN THE SONORA BURLESQUE:

> So, a U.S. Major appears in the last act, and closes the farce by signing an "agreement with Col. William Walker, (President of the Republic of Sonora.)" Upon what ground a United States officer recognizes Col. Walker as "President of the Republic of Sonora," is more than we are able to divine. In doing so, it strikes us, he plays but a sorry part in the stupid farce in which Walker has been so prominent an actor.[1]

For a few days, an erroneous report circulated that Walker had not, in fact, escaped Melendrez and had been killed along with more than a dozen of his followers. The *Daily Alta* took grim satisfaction, saying the death ends the great republic of Sonora, with all its sins of slavery-extension, robbery, and murder. It was unfortunate for Walker that he lived long enough to degrade his enterprise with crimes befitting only an abandoned pirate. Had he died early, like [Narciso] Lopez, a romance would have been attached to his name, which now will be followed by the curses of all wives and mothers. Happily, San Francisco has a prospect to be untroubled for some time by any imitators of his criminal career.[2]

Not relying solely on the sworn promises of Walker and his men, McKinstry kept them aboard a ship off San Diego until their transportation arrived. The *Southerner*, a two-masted wooden side-wheel steamer, picked them up as part of its regular San Francisco–San Diego run, steaming north on May 11 and arriving in San Francisco five days later after an uneventful trip. True to his word, Walker turned himself in to General Wool, and on May 25 a grand jury indicted him and two other men: Howard Snow, his navy secretary, and John Jarnigan, who by this point was not only his secretary of war but also Frederic Emory's replacement as secretary of state. The men were charged with violating the Neutrality Act.[3]

San Franciscans were of two minds about the filibusters. Some, as expressed in the *Alta*, dismissed Walker and his men as rogues or pirates. But others cheered them on. By the time of Walker's indictment, a jury had already convicted Henry Watkins, his former law partner and wrangler for fresh recruits, of violating the Neutrality Act; Emory had pleaded guilty; and a case was underway against Luis del Valle, the Mexican consul whom General Wool had arrested for his part in Count Gaston de Raousset-Boulbon's scheme to recruit French and German "colonists" to settle in Sonora, supposedly on behalf of Santa Anna. A jury convicted del Valle, but the government later dropped the charges when a second case against the French consul, Patrice Dillon, who had helped del Valle recruit French fighters, ended in a hung jury. Taken together, the trials "showed unmistakably the general loose feeling of society in San Francisco and California on the subject of filibusterism." The motives behind the prosecutions and whether filibustering itself could be considered a crime "were much discussed in private circles and by the public press."[4]

What was also discussed was yet another attempt by Raousset-Boulbon to invade Sonora. He dispatched several dozen men and followed them a few days later, arriving in Guaymas on July 1. He met with General José María Yáñez, head of the Mexican military outpost there, and offered to join his men with the Mexican forces, following the framework del Valle had established. But Raousset-Boulbon hadn't discussed this with his men, many of whom balked at joining Mexico instead of wresting territory away from it. Yáñez, similarly, distrusted the Frenchman. Suspicions grew into frictions, and gunfire erupted on July 13. After a few days of ineffectual intermittent fighting and negotiations, the French attacked Yáñez's troops garrisoned in their fort and in nearby buildings. But the ragtag filibusters were no match for trained soldiers, and the attack quickly dissolved, with most of the filibusters surrendering or running off. Some retreated to the Sonora Hotel, where Yáñez quickly launched an attack, slaughtering them all. Raousset-Boulbon, now without an army, surrendered. On August 13, acting on Yáñez's orders, soldiers escorted Raousset-Boulbon to a nearby beach, stood him before a firing squad, and killed him.[5]

Two months later and after a lengthy delay to contact witnesses, Walker's trial began in San Francisco. Presiding over the case was Judge Isaac S. K. Ogier, who had been the first district attorney for Los Angeles and who, as a state assemblyman, had introduced a bill that would have banned free African Americans from moving to California. Born in South Carolina, Ogier had practiced law in New Orleans in 1848 and 1849. It's unclear whether he and Walker had known each other there, but given the small legal community in the city, they likely at least knew *of* each other.[6]

Walker's old friend Edmund Randolph mounted the defense, aided by another lawyer, Calhoun Benham. It took a couple of days to seat a jury, because many of the summoned men were dismissed after expressing strong views on filibustering. Though only a handful of spectators were on hand for jury selection, when testimony finally began on October 16, the courtroom was packed. The US attorney, S. W. Inge, called several of Walker's men and friends—including Henry Crabb, his boyhood acquaintance—who described how the expedition came together, the meetings in Walker's rented rooms, the contents of the *Caroline* when she sailed, the expedition that followed on the *Anita*, and other details that painted a damning picture of Walker's intent. It also displayed how poorly conceived and run the campaign had been, including the fact that the filibusters were paid in Republic of Sonora scrip that was worthless and often slow in coming.

Walker rose occasionally to cross-examine witnesses. He pressed one, James Hamilton, to testify that the expedition had stolen no cattle until they came under attack at Ensenada, a battle in which Hamilton was wounded. Walker's point, though, was murky. Perhaps he was trying to paint the expedition's thievery as an act of retribution and compensation after being shot at and losing men to Melendrez's bullets. Ultimately, however, the prosecution's ten witnesses established the obvious—that Walker had arranged the expedition, and that while some men might have thought they were going to operate mines, most knew all along that it was intended as an invasion. After two days of testimony, the prosecution rested.

Walker began his defense around 11:00 AM on October 18, arguing that the prosecution and their witnesses had misconstrued the nature of the expedition. "I shall introduce evidence to show that at the time at leaving this port, my intention was to proceed to Guaymas and thence by land to the frontiers," Walker said. "And I shall also prove that it was only after we had got to sea and beyond the territory of the United States that this intention was changed so as to land at La Paz, and that previously to this, such was not my intention to proceed and land there in a hostile manner. This, gentlemen of the jury, is, in brief, the nature of my defense."

Walker summoned only three witnesses—his codefendant Snow; James Springer, who had accompanied him on his initial, unsuccessful excursion to Guaymas aboard the *Arrow*; and a man named William Godfrey—who testified that Walker first talked of going to Sonora to settle as ranchers and only turned to an invasion after they arrived at La Paz. Walker claimed the plans changed after they were attacked by the locals, starting the violent encounters that marked the rest of their experience. (He didn't mention that they had kidnapped the governor first.)

Inge went first in the closing argument, succinctly telling the jury that Walker's defense had refuted none of the testimony by the prosecution witnesses. Clearly, the plan all along was to invade Mexico, and Walker made the initial arrangements, including enlisting men and procuring weapons, on American soil. No other arguments or issues would, or could, matter, since the Neutrality Act left no wiggle room. Planning a hostile action from within the United States against a nation with which the United States was at peace was illegal. Nothing less than relations between nations was at stake.

Benham then rose on Walker's behalf and argued that the government had failed to prove that Walker conspired to attack Mexico. And even if he had, the Neutrality Act itself was unconstitutional, and thus Walker should be acquitted. Walker's crime, if he committed one, was not a crime against the United States but against Mexico, and Congress couldn't enact laws governing actions in another country. After a half-hour break, it was Randolph's turn. He, too, argued that no evidence tied Walker to the recruiting of invaders, and that Walker had only emerged as a leader once the *Caroline* sailed. "There was not a word proved to indicate that the meeting at Walker's room was not a prayer meeting, or anything else," he said, urging the jury to keep their "minds from wandering and following the acts of the defendant after he had left San Francisco," because they were not offenses under the Neutrality Act. Then Randolph, too, challenged the act itself as unconstitutional.

Besides, Randolph argued, Walker was motivated by the grandest of motives. "It was intended to drive back the savage Apaches," an effort first essayed by Raousset-Boulbon, who in his final effort "had fallen by the bullets of his executioners, on the sands of Guaymas." To oppose Walker, Randolph alleged, was to oppose decency, stability, and civilized society. "The government of the United States in a prosecution of this sort was, in fact, the ally of the savage" by seeking to imprison someone who sought to defend settlers against barbarous attack. "It is a strange partnership, surely—the army, and the navy, and the judiciary of the United States in league with the blood-red Apache!"

Walker was the last to speak. He, too, invoked his lofty intent to protect Sonorans against Indian attacks, painting the natives as aggressors. He argued that the federal government's decision not to prosecute Raousset-Boulbon after his first failed effort signaled that the government did not consider such expeditions a crime, so it was inconsistent to now target him for prosecution. Ultimately, Walker said, he and his men were emigrants, not invaders, and so had broken no laws.

Inge rose once more to offer a rebuttal of the defense. If the voyage of the *Caroline* was to bring miners to Sonora, then why was it loaded with firearms and not mining tools? The argument that Walker "was bound on an expedition of humanity . . . is not credible." Further, not only was the Neutrality Act constitutional, it was a wise and necessary law. Congress clearly had the authority to enact laws governing behavior in the United States, including ensuring its residents did not threaten the sovereignty of other nations.

With that, Judge Ogier sent the case to the jury, with one admonition: ignore the argument by the defense that it should nullify the Neutrality Act itself. "It has been suggested by counsel that, in this case, you were to be the judges of the law. I am constrained to believe the other way. The rule is laid down, and has been well settled by the adjudication of the federal courts, that you are not the judges of the law but are to take the law from the court." All the jurors need consider, he said, was whether the testimony they heard persuaded them that the crime had been committed. "If . . . the chartering a vessel and putting arms and instruments of war on board, the going out to sea, the leaving at night, and the hostile acts of the party after they had landed in Lower California, if these acts were sufficient to come to the conclusion in the mind of the jury that hostility was meditated before the expedition had set sail, then they might find the defendant guilty," Ogier instructed.

The jury left the courtroom to begin its deliberations. It returned eight minutes later: *not guilty*.

"When the verdict was pronounced, which the foreman did in a very emphatic tone," wrote the *Daily Alta* reporter covering the trial, "there was an audible manifestation of applause outside the bar, and many came up to shake Mr. Walker by the hand and congratulate him."

In the eyes of Walker's peers in San Francisco, it was no crime to plot the invasion of another country from US soil, no matter what Congress intended.

By the time of his acquittal, Walker had already resumed his career as a newspaper editor. He had been back less than a month when "the world-renowned hero of Sonora, is hereafter to reside in" Sacramento as an associate editor of the weekly *Democratic State Journal*, owned and edited by a couple of forty-niners: Benjamin F. Washington, whose great-grandfather was George Washington's younger brother Samuel; and Vincent E. Geiger, who would later stab a man and flee the country for Chile. But less than a week after that announcement, Walker quit for reasons unexplained and joined the *Commercial Advertiser* in San Francisco. By October, though, he was back with the *Democratic State*

Journal in Sacramento, where he wrote several editorials decrying extremism by both the pro- and anti-slavery forces in the state. Despite adopting the Louisiana legal codes, including slavery, as the law of his Republic of Sonora, Walker retained a view of the practice that was moderate for the times. He seemed less interested in whether the institution should stay or be abolished than in the tenor of the debate.[7]

Walker's brief connection with the *Commercial Advertiser* would provide the next step in his adventuring career. Among the paper's owners was a man named Byron Cole, who was also a partner in a new venture with William V. Wells and a handful of other San Franciscans called the Honduras Mining and Trading Company. The partners had come into possession of letters and other documents that led them to believe there was a fortune of gold to be mined along the Guayape River in the hilly Olancho region of Honduras, south of Trujillo and abutting Nicaragua's northwestern border. Few in the United States knew much about the region—even a reliable map was hard to find—and the company decided they needed to inspect it to verify the details they'd read. If the information was accurate, and the San Franciscans acted quickly and quietly, they could form the vanguard of a new gold rush—this one to the tropics rather than the semiarid foothills of the Sierra Nevada, and only a few days' travel by ship from New Orleans. Cole held several conversations about the prospects with Walker, seeking to persuade him to drop his ambitions toward northern Mexico. Central America, he argued, offered more natural resources, including verified deposits of gold, and weak governmental control.[8]

In fact, Nicaragua had recently fallen back into a civil war between the Granada-based Conservatives, led by Fruto Chamorro, and the León-based Liberals. A national election in 1853 produced no majority winner for the seat of "supreme director," with Chamorro receiving a plurality of 296 to Liberal standard-bearer Francisco Castellón's 193 votes. Two other candidates also received more than 100 votes. The results evidenced the geographic nature of the political divisions: Chamorro received no votes from León, and Castellón received one vote from Granada.[9]

The lack of a majority winner sent the election to the legislature, which selected Chamorro, who swiftly exiled the Liberal leaders, most of them—including Castellón—seeking refuge via the neighboring Liberal government of Honduran president General José Trinidad Cabañas. Chamorro convened a national assembly in January 1854, during which he pushed through a new constitution to replace the 1838 charter establishing the independent State of Nicaragua. The new constitution reflected core beliefs of the Conservatives, or Legitimists, who not only included the country's wealthiest landowners but also enjoyed the support of the influential Catholic Church. The document increased the minimum value of land possessions required before one could vote and apparently repudiated the concept of public lands, which under the 1838 constitution allowed those without property to grow subsistence crops on communal plots. It also placed significant new powers in the hands of the chief executive, whose title was changed from *supreme director* to *president*. It even changed the name of the country, from the State of Nicaragua to the Republic of Nicaragua.[10]

The new constitution, adopted on April 30, was only enforceable in Granada, but that didn't make it any more appealing to the Liberals, who came together quickly under longtime leader Máximo Jerez and began to fight. Liberal troops seized the Pacific port city of Realejo on May 5, then moved on to the village of Chinandega before securing their political base at León. On May 26, they reached the outskirts of Granada itself, rolling over Legitimist troops under the command of General Ponciano Corral at every encounter. Granada, though, was heavily reinforced, and the campaign stalled into a siege that would last more than a year. But the Liberals also established their own rival government at León, with Castellón, repatriated from Honduras, as its leader. So Nicaragua, long torn by the rivalry between two ersatz city-states, now had two national governments, neither of which could credibly claim political legitimacy or militarily control the country.

Chaos offered opportunity. Cole sold his stake in the *Commercial Advertiser* (after which Walker quit and returned to the *Democratic State Journal*), and he, Wells, and a third member of the company left San Francisco on August 15 aboard the *Cortes*, a seven-hundred-passenger steamship owned by Cornelius Vanderbilt. They arrived at San Juan del Sur on August 28, "our first experience of Central American peculiarities of climate being a tempestuous rain-squall, a significant foretaste of what might be expected for the future." The Americans made their way north to León and, bearing letters of introduction from mutual acquaintances, met with Castellón. Wells soon continued on to Honduras to investigate the potential for gold mining, while Cole settled in to persuade Castellón "that he should augment his forces by sending for 'the renowned Walker,' who he justly represented as one of the bravest and most capable of American adventurers."[11]

Castellón already had some Americans in his fighting force, including Charles W. Doubleday, who had arrived in Nicaragua from San Francisco just after the start of the siege of Granada. Doubleday came not as a soldier but as a rootless adventurer who had tired of the Sierra Nevada gold fields. Within hours of arriving at Realejo, Doubleday signed up with the Liberals in what he called their "efforts to establish by the sword that will of the people which had been declared through the ballot." He spent several days putting together a squadron of fighters from among the American and British fortune-seekers at San Juan del Sur. Doubleday spoke Spanish and had become a crack shot as a hunter, and he and his mercenaries quickly proved themselves to be capable fighters. Castellón awarded Doubleday the rank of captain. Given that positive experience with an American ally, Castellón agreed to Cole's overture as well, offering a twenty-one-thousand-acre land grant to a force of three hundred Americans under Walker's command, "provided they would engage in the Democratic cause and assist in the siege of Granada," for which they would receive military wages.[12]

Cole returned to California and reached out to Walker in early November. Even though a jury had acquitted the filibuster of violating the Neutrality Act over his Sonoran adventure, the terms of the Castellón offer gave Walker pause. It was clearly a contract for a military force, and if Walker organized an expedition under its terms, a new round of charges might stick. But he recognized one possible loophole: it was not clear which was the recognized government in Nicaragua. In fact, the US consul in San Juan del Sur was holding on to payments the Accessory Transit Company had deposited with him for the Nicaraguan government because he was uncertain which faction had the rights to it. So if the US consul wasn't sure which government was in control of Nicaragua, how could it accuse Walker of plotting against it from American soil? Still, Walker decided not to take the chance. He told Cole if he could obtain an invitation from Castellón for three hundred colonists to settle fifty-two thousand acres—more than double his original offer—with no mention of military service but with a guaranteed right to bear arms, Walker could proceed. Cole left San Francisco in late November, struck the new agreement with Castellón on December 29, and was back in Sacramento to present it to Walker in early February 1855.

Satisfied with the terms, Walker quit the newspaper, returned to San Francisco, and began raising money and men and putting together the logistics. He encountered Henry Crabb, who had joined a separate small group of Americans with a contract to provide five hundred men to the Nicaraguan Liberals through General Máximo Jerez—whose authority to negotiate such a deal was uncertain. Crabb, whose own ambitions were shifting toward California politics and a legislative seat in Sacramento, offered the Jerez contract to Walker, who turned it down in favor of the Castellón contract, he later explained, "not only because of its entire freedom from legal objections, but also because it was more reasonable, and had been given by an authority competent to make the bargain." Crabb's fellow interventionists eventually gave up on the Jerez proposal and joined Walker.[13]

Walker proceeded cautiously. He took the Castellón agreement to S. W. Inge, the federal attorney who had prosecuted him for the Sonoran expedition, and reported that Inge saw no conflict with the Neutrality Act. He also tracked down General Wool to apprise him of his plans, and reported that Wool "said he not only would not interfere with the enterprise, but wished it entire success." Wool remembered the encounter differently. He had received from Washington what he perceived to be a rebuke for his efforts to stop Walker's Sonoran expedition, informing him that, as a general in the US Army, he should limit his role to aiding civil authorities and not precipitate prosecutions. When Walker approached him with Castellón's contract, "I simply remarked, in reply, that, with the instructions which I had recently received from the Secretary of War, whether or not he was engaged in any such enterprise, I had no authority to interfere with him, certainly not until I was called upon by the civil authorities to aid in suppressing it."[14]

Walker, who had so easily attracted investors and adventurers for his Sonoran expedition, found that it "would be impossible to get more than a pitiful sum of money, and that . . . arrangements would have to be made on the most economical scale." He was further impaired by what he described as a "foot injury" (which some reports ascribe to yet another duel, though records are unclear) that made it hard for him to visit with possible investors. He managed to get $1,000 from Joseph Palmer of the Palmer, Cook & Company banking firm and began lining up men to join him.[15]

It's unclear whether he learned the lesson of Sonora and intentionally shied away from novice adventurers, but the core of his new venture consisted of experienced fighters, particularly veterans of the Mexican-American War. They included Achilles Kewen, who fought with López in Cuba; Timothy Crocker of the Sonora campaign; Frank P. Anderson, a veteran of the Mexican-American War; and Collier C. Hornsby, another Mexican-American War veteran and one-time sergeant at arms of the California legislature who had been involved with Crabb and the Jerez contract. In all, Walker put together an initial force of fifty-eight men—a far cry from the three hundred for which he had contracted with Castellón.[16]

Edmund Randolph and his law partner, Alexander Parker Crittenden, helped arrange the financing of a ship, but they had trouble finding a suitable vessel. In March, Randolph and Crittenden finally finagled an agreement with a man named Lamson, who owned the *Vesta*, "a leaky old brig which had weathered the waves for twenty-nine years." Most of its recent work involved moving lumber and other goods among San Francisco, Mendocino, and Humboldt Bay. The ship had collided with another vessel in January 1854, requiring significant repairs. Walker provisioned the ship for the voyage, and he and all his men were aboard at the Stewart Street Wharf on April 20, ready to set sail, when the San Francisco sheriff arrived with a writ. The ship's owner owed money to several vendors, who had placed a lien against the ship barring it from leaving port until the bills were paid.[17]

To enforce the lien, the sheriff placed several deputies aboard the ship, which led to a scuffle with some of Walker's men who were anxious to get underway. No one was arrested, but to ensure that the *Vesta* couldn't leave, the sheriff seized the sails. Once word got out about the unpaid bills incurred by the owner, vendors who had extended credit to Walker—in the form of stock in the Nicaraguan land grant—demanded cash instead and placed their own hold on the *Vesta*, further barring the ship from leaving port. Federal marshals enforced the writ by strategically anchoring the *W. L. Marcy*, a federal revenue cutter, next to the *Vesta*. Then the sheriff added his own complaint: the ship owed his office more than $300 for unspecified fees, and he would not let it set sail until the bill was paid. So there the *Vesta* sat at the end of the Stewart Street Wharf, filled with frustrated filibusters, under the watch of the sheriff's top deputy, J. B. Purdy, and blocked by a federal ship.

Walker tried to find a way out of the mess. After a few days, he determined that he and Lamson's creditors had a mutual friend: Henry Crabb. Walker met with his childhood friend and asked him to intervene with the Stockton-based vendors to whom Lamson owed money and vouch for his word and for the expedition: *there will be money, and the vendors will get paid.* Crabb, who had few doubts that Walker would wind up in control of thousands of acres of Nicaraguan land, quietly leaned on the creditors, who dropped their claim. Walker then pressured Lamson to intercede with the vendors from whom the expedition had bought supplies who were now demanding cash. "Lamson really controlled the action of the merchants who sold . . . the provisions, and when he was told it might not be safe for him to keep the passengers in San Francisco, he rather hesitatingly agreed to have the libel dismissed," Walker wrote later, the implication clear that Walker had issued the threat himself. Lamson persuaded the vendors to settle for the original credit terms, and that block on the ship was lifted as well.[18]

Walker still had the issue of the sheriff's bill and Deputy Purdy, who remained on the ship. But as soon as the other creditors' blocks were lifted, the *W. L. Marcy* no longer anchored as an adversary. Late at night on May 3, the *W. L. Marcy*'s captain returned the sails to the *Vesta* and deployed some of his men to help hoist them—all without anyone informing the sheriff. Walker had persuaded Purdy to join him below deck to look at some paperwork, and once there told him he would not be allowed to return to the main deck until the ship was underway. As long as the deputy agreed, he would be treated well; if he sought to climb to the deck, he would be restrained. Purdy acquiesced, and so was sitting in a cabin drinking champagne and smoking cigars in the early morning hours as the steam tug *Resolute* guided the *Vesta* from the wharf into the bay and the shipping channel. As the ships reached the Golden Gate, Purdy was brought up top and transferred to the *Resolute*, which steamed back to the wharf.

William Wells later memorialized the moment:

> As the tug had cast off, and the distance between the brig and her widened, and the headlands of San Francisco harbor began to dim, cheer upon cheer went up from the expeditionists, who gathered on the *Vesta*'s sides, and took, some of them, their last look upon the noble entrance to the bay. The moon shone brightly down upon a

foaming sea. They were afloat upon the broad ocean, bound upon an expedition in which they had staked each his all.[19]

The cheers and excitement died away and the men turned their attention to settling into their floating quarters. As the *Vesta* began rocking with the gentle swells of the open ocean, Captain Richard Eyre ordered his helmsman to head south.

The *Vesta* moved slowly down the coastline. The ship held sixty-two men, all but four of whom were enlisted in Walker's army of colonists, each carrying a rifle and most also with knives and with a pistol tucked into a belt or a holster. "They were most of them men of strong character, tired of the humdrum of common life, and ready for a career which might bring them the sweets of adventure or the rewards of fame," Walker wrote. But they were soldiers and not sailors, which meant the ship had only four real seamen aboard.[20]

No records suggest that the *Vesta* made stops at any other American ports on its journey south, and it seems unlikely that Walker would want it to, since it was unclear whether harbor authorities would let him leave again. The ship left US waters after several days of sailing and skirted Baja California—after the fiascos there and in Sonora, it's not likely Mexican officials would have been very receptive, either. After passing the tip of the peninsula, the *Vesta* headed southeastward along the mainland. At the Gulf of Tehuantepec, off Oaxaca in southern Mexico, the vessel "encountered a gale which tested her timbers—twenty-nine years in her sides—to the utmost. The bow of the old brig would open to the waves as they roared around her, and at times her decks were swept clear by the huge billows passing over her." Several of Walker's soldiers were pressed into service as sailors to help Captain Eyre keep the ship afloat until the storm, mercifully, passed.

More than five weeks after the *Vesta* left San Francisco, the adventurers got their first glimpse of Nicaragua as the twenty-nine-hundred-foot-high volcano of Cosigüina rose over the horizon. Still active, the volcano formed the southern edge of the Gulf of Fonseca, an island-strewn body of water shared by El Salvador to the west, Honduras to the north and east, and Nicaragua to the south. At the mouth of the gulf, the *Vesta* found itself becalmed. After bobbing on the waves for a few hours, Eyre and Walker dispatched a small boat to Amapala on the Honduran island of Tigre. Castellón had sent an American, Captain Gilbert Morton, to await the Americans at Amapala, and the small boat returned to the ship with him. Eyre didn't know the coast of Nicaragua, but Morton was intimately familiar with it, and he took over navigation for the rest of the journey.[21]

Walker had heard no news of Nicaragua and its civil war since leaving San Francisco, and given the amount of time it took for word to spread by ship arrivals, even that news was several weeks out of date. He also was unaware that the Legitimist government had been formally recognized by the United States (as Walker was sailing, the US envoy to Nicaragua, John H. Wheeler, sealed a trade pact with the Legitimists) and had filed a diplomatic protest. José de Marcoleta, the head of the Nicaraguan delegation to the United States, wrote to Secretary of State William Marcy that he had "with sorrow and astonishment, been informed" that "the so-called Colonel Walker, in company of several armed persons," had been allowed to sail for Nicaragua "in evident violation of the laws of both countries." Marcy replied that from the US government's standpoint, Walker and his men had left to join the Nicaraguan army, "which is not forbidden by the laws of the United States." So Walker's dodge of accepting an invitation rather than organizing an expedition got him safely around the Neutrality Act.[22]

As they sailed from Tigre, Walker questioned Morton on the state of affairs, learning that the war was not going well for the Liberals. The siege of Granada had fizzled, and the Conservatives began pushing back, eventually taking control of most of the country save the Occidental Department, the country's westernmost department, or state, which included León. And even there, the Liberals' hold was not secure. As the Granada siege crumbled and the Liberals retreated, they had lost faith in their military leader, Máximo Jerez, who had signed the mercenary contract Crabb offered to Walker. Castellón replaced him with General José Trinidad Muñoz, a Liberal hero who had put down one of the insurrections that united the warring political parties in the previous decade.[23]

Most mercenaries, upon learning that their prospective employers were losing the war, would question the wisdom of carrying on. But not Walker.

Joining an army that was winning offered little upside. Saving a lost cause was where a man could make his mark, his fame, and his fortune. Walker "felt that the more desperate the fortunes of the Castellon party were, the more deeply would they be indebted to the men who might rescue them from their danger, and the more thoroughly would they be committed to any course or policy the Americans might propose."[24]

The *Vesta* arrived at the narrow harbor at Realejo on the morning of June 16. Castellón had sent three men to greet Walker on his behalf: Charles Doubleday, who by this point had been made a colonel; Dr. Joseph W. Livingston, the former American consul at León; and a Liberal colonel named Ramirez. Doubleday was unimpressed at that first meeting, finding the diminutive Walker to be

> quiet and unassuming, as mild a mannered man as ever cut a throat or scuttled ship. . . . He was wholly unacquainted with the people and their mode of warfare, but during my short acquaintance with him he had developed an amount of willfulness in small things which augured a despotic character, which I was unwilling to subject myself to.

He would soon change his assessment.[25]

Though Castellón had arranged for rooms for the Americans at Realejo, he anxiously awaited meeting Walker in León, about twenty miles away. As the rest of the men settled in, Walker and Sonoran veteran Timothy Crocker set off under the guidance of Doubleday and Ramirez. They passed through Chinandega and then even smaller hamlets, encountering lounging Liberal army squadrons along the way. "You could perceive that the sergeants and corporals were keenly watching lest some of their new recruits might take advantage of the halt to slip away for a moment, and so escape the hated service." As the travelers neared León "they beheld spread out before them a vast plain which seems almost boundless in extent as you look toward the south; while gazing northward, you perceive the lofty line of volcanoes—Viejo on one flank and Momotombo on the other stretching from the Gulf of Fonseca to the Lake of Managua."[26]

Doubleday led his fellow Americans to Castellón's house. "It did not require many minutes to see that he was not the man to control a revolutionary movement, or to conduct it to a successful issue," Walker wrote later. "There was a certain indecision, not merely in his words and features, but even in his walk and the general motions of his body; and this trait of character seemed to be aggravated by the circumstances about him."

General Muñoz arrived a short time later, and the contrast was striking. "Muñoz had an air of conceit which affirmed a feeling of superiority on his part, to all around him. It was not difficult to see that they disliked each other; though Castellón concealed his feelings and opinions better than Muñoz." Walker didn't care for Muñoz, either, finding it arrogant that the Nicaraguan general, dressed in a full uniform, held forth with opinions on the merits of Winfield Scott and Zachary Taylor as American military leaders, "exposing his ignorance in every sentence, and showing the weakness of his character." Muñoz, for his part, seemed unimpressed with Walker, as well. He insisted to Castellón that if the American forces were to join the army, they must be divided up into small units and be deployed among his own troops.

After Muñoz left, Walker told Castellón that he had no intention of serving under the general and would lead his men himself—those who had arrived with him, and those he expected to follow later. Walker had studied maps of Nicaragua and devised a plan for a counteroffensive to recover lost territory. Once Walker and his men were accepted, they would march on the city of Rivas, a key part of the Conservatives' supply route. Rivas was also the main city of the Meridional Department, the location of the Accessory Transit Company's road from Lake Nicaragua to the Pacific Ocean. Controlling such valuable territory would allow the Liberals to collect more taxes with which to finance their war. It also would make it easier for other American mercenaries to join them, sailing on a Pacific Mail Steamship Company vessel to San Juan del Sur then over the transit road. Castellón, intrigued by the American's aggressiveness, agreed in principal, but said he wanted to make sure his minister of war, Buenaventura Selva, had no objections before he committed.

The next morning, Walker, Crocker, and Doubleday—whom Walker persuaded to join his detachment—traveled to Chinandega, to which the rest of the force had moved from Realejo, and waited for the final word from Castellón. It came on June 20. The Americans, who ostensibly had sailed for Nicaragua to become settlers with a fifty-two-thousand-acre land grant, were now Nicaraguan citizens and soldiers, members of La Falange Americana—the American Phalanx. Castellón gave Walker the rank of colonel, and left it to him to arrange his own officer corps and commissions. Walker split his men into two companies, each under a captain. He appointed Achilles Kewen his lieutenant colonel and, beneath him, made Crocker a major. Included in the order from Castellón was the good news that he did not expect Walker to seize Rivas alone. He ordered Colonel Ramirez to put together a force of two hundred Nicaraguans to augment the American force, and to place them under Walker's command as well.

Walker's Phalanx made its way back to Realejo to organize itself, procure supplies, and await the arrival of Ramirez's men. The Nicaraguan civil war was about to take another turn.

9 | ON TO SAN JUAN DEL SUR

IT TOOK WALKER THREE days to gather and load food and the tools of war aboard the *Vesta*, a process slowed because only small boats could navigate the narrow river from Realejo to the bay. Colonel Ramirez, a protégé of General Muñoz and a "morose and inconspicuous officer," reneged on Castellón's promise of two hundred men—fewer than half that mustered at Realejo, a development that didn't surprise Charles Doubleday, who had low regard for Ramirez. Doubleday warned Walker that Ramirez "was not only a man of inferior capacity and courage in the field, but was also a tool of Muñoz."[1]

Walker shrugged it off. "The reason for his indifference," Doubleday later recalled, "was his inordinate confidence in the ability of his handful of Americans to conquer, unassisted, any number of the enemy." That hubris worried Doubleday, who had fought against the Conservative forces for several years, while Walker's sole military experience "had been confined to the sage-brush nurtured inhabitants of Sonora, who were ready to fly at the sound of their own guns. He was evidently committing the grave error in a commanding officer, of undervaluing his enemy."

The *Vesta* set sail on June 23, and spent "four storm-tossed days" at sea. Doubleday was already suffering from dysentery, and the rough seas gave him the added misery of seasickness. The company doctor advised him to remain on the ship until his health recovered, but Doubleday refused. "No argument short of a clear presentation of the impossibility of my getting through would have deterred me from making the attempt." Walker ordered the *Vesta* to anchor off Brito, the small harbor town north of San Juan del Sur; Walker selected it believing that the Conservatives had reinforced San Juan del Sur, and he preferred not to have to fight his way to Rivas.

Amid rough seas, the invaders put to shore in small launches. The boat carrying Doubleday hit the beach with such force that he toppled overboard and "but for the active exertions of the men, I should doubtless have been drowned." It was near midnight before all the men reached dry land. As they set out, Walker and the Americans at the front and Ramirez and his men at the rear, a light rain soon turned into a steady downpour so thick the two local guides lost the trail. Walker halted the march and the men huddled under trees, soaked through and with their ammunition compromised by moisture, to wait out the storm.

Rain dogged the men all the next day, making the march slow and exceedingly uncomfortable, but they encountered no Conservative forces. Around nine o'clock on the night of June 28 they reached a hamlet called Tola, about nine miles from Rivas. Some of Ramirez's men familiar with the village relayed to Walker that the Legitimist government had a small *quartel*, or military barracks, at Tola. Walker sent a squadron of twenty men on horseback ahead to try to surprise the garrison. The rain that had made them so miserable now helped them, the roar of the torrential downpour obscuring the sound of their approach. It also drove the lone sentry from his post. The Americans found the rest of the small detachment playing cards inside a commandeered house and rushed in, guns blazing. Several of the Legitimist soldiers were killed or wounded while the others fled, giving the Americans a swift victory. But the escapees carried word to Rivas of the approaching force, confirming something the Conservatives already expected. A German wanderer who had been in Realejo while Walker and his men were preparing had carried the news to Granada, and the alert was issued to the troops at Rivas. General Ponciano Corral, the Legitimists' commander in chief at Granada, had already sent extra men to Rivas, boosting the force under Colonel Manuel Bosque's command to eight hundred trained soldiers, who also could count on help from sympathetic and armed residents. Bosque ordered a series of barricades made of looped-together logs to be erected on the roads leading to the plaza at the center of the city, hoping to slow down the Liberals' advance. And then he waited.

By morning, the weather had cleared, and the Americans—now dry, fed, and rested—set out for Rivas, with Ramirez and his men again trailing behind. Where the previous day the men occasionally had to wade through shin-deep mud, now the footing was firmer, if not completely dry, and the men made good time, slowly climbing the range that separated Lake Nicaragua from the Pacific. At a crest near Rivas "the advance guard reached a turn in the road [and] seemed to halt for a moment, involuntarily." The men had been ordered to move in silence but "an exclamation of surprise and pleasure escaped the lips of all" as they caught their first sight of the lake and the majestic Ometepe Island, formed by two nearly mile-high volcanoes. "The first glimpse . . . almost made the pulse stand still. . . . The dark forests of the tropics clothed the side of the volcano, which seemed to repose under the influence of the soft sunshine around it." The men were mesmerized.[2]

After a brief rest, the column moved on, reaching the road to Granada, which would enable Walker to attack Rivas from the north. Walker hoped that would give him an element of surprise, since the Legitimists would likely be watching more closely for an attack from the southwest, the closest point to where Walker had made landfall. About a half mile from the edge of Rivas, Walker ordered the men to halt and gathered his top aides together to outline his strategy and issue orders. Lieutenant Colonel Achilles Kewen and Major Timothy Crocker were to lead the attack—an audacious surge of men directly toward the heart of the city. Ramirez and his men would hold back, then follow to protect the Americans' flank while dispatching squadrons to seal off roads out of town, ensuring the Legitimists couldn't escape. Doubleday objected, arguing that it would be foolhardy to send Ramirez's troops out of sight until they had secured the plaza. Walker waved him off. "With the smile which we afterwards learned to understand the meaning of so well, he replied that I had not yet seen what fifty-six such men as he had, and so armed, could do." It then fell to Doubleday, fluent in Spanish, to inform the Nicaraguan colonel whom he distrusted of Walker's orders. Ramirez's eyes "sparkled as he perceived how favorable the disposition was for furthering his ulterior views." Doubleday sensed that Ramirez had no intention of engaging in a firefight with the Legitimists.[3]

Crocker and Kewen arranged their men two abreast in a line. They set out around noon, and once they neared the first barricade they charged in a screaming wave. The Legitimists fired a round of grapeshot from a twenty-four-pound cannon behind the barricade, but the rush had caught them by such surprise they hadn't time to aim, and the blast sailed wildly over the Americans' heads. They quickly overran the barricade as the Legitimists retreated to a second blockade. Retreat, though, had a purpose. The Americans were now well within Rivas, on a road lined with houses and shops. Legitimist soldiers, secreted in the buildings, opened a withering crossfire. Walker's troops scattered to the edges of the road, hugging the walls of the buildings for protection, and continued forward toward the plaza.

"We were now near enough to their stronghold to feel a cross-fire that, with better aim, should have annihilated us," Doubleday recalled, "and we also found that the more substantial nature of their defenses made further progress impossible, except by the slow and laborious method of picks and crowbars." But they had no such tools. Instead, they broke down the doors of buildings and sought cover inside as the vanguard of the invading force balked at the edge of the heavily reinforced plaza. Crocker, one arm useless from a bullet that had shattered a shoulder and bleeding from a graze wound on his chin, appeared before Walker to report that the men wouldn't go on.

Walker looked to the rear for Ramirez and his men, who were nowhere to be found. Instead, a fresh squad of Legitimist soldiers just arriving from San Juan del Sur suddenly appeared, sealing off the Americans. Shooting as they ran, Walker and his men reached a large adobe building near the top of a rise, kicked in the wide front doors, and slipped inside, the walls finally giving some protection from the bullets. "The men set about making the best arrangements for defense possible in such a place" by pushing heavy furniture into the doorway to slow any effort to overrun them.

They had just finished when the first rush came, an advance guard of enemy soldiers climbing bayonet-first over the barricade, some firing as they moved. Doubleday, Kewen, and a few others slashed at the bayonets with swords as fellow Phalanx members began firing from behind, killing and wounding the first couple of lines and sending the rest in retreat, leaving the dead and the dying Legitimists at the barricade.

Battle of Rivas. *Courtesy of Anne S. K. Brown Military Collection, Brown Digital Repository, Brown University Library*

But the Conservatives' forces had caused damage. "As the fire of our men released us from the pressure of the enemy, Lieutenant Colonel Kewen, Walker's second-in-command and a veteran of López's adventures in Cuba, staggered forward, clutching the air with his hands." Doubleday "caught him and laid him gently on his back. There was no need to ask how badly he was hurt, for the purple stream issuing from his lips, and a red spot in the centre of his breast from which too the blood flowed rapidly, told me . . . he had been shot through the lung, and smilingly sank in death."

Crocker, Walker's third-in-command, also had been killed, as had more than a dozen other of Walker's force, with more wounded. Still they fought on, firing over the barricade and through windows, as the Legitimist soldiers poured bullets into the building through the same gaps. One slug struck Doubleday in the side of the head, lodging near his ear and dropping him to the floor. "I remember a flickering sensation as of a struggle to keep down to the earth in opposition to a gravitative impulse upward, and then I distinctly heard Captain Hornsby say, 'He's gone,' and Colonel Walker reply, 'It is a pity.'" Doubleday bled profusely but was stunned more than damaged—the bullet had cracked but not penetrated his skull—and after a few moments, he was back on his feet.

Walker was down to about thirty-five men healthy enough to fight, and he no longer harbored any hope that Ramirez would come to their rescue. The Legitimists, sensing that they had the Americans at their mercy, continued to press. They ignited the thatch-and-wood roof of the adobe and began maneuvering a cannon into position to blast through a wall. Doubleday suggested to Walker that rather than wait to be annihilated, they mount a quick counterattack and try to shoot their way to a ravine visible beyond the plaza, which would give them cover as they tried to escape Rivas. Walker agreed, and those who could still run gathered at the edge of the barricade. At a signal, they emerged en masse, scrambling over the stacked furniture, yelling and shooting as they ran right into the heart of the enemy soldiers "with such impetuosity that we were firing our revolvers in our opponents' faces and thrusting our way through their ranks before they had any notion of what we were about." By dashing through the line of attackers, the Americans also made it difficult for the Legitimists to fire without shooting each other. One of the Americans fell, mortally wounded, but the rest, still firing, reached the ravine and quickly followed it out of Rivas. Staying away from roads and cutting through cacao plantations, they reached the village of San Jorge about a mile and a half away. There, confident that the Conservatives had decided not to pursue them, they finally had a chance to rest and take stock.[4]

The battle had lasted about four hours, and it was a disaster. Among the dead (Walker put the total at eight; others counted at least sixteen) were his top two officers, Kewen and Crocker, the latter of whom Walker seemed to have formed a deeper bond with than with others. He may have seen something of himself in Crocker. "The death of Crocker was a loss hardly to be repaired," Walker later wrote. "A boy in appearance, with a slight figure, and a face almost feminine in its delicacy and beauty, he had the heart of a lion; and his eye, usually mild and gentle, though steady in its expression, was quick to perceive a false movement on the part of an adversary." He described Crocker, despite his lack of military experience, as "invaluable," and said that after "many a trying hour . . . the fellowship of difficulty and danger had established a sort of freemasonry between [us]."[5]

The deadly tenacity of Walker's Legitimist opponents forced a reconsideration by white supremacists who viewed the dark-skinned Central Americans as inferior people and fighters. "This has been no boys' play, as the list of killed and wounded sufficiently displays," the *Alta California* noted in a later description of the rout.

> And we may add that however contemptible these natives may be physically and morally, they are now an enemy by no means to be despised, having been engaged in active warfare for the last thirteen months with guns constantly in their hands. They do not now throw away their shots as before, and make really formidable soldiers, living for days upon plantains, running barefoot through the country, acclimated and capable of enduring every fatigue.[6]

Walker would later learn that the wounded men they left behind had been summarily executed, their bodies stacked in a heap with the other dead and burned. The attack on Rivas was doomed from the start. Even if Walker had been able to maintain the element of surprise, he would still have been recklessly leading his men into a clash with a far superior force able to fight from behind barricades and inside houses. It also became clear that Colonel Ramirez had recognized the plan's futility and treacherously withdrawn his forces' support—possibly on the orders of General Muñoz, since Doubleday had warned that Ramirez was the general's "tool." As soon as the American Phalanx moved into Rivas, the colonel had marched his men south to Costa Rica, abandoning Walker's men to their inevitable defeat. The Americans were, militarily, children at play, and the men now gathered at San Jorge were lucky to have survived it.

———

Staying alive became Walker's immediate goal. The best option, he thought, was to make for San Juan del Sur and from there try to reach the sanctuary of the *Vesta*, so after a brief rest at San Jorge the men set out. Walker insisted on a brisk pace, fearing the Legitimists would guess their destination and try to cut them off. With Ramirez's betrayal fresh in his mind, he also distrusted the Nicaraguan guide, a Liberal captain named Mayorga, who was leading them over obscure trails to the transit road and then the coast. Walker directed the Spanish-speaking Doubleday to inform Mayorga that "if he should lead us into an ambush, his life would pay the forfeit, since every man had orders, in that event, to shoot him." Mayorga protested that he couldn't be held responsible if the Legitimists attacked, but Walker wouldn't relent. As Mayorga led, Walker and Doubleday flanked him, each with a pistol drawn to reinforce the threat—and to keep Mayorga from running off.[7]

The bedraggled force looked more like a parade of tramps than soldiers. They'd been moving or fighting for days and were covered in filth and, in many instances, blood, some with arms in slings or relying on makeshift crutches. Unshaven, some missing clothing, including boots, they worked their way south, slowed by both the wounded among them and the briars and thickets that obscured hard-to-follow trails.

At midnight, they reached a clearing and a small cattle ranch, and Walker called a halt. They rousted the rancher, his wife, and their sons. Using the parents as hostages, Walker directed the sons to butcher an ox and prepare breakfast for the men while they slept. Doubleday, to his own surprise after two sleepless nights, remained awake and "sat the long night through, occasionally chatting with the old farmer and his wife, the latter of whom seemed anxious to know whether we would not kill them before leaving in the morning."[8]

As the ravenous men awakened and dug into the breakfast, the Phalanx's surgeon, Dr. Alex M. Jones, approached Doubleday and examined the wound in his head, then "extracted the ounce ball from my skull, near the ear, using a jack-knife and his fingers." Refreshed, the men set out for the transit road that they discovered, to their relief, was only a couple of miles away. Taking the road, though, involved risk, since the Americans would not be the only travelers. A chance encounter with Legitimist troops wasn't the only concern. Any traveler could tell easily that they were Americans engaged as a fighting force—despite their lack of uniforms, the rifles, cartridge boxes, and red ribbons streaming from their hats were a telltale giveaway—and tip off the Legitimists where to find them. An added problem was the nature of the road itself. It was smooth and wide enough for carts, but the surface was crushed white gravel, which lacerated the feet of those whose boots had disintegrated during the sodden marching. That included Doubleday, who now was bleeding from both the skull and the soles of his feet.

After a few hours on the trail, at the sound of approaching horses, Walker ordered the men to hide in the brush, where they watched a treasure train—a horse-drawn cart protected by gunmen—pass by, bringing gold and specie from the Pacific route to the Atlantic and, eventually, New York. The decision to hide rather than confront and, possibly, attack, suggests how rattled Walker and his men were in the aftermath of their first battle.

Back on the road, they soon encountered a solitary American horseman named Dewey, whom Doubleday had fought alongside in pre-Walker battles. Dewey informed Walker that there were no Legitimist forces at the beachside military barracks at San Juan del Sur, which emboldened Walker to increase the pace of the march. Doubleday, slowed by illness, wounds, and lacerated feet, soon fell behind, and began looking for a hiding spot along the road to rest and recover as the Phalanx continued without him. Dewey noticed Doubleday's predicament and, circling back, helped "me up behind his saddle, rescued me from the inevitable fate which awaited those who from wounds or exhaustion were left behind"—execution if discovered by the Legitimists.

The motley band of invaders entered San Juan del Sur just after sunset. Walker commandeered a Costa Rican schooner, the *San José*, and the men were ferried aboard, the last clambering over the rail as darkness settled. Walker's plan was to set sail in search of the *Vesta* or, failing to find her, force the captain of the *San José* to take the Phalanx back to Realejo. Walker's men roamed the ship searching for places to stretch out and sleep. Because the ship couldn't set sail until the tide turned, Walker and a few others kept watch, scanning the shoreline for signs that the Legitimists might have caught up to them.

A flash of light broke the darkness, which they soon concluded was from a fire in the abandoned beachside barracks, a blaze that seemed to be spreading quickly. Walker dispatched a boat to shore to find out what had happened, and received the return news that Dewey, Doubleday's savior, and another American, a fisherman named Sam, had torched the empty army barracks as an act of personal revenge against the Legitimists. Fortunately, the fire was contained to the barracks complex, but that was due only to the relatively calm breeze. Stronger winds could easily have engulfed the town of wood-frame buildings.

The arson angered Walker, who feared the townspeople would blame the Phalanx for endangering their homes and businesses. He sent men back to shore to arrest Dewey and Sam. The detachment returned with the two men aboard a second boat, Sam's fishing launch, which they tethered to the stern of the *San José*. They persuaded Sam, who was stumbling drunk, to board the *San José*, but the more sober Dewey, armed with two revolvers, refused to leave the launch. After some jockeying, he hid in a low spot of the boat, out of the line of fire of the two sharpshooters Walker had stationed at the ship's stern with orders to shoot Dewey if he tried to cut the towline.

Walker convened a brief trial of Sam, who in his drunkenness had already admitted he and Dewey set the barracks afire. Walker ordered him shot and a note attached to the body explaining that he had been executed by the Phalanx as punishment for his crime, and dispatched a detachment to take Sam ashore and carry out the sentence. But once on land, Sam slipped his shackles and fled; his captors returned to the ship but Walker and Doubleday doubted their story and presumed they let him go, which Walker feared would fuel belief in the village that his own men had torched the barracks.

As the tide turned and the morning breeze picked up, the *San José* weighed anchor and began drifting seaward, towing the launch that still sheltered Dewey and, they were surprised to learn, Sam's wife, who the Americans didn't know had been hiding on the launch. As the two craft moved out to sea, Dewey grabbed Sam's wife and, using her as a shield, moved toward the front of the launch and the towline. Walker ordered the sharpshooters to pick their moment and avoid hitting the woman, an opportunity that came as Dewey exposed himself reaching for the rope. Two rifles cracked and bullets tore through Dewey's body, knocking him backward into the shallow hold; one of the bullets also struck the woman in the thigh. Soldiers pulled the launch to the *San José*. Sam's wife was taken aboard and treated (she eventually recovered); Walker's men sewed Dewey's body up in a sail and dropped it overboard.

Walker saw his efforts to hold his two fellow Americans accountable for their crimes against the people of San Juan del Sur as an act of nobility:

> The Nicaraguans conceived from these events a respectful idea of American justice. They saw that the men they had been taught to call "filibusters," intended to maintain law and secure order wherever they went; that they had the will to administer justice, and would, when they had the power, protect the weak and the innocent from the crimes of the lawless and abandoned.

It was a romanticized and distorted mirror into which Walker gazed.[9]

A few hours after leaving San Juan del Sur, the *San José* encountered the *Vesta* cruising offshore, and Walker and his men transferred back to their original ship. The vessel anchored off Realejo early on July 1. Doubleday had sailed there separately in command of Sam's fishing launch, and, suffering from fever he ascribed to his head wound and exposure, was hauled by cart to the home of a doctor friend in Chinandega, where he spent several weeks healing and regaining his strength.

Walker used the time at sea to write a report on the battle at Rivas in which he denounced Colonel Ramirez but also attributed his duplicity "to the inspiration, if not orders, of the commander-in-chief," General Muñoz. Walker threatened that "unless the course of Muñoz was inquired into, and cleared of the suspicions hanging about it, the Americans would be compelled to leave the service of the Provisional Government" and sell their services elsewhere in Central America. He didn't go into details, but his backup plan was to offer aid to Honduras's Liberal president, General José Trinidad Cabañas, who had sheltered Nicaragua's Liberal leaders after the Legitimists exiled them, and who was fighting a war with Guatemala.[10]

Castellón thanked Walker and his men for joining the Liberal cause and, without mentioning Muñoz, urged them to stay on. He sent Joseph Livingston, the former US consul, to the *Vesta* to reinforce the message and to pass along Castellón's fears that the Legitimists were planning an assault on León to drive the Liberals from their last main stronghold.

Walker held firm. Emissaries ran back and forth. Castellón eventually traveled to Realejo, met briefly in person with Walker, and wore him down. Leaving the wounded in Chinandega, Walker and his healthy fighters—reprovisioned under Castellón's orders—struck out for León, where Castellón arranged a meeting with Walker and Muñoz. If the intent was to clear the air, it didn't work—the treachery at Rivas went unmentioned. Instead, they discussed reported movements of Legitimist troops and general plans, but their mutual distrust was manifest. Muñoz, in fact, had written privately on July 2 to the president of El Salvador, who was trying to mediate a truce between the Liberals and Legitimists, that he refused to "accept the Yankees," and was suspicious of their motives and true loyalties.[11]

The feared attack on León by the Legitimists faded away as reports of troop movements dwindled. The Liberals similarly fell into inaction as Castellón, Muñoz, former military commander Máximo Jerez, and war minister Buenaventura Selva struggled to find common ground with Walker. Muñoz again sought to dismantle the Phalanx, recommending the Americans be divided into units of ten and assigned to separate divisions of the Liberal Army, which would then march along separate routes to Granada, striking at the Legitimist heart. Walker again refused to divide his men or to give up command of them.

Walker still believed that controlling the transit road would be crucial to controlling the country, so he urged a second, larger attack on Rivas. But the Liberal command rejected that idea, fearing that sending troops back to Rivas would leave León, Chinandega, and Realejo open to Legitimist attack. Walker did win one point, though. The original intermediary between him and the Nicaraguans, Byron Cole, talked Castellón into offering the Phalanx a new contract. Dropping the facade that his men were a society of emigrants, Walker agreed to recruit a contingent of three hundred American fighters to be paid $100 a month, and awarded five hundred acres of land at the end of their service. Since the agreement was being negotiated from Nicaragua, Walker couldn't be accused of violating the Neutrality Act by signing it. Cole also, surprisingly, gained for Walker the authority to "settle all differences and outstanding accounts between the Government and the Accessory Transit Company."[12]

The Legitimists, meanwhile, had a very good reason for their scaled-back troop movements. In March, their president, Fruto Chamorro, had died of dysentery, a development the Legitimists kept hidden for weeks, fearing its impact on the war. A month after his death, fellow Legitimist politician José María Estrada assumed the presidency, with General Corral still leading the military efforts, aided now by José Santos Guardiola, a Honduran general with a reputation for brutality from his involvement in massacres a decade earlier. Castellón and Muñoz had been negotiating with Corral and, by extension, Estrada, but those talks broke down over how a new joint government might be formed. Before the fighting could resume, however, a wave of cholera swept through both armies, though it skipped the American battalion, which likely gained some protection by its isolation from the Nicaraguan troops.

With illness raging and no one able to settle on a course of action, little occurred for several weeks. Walker decided to move his men from León back to Chinandega, where they would have easier access to the *Vesta* in case they ultimately decided to go to Honduras. Castellón and Muñoz didn't want the Americans to leave. When Walker ordered a collection of oxcarts to help transport the Phalanx's equipment, Muñoz instead moved some 350 of his own troops into barracks across from the Americans' quarters. Walker was alarmed: "Had Muñoz been able to take the Americans unawares, he would, in all probability, have disarmed them and sent them out of the country." Walker sent word to Castellón that if Muñoz's men weren't removed he "would consider the force hostile and act accordingly." Muñoz withdrew, the oxcarts arrived, and the Americans repositioned themselves at Chinandega.[13]

Still, no military plan gelled. Walker and Castellón continued corresponding about the role of the Phalanx. Walker decided to again attack the Meridional Department, to gain control of the transit road "in order to recruit from the passengers to and from California, and to have the means of easy and rapid communication with the United States." And he would do it with or without Castellón's blessing or Muñoz's military support. In fact, Muñoz had already marched with six hundred men for the northern border area near Honduras to counteract a reported move by the Legitimist troops under Guardiola to connect up with sympathetic Honduran forces for a joint offensive against León. As Walker prepared his own march to the south—buying or commandeering firearms and ammunition—he persuaded José Maria Valle, a Liberal colonel and indigenous Nicaraguan (and a rival to Muñoz) known popularly as El Chelon, to join his effort to secure the transit road. Valle, who walked with a pronounced limp thanks to a shattered leg bone suffered during the siege of Granada, brought with him about 165 men. Walker, too, was adding to his roster as Americans and a few Nicaraguans joined, bringing his total back to about fifty—though by now cholera was beginning to spread among his force.

On August 18, General Muñoz and his army confronted Guardiola's Legitimists at El Sauce, a village some thirty-five miles northeast of León. The battle lasted several hours, and at its conclusion, Guardiola retreated with his men to Granada, leaving scores of dead behind. The Liberal troops also suffered severe casualties, including, crucially, Muñoz, who during the battle was shot in the back by one of his own men, José María Herrera, a Honduran artilleryman who was sympathetic to Walker and bore a deep grievance against Muñoz over his actions during the 1840s civil wars. Muñoz died a few hours later.[14]

Castellón told Walker that with Muñoz gone, so too were the frictions in the high command, and he urged Walker to return with his men to protect León. Castellón feared that once the Legitimists learned of Muñoz's death, Guardiola would try to seize León, and Castellón wanted all the troops he could muster to protect his government. The message reached Walker on August 23, as the *Vesta* was about to set sail. Emboldened by the addition of Valle's troops and cognizant that the death of Muñoz gave him more power, Walker rejected Castellón's request and set off for San Juan del Sur, with most of the men aboard the *Vesta* and the rest crammed onto a small ketch, the *Esperanza*. "After getting to sea the cholera was less severe among the troops, and few died between the time of leaving Realejo and the arrival of the brig at San Juan del Sur." Foul weather—"baffling winds"—separated the ships and slowed their progress, but they finally arrived August 29 to find the southern port abandoned by the Legitimists.[15]

At the port town, Walker was surprised to find a former acquaintance from California, Parker H. French. A swindler by nature, French had used forged documents in 1850 to entice four hundred people in New York City to pay him $250 each to lead them to California. The trek ended in disaster when the forgeries—from bank drafts to government permission to take provisions from forts along the way—were exposed as the migrants neared El Paso, forcing French to flee into Mexico. There he lost much of his right arm in a gunfight with some of the men he had swindled. French eventually reached San Francisco, where his mere name was "suggestive of unfairness and dishonesty." He went on to open a short-lived newspaper in Sacramento and served for a brief time in the state legislature representing San Luis Obispo. Two men sued him for unpaid loans of $1,800 and $1,300, respectively, posing the question of why someone would loan money to such a notorious con man in the first place. In January 1854, French punched former California governor John McDougal over an insult to a third man.[16]

When Walker was in San Francisco preparing his expedition to Nicaragua, French had met with him several times, offering services and connections. He claimed a close relationship with Cornelius K. Garrison, a former Mississippi riverboat captain and Panama banker whom the Accessory Transit Company had hired as its representative in San Francisco, and said Garrison would help the expedition, but nothing came of it. French, though, pledged that he would follow Walker with more men, and in July 1855—two months after Walker's departure—French was posting ads in San Francisco newspapers seeking recruits for the Central American Colonization Society, which, without naming Walker, intended to take advantage of the "unsettled state" of Nicaragua by taking title to purportedly unclaimed lands, though French also urged colonists "to go armed." The planned departure date was July 20.[17]

Despite the newspaper ads and claims of more than a hundred subscribers for the venture, French departed alone aboard the *Uncle Sam* on July 16, a trip described as "a peaceable tour of observation." Two weeks later, he reported from Rivas that the Legitimists had placed him under arrest, allowing him to roam but not leave the city, though he said he expected to be escorted the next day—August 1—to Granada.[18]

He blamed Walker's presence in the country for his predicament. "These people are very much exasperated against the whole American race, since the late attack upon them by Walker and his party," French wrote. "They now look upon us with hatred and aversion. Although I am their warm friend, and desire to serve them, yet they distrust me and fear treachery; hence I am hedged around with difficulties I never anticipated."

Yet at San Juan del Sur at the end of August, French eagerly sought a meeting with Walker, telling his fellow American that he had been in Granada to "observe the strength and defenses of the place." Walker suspected French was playing both sides, but still, he commissioned him to return to San Francisco and recruit seventy-five more soldiers to help meet his contract with Castellón for three hundred American fighters. Other supporters were already putting together small squadrons, so it was inevitable that Walker's army would grow.[19]

Still troubled by the rout at Rivas, Walker felt the Phalanx needed to make a statement as a military force. Around midnight on September 2, he set out on the transit road for Virgin Bay, the southern terminus of the Lake Nicaragua steamers operated by the Accessory Transit Company. To Walker, the march had no significant intent other than as a show of force to the Nicaraguans, and to his own men. "The object in marching to Virgin Bay had not been to occupy the place, but to prevent the enemy, as well as the people of the Department, from supposing" that the Phalanx and El Chelon's small army "intended to remain entirely on the defensive" by holing up at San Juan del Sur. Successfully marching the length of the transit road would also let Walker's force "acquire confidence by seeing its ability to pass through the country without the fear of an attack from the enemy"—unless, of course, the enemy attacked.

Walker placed himself at the head of the column, followed by his men and then El Chelon's contingent. The group included a couple dozen horses and two horse-drawn wagons—confiscated from the Accessory Transit Company—which held the ammunition, extra arms, and blankets and other supplies. A few hours into the night march brought them to the Halfway House, a small inn, where they took a break for a few hours before resuming, arriving at Virgin Bay around 9:00 AM.

With so many people wandering the countryside, no military movements of that size went without notice. Guardiola had left Granada for Rivas, intending

The Halfway House on the transit road. *Frank Leslie's Illustrated Newspaper, August 16, 1856*

to attack the Americans at San Juan del Sur. As Walker's men rested at the Halfway House, Guardiola and his force were encamped less than two miles away. When he arrived at the Halfway House himself the next morning, Guardiola learned that the Americans had passed through en route to Virgin Bay, so he changed course and pursued them.[20]

Unaware of the pending attack, Charles Doubleday ordered breakfast for the troops from several Virgin Bay hotels and serving houses, none of which was large enough to handle feeding the men alone. As they finished up, sentries along the transit road opened fire on an approaching column of Legitimist troops, falling back as they fired, a tactic that served the dual purpose of slowing the attackers' progress while signaling the rest of Walker's force.[21]

Walker ordered the squadron's drummer to tap out the call to arms, and the men hurriedly fell in as the Legitimists advanced in three groups, one moving rapidly up the transit road and the others approaching on parallel routes through the brush, one hoping to reach the lake on the east and the other to control a slight rise to the southwest and thus contain Walker with his back to the lake. Walker's Phalanx moved down the road to fend off the attackers advancing there, while Valle divided his men into two groups to counter the forces moving through the brush.

Estimates vary of how many Legitimist fighters were involved, but they outnumbered Walker and Valle by a margin of better than two to one. Yet Walker had three elements in his favor. First, most of the Legitimists carried relatively inaccurate muskets, while the Americans, at least, carried more powerful and accurate rifles, with which most had experience. Second, the attackers were moving down the open road or through thick brush; Walker and El Chelon had buildings for protection (much like the advantage the Legitimists enjoyed at Rivas). And third, in a stroke of luck for Walker, Guardiola "was unable to use" a six-pound cannon "through some defect in the carriage."

As the Legitimists rushed down the road, part of the Phalanx moved to meet them and, nearing range, "made a slight oblique and halting movement" to widen their attack line, then opened fire. The charging edge of Legitimist troops "went down like grass before a scythe, their bodies and the severity of the fire abruptly checking their advance." The Legitimists, still in the open on the road, fired a return volley that was wild yet effective. Walker dropped to the ground, struck by two bullets. One creased but didn't penetrate his throat, leaving him bleeding from the neck. The other struck him full on in the chest but hit a wad of letters from Castellón and other papers in a pocket, bruising Walker deeply but not seriously wounding him. The Phalanx continued its rifle fire, the accuracy overwhelming the loose fire from the Legitimists, who soon broke ranks and retreated, leaving the dead and the wounded splayed about the crushed-gravel road.

The attackers pressed on the remaining two lines, one to the left of the Liberal troops and the other seeking to push the Liberals from the slight rise to the right. Doubleday joined a small contingent Walker deployed to aid Valle's men in keeping Legitimist troops from reaching the Accessory Transit Company's two-story office and warehouse building adjacent to the wharf, which would offer them protection and an angle from which to fire at the rear of the Liberal forces.

As Doubleday neared the fighting, he spotted a Legitimist in a white jacket atop a horse, and he and another Liberal took aim and fired, knocking the

Virgin Bay. *Frank Leslie's Illustrated Newspaper, April 19, 1856*

commander off his mount. The added Liberal rifles sent the Legitimists scattering, firing as they went. Doubleday felt an "exceedingly sharp, stinging sensation" in his side and fell to the ground just as the Legitimists, in a surprise move, reversed course and charged, passing "over the ground on which, for some seconds, I lay, unable to rise. When I at last succeeded in staggering to my feet, their white uniforms intervened between me and the houses from behind which our men were firing." Doubleday at first was certain a bullet had gone "plumb through me," but he shared a touch of Walker's luck: the bullet had hit "the broad buckle of my sword-belt with such violence as to produce a contusion of great severity, from which I suffered much afterwards."

Doubleday managed to dodge back through the Legitimists to rejoin his comrades as they launched a counteroffensive, reinforced by the arrival of yet more of Walker's contingent, who unleashed "well-directed fire from behind the fences and palisades on the left of the village," with more shots coming from men "deployed at irregular intervals along the beach."

That turned the tide:

> The Americans were scattered about the place in squads, eight or ten
> natives [Nicaraguans] being with each party. So they fought, running

from place to place, wherever they could get the best chance at the enemy, or wherever the latter tried to charge in, which they did several times, but were repulsed by the deadly shower of bullets from the American rifles.

The Legitimists, who had closed to within thirty-five yards of the Accessory Transit building, fell back. "Soon the firing grew feebler and feebler," and then Valle appeared on the road leading oxcarts of ammunition seized from Guardiola's destroyed force. Estimates of the Legitimist dead ranged from eighty to one hundred men, while Walker lost none, though fourteen were wounded, four of them severely.[22]

So Walker, who had foolishly rushed his men into battle at Rivas and been so badly beaten, managed to fight off a much larger Legitimist force at Virgin Bay, and against the Legitimists' top commander. Walker's victory didn't arise from any master military strategy. His men had the better weapons and the better position. But it was a victory nonetheless, and the Americans had proven themselves a force to be reckoned with.

10 | THE WAR FOR NICARAGUA

THE DAY AFTER THE BATTLE AT VIRGIN BAY, Walker marched his troops, including his wounded men and the captured Legitimist weapons and ammunition, back to San Juan del Sur. They left at midafternoon, stopped again at the Halfway House, and arrived the next morning. Walker then sent the Liberal leaders in León his report on the battle—though it's unclear whether Francisco Castellón learned of the victory before the cholera wave sweeping Nicaragua claimed him as well.[1]

Castellón's successor, Nazario Escoto, a member of the Liberals' senate, warned Walker that the cholera epidemic made it difficult to find more Nicaraguan recruits—particularly since Walker refused to accept men who had been conscripted by force, a tradition in Central American armies. Walker preferred to fight with willing soldiers, whether their motivation was to defend their native turf, exact revenge for Legitimist atrocities, or simply seek adventure. And as word spread of the victory at Virgin Bay, volunteers began arriving in San Juan del Sur. Some came from the Liberals' traditional support base— rural Nicaraguans who distrusted the Legitimists' conservative policies—but others were deserters from the Legitimist forces who had been pressed into military service against their will and now sought their revenge by joining the Liberal forces. Walker also found fresh fighters for his Phalanx among American adventurers crossing the isthmus in both directions. And he had recruiting agents among his men, who sent letters home with glowing reports of the war and the chances for establishing new lives in a new land—letters that newspapers occasionally reprinted, including one advising a friend to reject an unspecified job offer:

> You speak in your letter of an appointment you are confident of get-
> ting. Very good. If you get it, it will last you a year. Here, however, is
> an opening for something that will last perhaps a lifetime. Three or
> four more months will finish the war, and then there will be a chance
> for Americans in the country; but of this fact be assured, it will not
> be as it was in California, the first last and the last first. This will be
> no country for those who come after the fighting is over.[2]

Walker kept his men in San Juan del Sur for about a month, building and training his force. On October 3, 1855, the first group of men specifically recruited to fight for Walker arrived from San Francisco: thirty-five fighters led by Charles Gilman, who had lost a leg in Walker's Sonora campaign. "Gilman was a man of strong mind, with all the sentiments of a soldier," Walker said. A stream of additional recruits followed, swelling the American contingent to nearly 120 fighters, whom Walker placed under the command of Collier Hornsby, with Gilman as his second. He also divided them into three companies, each led by a captain: John Markham, A. S. Brewster, and George R. Davidson.[3]

During this period of preparation, Charles Doubleday spent extended periods of time with Walker, his experience in Nicaragua making him a valuable aide and strategist. Bit by bit, Walker let his adviser in on his long-term ambitions. "We took long walks on the beach," Doubleday recalled, "the rhythmic wave-beats seeming to emphasize the gigantic plans of empire he unfolded." Walker's first step had nearly been accomplished—proving himself indispensable as a military commander to the Liberal political leadership. Routing the Legitimist troops was the path forward, and he intended to go on the offensive shortly. Once the Liberals had won, Walker and his American-heavy army would be positioned to seize control of the country and then expand into neighboring jurisdictions, eventually reestablishing a unified Central American States "with himself, of course, as the central figure." Seeking the blessing of the Roman Catholic Church would be crucial, as well. Once united, the Central American States would move on Mexico under the pretext of old boundary disputes. The ultimate goal: establishing a new slave-based economy in Central America, Mexico, and Cuba, and aligning it with the United States. Since

Walker and his men were now all putatively Nicaraguan citizens—something achieved simply by declaring it—England couldn't accuse the United States of violating the Clayton-Bulwer Treaty.[4]

It was an audacious plan. Doubleday was both skeptical and appalled. From a pragmatic standpoint, the majority of Nicaraguans were the descendants of native peoples, African slaves, and Spanish conquerors and settlers. Slavery had been abolished for decades, and the idea that Nicaraguans would welcome its return, especially since it would potentially make most of them mere chattel, was delusional. Doubleday, who opposed slavery and believed in popular sovereignty, objected. "I listened to this conspiracy against the popular liberty, for which I had entertained a romantic attachment, and my heart was sad. He was ambitious of power, while I was merely philosophic."

The two men quarreled. Walker "was offended—he could now afford to be, for there were plenty of able men willing to do his bidding. I tendered my resignation, well knowing that, as victory was assured, I could be spared." Walker, who had initially sought to negotiate Doubleday's continued service, accepted it. Doubleday left on the next ship for Panama.[5]

———————

In the aftermath of Walker's victory at Virgin Bay, the Legitimists had lost confidence in Guardiola and consolidated his troops with those General Corral controlled at Rivas. In late September, travelers to San Juan del Sur reported that Corral had set out from Rivas planning to track down and attack the American and Liberal forces. Walker decided to catch Corral en route, hoping an aggressive move delivered with an element of surprise would give him an advantage. Walker moved out along the transit road, leaving some men hidden on a hill a little over a mile and a half from San Juan del Sur, and the rest on a hill near Virgin Bay. That way, whichever location Corral approached, he would be stepping into an ambush.

It was foul weather for such a strategy, though. "The night was dark and dismal, the rain falling now slowly and like a heavy mist, then rapidly and in drops nearly as big as a revolver bullet," Walker later wrote. "But the men stood to their places, sheltering themselves under the large trees which cover the sides of the hill, and being careful to keep their cartridge-boxes dry, drawing them, for this purpose, to the front part of the belt, and bending over so as to protect the precious powder with their bodies."[6]

Corral had indeed left Rivas. But when he, in turn, learned that Walker had marched from San Juan del Sur, Corral feared that the Americans were headed for the now lightly defended city from which he had just departed. So Corral turned around, which meant Walker's men had suffered through the night rain for nothing. They returned to San Juan del Sur in the morning. The venture was not a complete waste, however; Corral's decision to hurry back to Rivas told Walker that he "had only to leave San Juan del Sur, apparently for Rivas, in order to paralyze any advance movement his opponent might make." Also, from intercepted letters, Walker learned that with Corral and his troops based at Rivas, the Legitimist capital of Granada was lightly defended. So Corral was right to worry about leaving a city unprotected.

Walker hatched a plan. He sent a request to Escoto, the Liberals' new leader, to deploy forces based at León on a march toward Managua as a decoy to draw even more Legitimist troops out of Granada and perhaps from Rivas as well. Meanwhile, Walker picked up some added artillery: a small, brass two-pound cannon sent from León, and a new iron six-pound cannon obtained from the *Queen of the Pacific*, a clipper ship at anchor off San Juan del Sur. And he was still adding men—American travelers deciding to delay their trip for the sake of adventure, more recruits from San Francisco, and Nicaraguans joining Valle.

On October 11, Walker and the combined force set out on the transit road for Virgin Bay, arriving at around sunset. Walker ordered sentries posted on the roads and at the wharf to stop anyone from leaving the town, fearing a traveler would reveal their presence to Corral. Walker picked the eleventh because he knew the Accessory Transit Company lake steamer *La Virgen* was scheduled to dock that evening to transfer local lake freight and passengers, ultimately heading for Granada. And Walker needed *La Virgen* for his plan.

As *La Virgen* anchored, Walker sent Hornsby, the commander of his American forces, and a contingent of men aboard a small launch to draw up alongside the steamer. Aboard the larger vessel was Joseph N. Scott, a stout, six-feet-tall man in his midfifties with iron-gray hair, who was the main agent for the Accessory Transit Company's river and lake steamers. Scott, uncertain of the motives of the men in the launch, ordered the pilot to move it away from *La Virgen*, but Hornsby shouted out, "I am on board, and you are too late." As Walker's men streamed over the sides and onto the deck, Hornsby ordered the fires feeding the boilers to be extinguished and posted guards on the deck and in the engine room. Hornsby warned Scott that if anyone sought to hoist the anchor or start the steam engine, "he would shoot him down." Scott replied that "I would obey such orders only by force," and Hornsby repeated the threat, and told Scott that he should consider himself taken prisoner.[7]

Scott wrote out a protest against the seizure of the ship, arguing that the Accessory Transit Company was an American business, its ships protected under US jurisdiction, and that Walker had no authority to take it over. But Walker rejected that argument. The Accessory Transit Company was the creation of the Nicaraguan government and existed under the charter that government had granted. The Liberals were at war with the recognized government, so the ship was fair game. "Even, however, had the property been that of a neutral, and not of a subject, it would have been permissible to use it temporarily for the purpose of transporting troops."[8]

Scott went ashore to meet with Walker, who told him that he needed the ship for a few days, and that afternoon Walker "commenced embarking soldiers, baggage, and ammunition." Scott estimated the force numbered about 200 Americans and 250 Nicaraguans. It took several hours for the men and supplies to be ferried aboard, so it wasn't until after 6:00 PM that Walker ordered the engines fired. Once *La Virgen* was a few miles out into the lake, Scott asked Walker "in what direction he wanted the boat to steer. He said toward Granada."

Walker, though, didn't want to go to Granada proper. After consulting with the ship's captain, Thomas Ericsson, who knew the lakeshore better than Scott, Walker directed the ship to a beach about three miles north of the port. As *La Virgen* steamed northward, the men hid below deck under instructions to be quiet lest they draw attention from shore or another boat. As the ship navigated closer to shore, as it would on a normal run, "scouts of the enemy could be plainly perceived at intervals along the beach. On approaching Granada the lights on the steamer were extinguished, the canvas curtains were let down from the roof of the upper deck." Ericsson steered the ship at a distance around the fort at San Pablo, on the Isletas de Granada south of the city, "so as not to be seen by the sentries stationed there," passed Granada itself, and then anchored off the beach. "A line was made fast to a large tree on the beach, and the disembarkation was effected by pulling an iron launch from the steamer by means of the cable fastened ashore."[9]

Walker ordered a force of ten armed men to remain on *La Virgen* to ensure that it didn't steam away, and then began overseeing the transfer of the bulk of his force ashore. The last of the men, equipment, and two horses—one for Valle, the other for the one-legged Gilman—alit at about 3:00 AM. In the darkness, Walker organized the men into columns, a task made more difficult by the jungle encroaching on the edge of the narrow beach, and they finally struck off, moving as quietly as they could manage across terrain few of the men had ever trod before. A Granada native among the Nicaraguan force served as a guide, and as the sun rose, he gained his bearings and led the invaders to a roadway, where travelers told them the city was quiet and seemingly unprepared for an attack.

As the sun edged above the trees, the first of the "armed to the teeth" Phalanx reached huts at the edge of the city and quickly realized how exposed the Legitimists had left it. In a flash, they overwhelmed lightly manned barricades and made for the central plaza. The few Legitimist soldiers left behind fled, with some opening fire in a vain effort to stop the takeover. But it didn't last long. Walker lost no men; Valle lost a drummer boy; the Liberals found three dead Legitimist soldiers. The attackers quickly seized several key figures in the Legitimist government and power structure, though Walker had to intervene forcefully to keep Valle from killing some of the higher-profile captives—men the Liberals had been fighting, in various ways, for years. The invaders seized "18 or 20 cannons, most of which we spiked so if the enemy gets them, they are useless"—an odd decision, since the Americans could have used the weapons themselves. "We intend to stick to Granada and hold it, too," John Brenizer, a Tennessee doctor who had moved to Nicaragua to practice medicine before joining Walker's army, wrote home. "The enemy is 12 miles from here. They say they are nine hundred strong with two field pieces headed by Gen. Corral. . . . We are ready for them—if they come, we will teach them a bloodier lesson than our little army taught them at Virgin Bay."[10]

Walker immediately issued a proclamation briefly recounting the taking of the city, and noted that it was done with relatively little violence. "All those families who were expecting incendiarism, robberies, assassinations, shootings, and unutterable immoralities, as the lying Legitimists had repeatedly foretold, have seen and witnessed quite the contrary." Walker insisted that he intended to establish order, not usurp it.[11]

The ease with which Walker seized Granada, the seat of the Legitimist power, was remarkable, but as at Virgin Bay, it had little to do with the skill of Walker's fighting force. Corral had erred grievously in concentrating his forces at Rivas; the city was between the transit road—and thus Walker—and Granada, but Corral failed to contemplate an attack by water. So while he was at Rivas with his eyes cast southward toward the transit road and San Juan del Sur, Walker, shrewdly recognizing the vulnerability, had sailed around and come in from the north.

To Walker, Granada was valuable more as a bargaining chip than as a territory worth holding. His main goal continued to be securing control of the transit road, which was his lifeline to the United States for communications and fresh recruits. And he recognized the danger of overextending his men by trying to secure scattered cities. But sitting in the Legitimist capital gave him more leverage in potential peace talks with Corral. It was unclear, though, how much authority Walker had to negotiate on behalf of his patrons in León. The Liberals had their own government and chain of command, but Walker had set himself and his men apart from their oversight and actively pursued his own political agenda in sync with Castellón's desire, before he died, "of introducing an American element into Nicaraguan society." It's doubtful, though, that Castellón had intended to turn his country over to American interlopers.[12]

Before they moved on Granada, Walker's men had intercepted some letters between Corral and another Legitimist general, Fernando Chamorro (younger brother of Fruto Chamorro, the late president), which detailed the tenuous state of Granada and had persuaded Walker that the city could be taken. But Walker had also, after reading the letters, sent them on via courier to Corral, with a note that Walker had read them. It was a bit of psychological gamesmanship "making the Legitimist general feel that his condition and prospects were not unknown to his adversary." Walker also suggested to Corral that Nicaraguans—Liberals and Legitimists alike—were tired of war. Corral replied with a direct note to Walker at Granada "acknowledging the receipt of the letters" and included "a small slip of paper containing some cabalistic signs" that Walker speculated might have been some sort of Masonic code (Corral was a Mason). Walker shared the note with his top aides, one of whom—also a Mason—transcribed the symbols. "Corral desired by them to know whether he could communicate confidentially with Walker. Here the correspondence ended; and it had served the purpose of showing that Corral was not indisposed for peace even in the then condition of affairs."[13]

Walker sent two delegations to Rivas to meet with Corral. One traveling by land included several local Granada officials; its aim was to persuade Corral that it was in the best interests of Granada itself to seek peace, if for no other reason than to avoid the destruction of the city, home to many top Legitimists and their families. The second delegation traveled aboard *La Virgen*, still under Walker's control, to a landing near Rivas, and then proceeded on to the city. That group included the US minister to Nicaragua, John Wheeler, a supporter of the Americanization of the isthmus (which conflicted with formal US policy), and Juan Ruiz, a former Legitimist minister of war whose presence was demanded by the leading families of Granada to persuade Corral that it would be better to negotiate with Walker "and thus get rid of the hated Leoneses," or Liberals. But Corral rejected both overtures and, for a time, held Wheeler captive.[14]

Four days after Granada fell, Parker French and a fresh contingent of more than eighty-four men arrived in San Juan del Sur, under the command of Birkett Davenport Fry, a Sacramento lawyer and veteran of the Mexican-American War. Without orders, French and Fry marched from San Juan del Sur to Virgin Bay, encountering no Legitimist resistance en route. French decided to seize a lake steamship and attack Fort San Carlos, which guarded the transition from Lake Nicaragua to the San Juan River and the northern leg of the transit route. *La Virgen*, which Walker had released, was again at anchor off Virgin Bay, and French and his men boarded, ostensibly as passengers, along with the usual load of migrants crossing the isthmus.[15]

Scott, the Accessory Transit agent, sought to weigh anchor, but French asked him to keep the ship where it was until another load of baggage arrived. It wasn't packages but a cannon, which was quickly moved aboard the steamship, and *La Virgen* set off. As the ship neared Fort San Carlos, French ordered it to stop. Scott, who had a schedule to keep, refused. He was told, he later recalled, that if he didn't stop "they would blow the top of my head off." The ship anchored and French ordered Ericsson, the ship's captain, and two other men to carry a note ashore for the commander of the fort, demanding that he surrender it to French and his men. A half hour later, French got his answer in the form of a cannon shot at the ship, but the ball fell a few hundred feet short. French allowed *La Virgen* to steam farther away "close under the land out of the range of the fort" as cannons fired several more shots, then ordered the ship stopped again. He deployed two launches with men to make for shore, intending to sneak around and take the fort while the Legitimist soldiers focused on *La Virgen*. As the launches neared shore, though, a violent rainstorm opened up, drenching the men and rendering their exposed ammunition useless. The hapless landing force returned to the ship, which French then directed to return to Virgin Bay. Ericsson and his two companions remained at the fort as prisoners.[16]

French's decision to use *La Virgen* to challenge Legitimist troops at Fort San Carlos had a disastrous effect: the Legitimist forces now considered the Accessory Transit fleet to be the enemy. Just hours after the confrontation with *La Virgen*, the *San Carlos*, another Accessory Transit ship, steamed from the river en route to Virgin Bay. As it passed the fort, the Legitimist commander signaled the ship to stop and anchor. Five minutes later a twenty-four-pound cannon shot "struck her forward, passing through and damaging her machinery," then carried through to the upper deck, where it struck and instantly killed a passenger, Mrs. Alexander White of Alameda County, California, and blew away the legs of one of her children, who died five or six hours later. Another of her children lost a foot but survived. Following the cannon blast, soldiers at the fort opened fire with rifles, more than fifty shots sweeping the deck and the ship's pilothouse, wounding more than a half dozen crew and passengers. Once the guns fell silent, the captain, named Slocum, took a launch ashore and demanded to know why the fort had fired on his ship; the commander told him about the ultimatum from *La Virgen*. Slocum persuaded the Legitimists that he had no filibusters aboard the *San Carlos*, and after eight hours the ship proceeded to Virgin Bay, where the American mother and child were buried.[17]

The next day, October 19, a force of more than one hundred Legitimist soldiers and French adventurers led by officers on horseback swarmed the Accessory Transit facility at Virgin Bay, where hundreds of travelers were awaiting ships to carry them north across the lake. In the eyes of the Legitimists, that made them part of the opposition and possibly volunteers for Walker's army. The soldiers opened fire, sending bullets through the panicked crowd. Five people died on the spot and at least another nine were wounded. One bullet struck Theron Wales, a passenger, in the upper arm as he stood inside the Accessory Transit office. Clark Hite, another passenger, escaped getting shot, but soldiers robbed him of his gun, his ticket, and forty-four dollars in cash. Jonathan G. Kendrick similarly was robbed—but only after a bullet blasted through his shoulder. As he lay prone, soldiers rifled his pockets and left him for dead, though he recovered. The Legitimists also ransacked the Accessory Transit offices and took several prisoners, including Courtland Cushing, a former US attorney and judge now working as an agent for Accessory Transit; he was later ransomed for $2,000.[18]

Walker condemned the actions of French and Fry: "It was a most foolish if not criminal act, to take the passengers on the boat destined for such an expedition, and no benefit could be expected to result from an undertaking commenced under such circumstances." But the usually taciturn Walker was more, and uncharacteristically, outraged by the ensuing atrocities committed by the Legitimists. "Such conduct on the part of officers, acting under color of the Legitimist government, called for retaliation and punishment in order to prevent its recurrence."[19]

Walker ordered the public execution of one of his prisoners, Mateo Mayorga, on Granada's main plaza. Mayorga served in President Estrada's Legitimist cabinet and "was, therefore, morally responsible for the outrages and barbarities practiced by those holding a military commission from the Legitimist authorities." Walker delegated the execution to the Liberal troops, who were only too happy to comply. Walker then sent Pedro Rouhaud, a French citizen who had lived in Granada for years, as an emissary to General Corral, who had left Rivas for Masaya, about ten miles northwest of Granada. Rouhaud informed Corral of Mayorga's execution and Walker's reason for it, and passed along a warning from Walker that "all the Legitimist families of the city would be held as hostages for the future good conduct of Estrada's officers toward

American women and children, and toward non-combatants generally." Most of Corral's top officers had left their families behind in Granada, about ninety persons in all, and they were now at the mercy of Walker. With Mayorga's blood staining the Granada plaza, it was a brutal and effective threat. Corral, who had rebuffed Walker's earlier overture for peace negotiations, now agreed to talk.[20]

Walker and Corral met on the outskirts of Granada on the morning of October 23, and then rode together to the government plaza in the heart of Granada, a trip Walker later wrote about:

> As they passed, the doors and windows of the houses were filled with women and children, dressed in the bright colors affected by the people of the country and smiling through tears at the prospect of peace. On the Plaza, the whole democratic force was drawn up to receive the commanding-general of the Legitimists; and arms were put into the hands of many of the California passengers, and they were drawn up in as good array as possible, to impress Corral with an idea of the American strength of the democratic army.[21]

Corral had the full authority of the Legitimist government to negotiate an agreement. But anything Walker agreed to beyond the scope of his own troops and their occupation of Granada would have to be sent on to León for approval by the Liberal government. Walker let Corral take the lead in the discussions, and the Legitimist mapped out a provisional government between the Legitimists and the Liberals that placed Patricio Rivas, a Legitimist bureaucrat who had not been very involved in the war with the Liberals, as the chief executive pending an election within fourteen months. It also awarded Walker the rank of brigadier general in a combined army of Legitimist and Liberal soldiers, with the existing ranking officers of both armies retaining their positions in the merged force. Legitimist generals Tomás Martínez and Florencio Xatruch would be in charge of the forces in Managua and Rivas, respectively.[22]

The Liberals accepted the terms. War was over, but peace would be elusive. Under the terms of the agreement, the Nicaraguan troops—most of whom had been conscripted against their will—were free to muster out. Walker and his American filibusters became the core of the army, which had been growing even as it was fighting the Legitimists. Each ship from the United States seemingly carried more armed men seeking adventure and fortune under Walker's leadership. When French and Fry departed San Francisco on October 6 with at least eighty-four men aboard the *Uncle Sam*, they had to leave behind more than two hundred other men—mostly hard-edged miners who struck out in the gold fields—who were stranded on the dock and on a sailing ship they had boarded in hopes of transferring to the fully booked *Uncle Sam*.

Two weeks later, more filibusters set sail from San Francisco aboard the *Sierra Nevada*. They included Edward J. C. Kewen, a poet, a lawyer, California's first attorney general, and the brother of Achilles Kewen, killed in the disastrous attack on Rivas; Adolphus Sutter, son of John Sutter, whose mill was the site of the first gold discovery that set off the gold rush; Edmund Randolph, Walker's old friend and confidant; Frank Turk, a former vice mayor of San Francisco; and others drawn from a range of San Francisco classes. And when news reached other US ports that Walker's presence had been the determining factor in the civil war, recruitments came together there, as well—in New York City, particularly, but also New Orleans, drives propelled by promises of land for settlers willing to defend the new Nicaragua.

Those would prove to be the seeds of yet more conflict—a consuming regional war that would make Walker's quick and violent rise to power seem like a holiday excursion.

11 | PRESIDENT WALKER

A GOVERNMENT, OF COURSE, needs money to operate, and the new Nicaraguan government had little to none. The Legitimists had drained their treasury fighting the Liberals, and the Liberals had drained theirs fighting the Legitimists. What cash the new provisional government did have went to keeping the fighting men paid and fed, but the peace agreement also required the new government to cover bills the Legitimists still owed to their troops. When it couldn't raise the money, General Corral "became impatient, clamorous, and threatening." Despite the peace treaty, the new government was, at best, precarious, and fears grew that it would fall apart if President Rivas reneged on this financial promise.[1]

Now American corporate intrigues crossed paths with Walker's ambitions. C. J. MacDonald, a Scottish-born friend and confidant of Cornelius K. Garrison, Accessory Transit's agent in San Francisco, had arrived in San Juan del Sur aboard the *Cortes* on October 3, 1855. Walker's shady comrade Parker French had not been lying about being acquainted with Garrison; the agent also knew Charles Gilman, the Walker loyalist who had lost a leg in the invasion of Baja and who was now a colonel in the Nicaraguan force. French introduced MacDonald to Walker, and MacDonald was at Granada on October 23 when the agreement was reached to end the war. MacDonald's mission was to serve as Garrison's eyes and ears in Nicaragua and ensure that valuable shipments from San Francisco—including fortunes in gold—crossed the isthmus safely.[2]

MacDonald learned of the financially precarious position of President Rivas's government, and in a discussion with French, someone mentioned the large sums of money the Accessory Transit Company carried for clients. It was a subject with which MacDonald was intimately familiar, since he was apprised of all shipments Accessory Transit handled. French said later he was uncertain who first mentioned the money in transit, but MacDonald agreed that the Accessory Transit Company was as much at risk from renewed war as the provisional government, and he agreed to divert $20,000 worth of gold from a shipment belonging to the Palmer, Cook & Company banking firm. French relayed the offer to Walker, who initially refused, because he didn't know what authority MacDonald had to make it. MacDonald produced a "vaguely drawn" document from Garrison declaring him his representative, though it "did not cover any such contingency as this." Charles Gilman vouched for MacDonald in a private conversation with Walker.[3]

Sorely in need of the cash, Walker decided to accept and sent a contingent of men to the *San Carlos* to get the gold. Joseph Scott, the same Accessory Transit agent who had resisted the filibusters' takeovers of *La Virgen*, refused to turn over the shipment. Instead he traveled to Granada to protest directly to Walker, arguing that he would only surrender the gold with an order from Charles Morgan, the president of Accessory Transit. Walker sent men to seize the gold anyway. When Garrison later learned what his man in Nicaragua had set in motion, he "seemed very much excited and spoke with a good deal of bitterness," suggesting that MacDonald acted on his own, and for his own undisclosed reasons.[4]

Walker faced other problems as well. With the fighting over, his men had a lot of idle time on their hands, which many of them spent getting drunk. Patrick Jordan, a native of Ireland, had left San Francisco with Walker aboard the *Vesta*, fought in the failed attack on Rivas, took part in the battle at Virgin Bay, and was there for the coup de grâce at Granada. Like most of Walker's men, he was less a disciplined soldier than an opportunistic adventurer. On November 1, Jordan got drunk, grabbed a rifle, and, for some unexpressed reason, threatened to shoot two colleagues before firing the gun at an unidentified Nicaraguan man. The bullet ripped through the man's arm and torso and lodged in his spine.

Walker ordered Jordan's arrest. A hasty court-martial found Jordan guilty and ordered him discharged from the army then booted out of the country. But ten hours after the shooting, and shortly after the court-martial had delivered its verdict, the victim died. Walker ordered Jordan to be shot. Jordan's fellow soldiers carried out the sentence at daybreak on November 3, moments after "poor Patrick" delivered a short speech "to his companions, in which he warned them against the evil effects of liquor, acknowledged the justness of his sentence, and said that he knew our preservation depended upon his execution in a great measure." Jordan recognized that Walker needed to show the Nicaraguans that he would treat seriously violations of decency and law committed by his men—a lesson not lost on his troops, either. And Walker needed to preserve the Nicaraguans' faith in him and his men, because the next day nearly all the locally conscripted soldiers mustered out and returned home, increasing the new government's reliance on the Phalanx.[5]

The presence of the Americans, and Walker's role in ending the war and now leading the military in peacetime, disturbed the Legitimist upper echelon. They initially believed they could isolate Walker politically. But when President Rivas, under Corral's tutelage, began filling his top administrative positions with Legitimists, Walker objected. Stacking the new government with officials from one camp would eventually lead to more friction and potentially war, he argued. Walker managed to get former Liberal general Máximo Jerez appointed as minister of relations, a counterweight to Corral's appointment as minister of war. Fermin Ferrer, a Spanish immigrant with inherited estates in Nicaragua who was a moderate Legitimist sympathetic to the American presence, emerged as a consensus appointee to oversee the treasury. Parker French received an appointment as "minister of hacienda," akin to an interior secretary—which, given French's history as a con man, was a risky choice.

Despite the balanced mix of interests among the cabinet members, the Legitimists feared the Americans threatened Nicaraguan sovereignty. Their experience with the Accessory Transit Company soured them on any idea that trucking with the Americans would lead to more trade and riches for Nicaraguans. The Legitimists had agreed to end a war they'd been winning to preclude the massacre of their families, so they felt no loyalty to Walker or, by extension, to President Rivas, whose elevation wouldn't have occurred without Walker's military adventurism and threats against the hostage residents of Granada. The Conservatives' suspicions increased when Walker directed Martínez at Managua to reduce his force size, and gave a similar notice to the garrison at Rivas. Such moves would only increase Walker's power, they realized, and they began to understand that they shared more in common with their traditional Liberal rivals and with neighboring Costa Rica and Honduras than with Walker. Some, at least, believed Walker's presence was a cancer that if not checked would eventually consume the entire isthmus.[6]

One such believer was Corral, and even as he worked with Walker to establish the provisional government and make plans for a national election, he sought ways to counter the American's power. On November 5, two days after Jordan's execution and five days after Patricio Rivas took the oath as president of the provisional government, Walker ally José Maria Valle intercepted a courier ferrying a packet of letters from Martínez to former Conservative military leader Guardiola, now a rising political figure in Legitimist-run Honduras. Martínez's communication was, in effect, a cover letter to explain the rest of the packet—forwarded letters from Corral "who does not write much on account of the insecurity; but you already understand all he wants to tell you, and it is enough if you consider the sufferings of the man who has been forced to the sacrifice to do what he has done, and to whom they already deny what was offered to him." The implication was that somehow Walker had broken an unspecified promise to Corral. "We all confide in you, and only you," Martínez went on, "to redeem this beautiful section of Central America. We hope that you and the real friends of Honduras will not be indifferent to our disgrace."[7]

One of the enclosed Corral letters was addressed to Pedro Xatruch, a Guardiola ally and general in the Honduran army, and brother of Florencio Xatruch, the former Legitimist general overseeing the troops at Rivas. It contained a succinct plea for help: "We are badly, badly, badly off. Remember your friends. They have left me what I have on, and I hope for your aid." Another letter was addressed to Ana Arbizu—Guardiola's wife—with the envelope marked PRIVATE. Upon opening it, Walker discovered that the letter inside was actually addressed to Guardiola: "It is necessary that you write to friends to advise them of the danger we are in, and that they work actively. If they delay two months there will not then be time. Think of us and of your offers. I salute your lady; and commend your friend who truly esteems you and kisses your hand, P. Corral." Then, in a postscript: "Nicaragua is lost; lost Honduras, San Salvador, and Guatemala, if they let this get body. Let them come quickly if they would meet auxiliaries."[8]

Walker interpreted the "they" in "if they get body" to mean Walker and his men, and "body" to mean if the American force grew larger. "Friends" referred to other Legitimist governments in different Central American states, and "your offers" clearly implied the letter was among a series of communications that, Walker quickly realized, were invitations for a coup or an invasion.

Walker acted swiftly. He dispatched some of his men to the roads leading out of Granada with orders to allow no one to pass, and sent others to summon the Legitimist leaders and top appointees of the new government—including Corral and President Rivas—to a meeting at Walker's quarters, without letting on why. That all the officials, including the president, attended despite the short notice evidences the sway Walker held over them.

Once the leaders were assembled, Walker produced the letters, read them aloud, and accused Corral of treason "by inviting the enemies of the State to invade Nicaragua," Walker later wrote, "and conspiring with them for the purpose of overturning the existing government." Corral offered no denials. The Legitimists seemed stunned, the Liberals smugly satisfied. Jerez directed that Martínez be summoned to Granada, but by the time the message arrived Martínez had already learned of the unmasking of Corral and fled, eventually reaching Honduras.

Since "there was no existing civil tribunal before which to arraign" Corral, Walker convened a court-martial for the next day, deciding a military trial was appropriate for a general accused of "high treason" and conspiring "with the enemies of the state to overthrow the existing government of Nicaragua." Colonel Hornsby presided over a panel of six other filibusters, with lawyer Birkett Fry assigned as prosecutor and swindler Parker French as defense counsel. Walker was the main witness. The hearing was brief; with the letters in Walker's hands, Corral had no plausible defense and pleaded for mercy for the sake of his family. The court found him guilty and sentenced him to be shot the next day, but also recommended that Walker, who needed to sign off on the death warrant, grant clemency. Corral enjoyed wide support in Granada, and intense lobbying began, including a tearful meeting with Corral's daughters and other women of the city, to spare Corral's life.

They failed to move Walker. He and Corral had taken oaths just days earlier, at Corral's insistence before a Catholic cross (even though Walker was Protestant), to protect and defend the new government of Nicaragua. Walker wrote that he

> considered the question of policy as clear and unequivocal as the
> question of justice. Not only did duty to the Americans in Nicaragua
> demand the execution of the sentence, but it was politic and humane
> to make their enemies feel that there was a power in the State capable

and resolved to punish any offences against their interests. Mercy to Corral would have been an invitation to all the Legitimists to engage in like conspiracies.

In short, Walker intended to make an example of Corral, much as he had with the drunken murderer Jordan—and earlier with Mateo Mayorga, whose execution had brought the Legitimists to peace talks in the first place.

A little before 2:00 PM on November 8, the day after the court-martial, the bells of Granada's main cathedral began ringing as a small group of men entered the main plaza. Corral was in front, with a priest bearing a small cross to one side and Corral's friend the French consul Pedro Rouhaud on the other, all trailed by American soldiers. Corral's face "bore the marks of extreme mental suffering. He took his seat in the fatal chair, which was placed with its back to the wall of the cathedral." Corral took a handkerchief from his pocket, tied it around his own eyes, lowered his hands in the position of prayer, and said, "*Pronto*"—quickly. The one-legged Gilman, standing next to the firing squad ten paces from the chair, read the death proclamation and ordered the men to fire. Corral's lifeless body toppled to the ground, his blood seeping into the packed Nicaraguan soil.[9]

Execution of Ponciano Corral. *Courtesy of Library of Congress Prints and Photographs Division, LC-USZ62-60912*

If Walker thought the execution would send a positive signal that Nicaragua would be run under the rule of law and that treason would be punished to protect the nation, he sorely misread the body politic. Corral's execution, in fact, confirmed for many that Walker was a man to be feared, that he embraced no humane sense of justice, and that the October treaty was more a pact with the devil than a blueprint for peace.

John Wheeler, the US minister to Nicaragua, found himself in a diplomatic bind. His orders from William Marcy, the secretary of state, barred him from meddling in Nicaragua's internal affairs. But the civil war had ended with a provisional government that included two Americans in key positions of power: Walker and French, whose ambitions appealed to Wheeler. Needing guidance from Washington, the minister sent two letters to Marcy a week apart. The first, on October 23, included affidavits from survivors of the Legitimist attacks on the *San Carlos* and at Virgin Bay. The second reported optimistically on the founding of the new provisional government.[10]

"As soon as the departments are filled, the republic will be under another set of rules than those recognized by the United States, and if no event of importance intervenes to call for any diplomatic action on my part I shall await instructions from you," Wheeler wrote. "By that time, too, it will be ascertained if the people of Nicaragua have now substantially made another change or whether it be only a successful foray of arms, ultimately to be overcome by a superior force."

But Wheeler had faith in Walker, with whom he had spent time and conversed over the previous several weeks. In fact, Walker, President Rivas, and Parker French had dined at Wheeler's residence the night before the Corral letters were discovered. Wheeler told Marcy that "it is confidently believed that the present condition of things will be permanent, and that substantial peace, for the first time in thirty years, reigns in Nicaragua; that at least three of the five Central American States will form a federal union (San Salvador, Honduras, and Nicaragua) under one president."[11]

Marcy replied that US policy recognized that each nation had a right to handle "management of its own internal affairs" but that the United States also held a responsibility to protect its own citizens even when in other nations, such as the victims at Virgin Bay, and the right to demand that "perpetrators of these crimes . . . be punished, the sufferers indemnified, and the families of the murdered provided for." But who were the authorities? "In the present condition of affairs there, it is difficult to decide who has the responsible government on which the demand for satisfaction can be made."[12]

Marcy, speaking for President Pierce, also made it clear that the US government had no illusions about Walker. "It appears that a band of foreign adventurers has invaded that unhappy country, and, after gaining recruits from among the residents, has by violence overturned the previously existing government, and now pretends to be in possession of sovereign authority." But such pretension was insufficient to recognize the new government. "It appears to be no more than a violent usurpation of power, brought about by an irregular self-organized military force, as yet unsanctioned by the will or acquiescence of the people of Nicaragua. It has more the appearance of a successful marauding expedition than a change of government or rulers." And Marcy noted that Wheeler had already erred by serving as Walker's messenger to Corral after the Phalanx took over Granada, an act that had led to Wheeler's three-day detention by the Legitimists. Marcy warned Wheeler not to make a similar mistake again. "You will observe great circumspection in your conduct."

By the time Marcy's letter reached Wheeler, however, the minister had already broken the orders. On November 10, Wheeler showed up at the Government House, the offices of the new administration in Granada, where he was "officially received as the minister of the U.S.," and delivered a brief speech congratulating President Rivas, noting the shared interests of the two countries and reasserting the Monroe Doctrine. "Our true policy is to declare and to maintain that the people of the American republics can govern themselves; that no foreign power shall be allowed to control, in the slightest manner, our views, or interfere in the least degree with our interests." Rivas replied with similar diplomatic comments, citing the American colonies' move to independence eighty years earlier as an influence on "Spanish America" and decreeing that Nicaragua and the United States "have considered themselves identified by such peaceful interests, and every day their mutual welfare becomes more immediately connected."[13]

Guatemala and El Salvador, though, agreed with Marcy's assessment that Walker threatened regional peace and sovereignty. Antonio José de Irisarri, who held a dual ministerial appointment in Washington from those two nearby countries, complained to Marcy about the US government's failure to stop Walker. (The chargé d'affaires for Costa Rica sent a similar letter.) Irisarri dismissed the "absurd and impolitic" claim by Walker and others that they had a right to seek their fortune where they chose and could even overthrow governments. "All nations, whether civilized or otherwise, must resist" such invasive expeditions "because it is better to cease to exist than to be at the mercy of such interlopers." And while the US policy against filibusters was known, "this disapproval has not prevented the overthrow of the legitimate government" of Nicaragua "with the assistance of these foreigners." Further, the US government "has not prevented these same foreigners from barbarously murdering the loyal defenders of the established government." Irisarri also accused officials for the Accessory Transit Company with encouraging and working with the invaders—which, while a popular belief, was not true. Walker treated Accessory Transit as a conquered supply chain, using its ships as needed without paying fare or freight charges while disrupting the regular transit business. Irisarri asked the United States to stop reinforcements from leaving America to join Walker. "El Salvador and Guatemala cannot lay down their arms until they have driven from Nicaragua the intrusive rulers of the country," he warned, adding that more recruits from the United States would only make the looming war longer and bloodier—and the US government would bear some of the blame.

Marcy wrote back that the United States understood the frustration but that the filibusters had not left with the cooperation of US or California authorities, and that given the number of men traveling to and from the California gold fields, it was impossible to figure out who was truthfully heading home and who was aiming to join Walker.

Marcy also undercut Wheeler's recognition of the Rivas government. "In recognizing the new government in Nicaragua, the minister of the United States in that country did not act pursuant to the instructions of this department," Marcy wrote. "On the contrary, express instructions have been given to him to abstain from doing so, though these had not reached him when he acted in that matter." But Marcy also offered something of a philosophical defense of mercenaries, arguing that while the United States preferred other nations change leaders and governments through "peaceful means, the United States do not feel called on to interpose against the employment of others for that purpose" so long as laws are followed.

Mixed in with the letters was an announcement by President Rivas, clearly controlled by Walker, that he had recalled his minister to the United States and replaced him with French, in part to remove the Legitimist loyalist as the liaison between the Rivas government and Washington and in part to get French out of Nicaragua. Walker had come to realize French "was utterly unfitted" to run a government ministry whose responsibilities included contracting for goods and services. "His rapacity made him dreaded by the people of the country, and, as a matter of policy, it was necessary . . . to get rid of him." José de Marcoleta, the Legitimist minister in Washington, refused to recognize the provisional government or the letter removing him. The communications from "the spurious authority" that sought to replace him with French were from

> a pretended, intrusive, and usurping administration, brought into existence by fraud and treason, created and subjected to the pressure and influence of the bayonets of a savage horde of pirates, imbued and stained with the noble and innocent blood of illustrious Nicaraguan patriots, inhumanly, cruelly, cowardly, and shamefully assassinated and immolated on the altars of the country.[14]

Marcy and the Pierce administration agreed. When French arrived in Washington, they would refuse to accept his credentials.

———————

Scott, the Accessory Transit agent, left from Greytown on November 24 on a business trip to New York City. He was traveling aboard the company's *Northern Light*, a 253-foot-long, three-decked wooden side-wheel steamer that could hold up to 900 passengers, 250 of them in first-class cabins. It was the same vessel that was carrying French back to the United States; he planned to do some recruiting and weapons shopping in New York before presenting his diplomatic credentials in Washington. Also aboard was Captain W. H. Williamson, another member of Walker's army. After an uneventful trip, the ship pulled into pier 3 on the North (now Hudson) River, on the Lower West Side of Manhattan, on December 11.

Just before Scott left Nicaragua, President Rivas—apparently at Walker's direction—had issued a proclamation inviting Americans to settle in

Nicaragua. The government would give 250 acres of land to each single settler, and an additional 100 acres to families, with all of their possessions and farming tools imported without tax. Scott's arrival in Manhattan and the Rivas proclamation made the newspapers. One of the announcements came in a long letter to the editor published in the *New York Daily Times* that lauded Walker and the peace he had brought to Nicaragua after thirty-two years of strife. It also extolled French for procuring money to launch the new government "as if he possessed the magic wand, or the Cave of Sesame," presumably referring to the $20,000 confiscated from the Accessory Transit ship. The letter-writer was Joseph Male, who was traveling with French and edited the recently launched *El Nicaraguense*, an English- and Spanish-language newspaper published by the Rivas-Walker government. Male was, in essence, Walker's propaganda minister.[15]

Scott spent most of the ensuing days in meetings at the Accessory Transit office at 2 Bowling Green, a few doors from the Atlantic Steamship offices and three blocks from the pier. At French's urging, Scott introduced him to the officers of Accessory Transit, a meeting that, in fact, had been requested by Walker. Whatever future success Walker might achieve in Nicaragua, he believed it would involve the steady supply of men and weapons from the United States via the Accessory Transit Company.

And French had some cards to play in pursuit of that goal. Under the contract that had granted Cornelius Vanderbilt exclusive rights to build a canal and a transit system across the isthmus (later separated into two contracts when Vanderbilt abandoned the canal), Accessory Transit was to pay the Nicaraguan government $10,000 a year for the twelve years the charter would be in effect, plus 10 percent of the net annual profits from moving passengers from sea to sea through Nicaragua. But the company didn't make the $10,000 payments, arguing that the wording of the charter meant the money was not due until the twelve years were up. And it had not paid the percentage of its profits because, it argued, the Nicaragua part of the transit system was not making any money. The company intentionally maintained no records in Nicaragua that the government could use to prove the company was lying; it kept all the books in the US ticket offices. Chamorro's Legitimist government had sent a two-man delegation to New York in the spring of 1855 to present a demand of $35,000 to settle the claim. The company offered $30,000, which the Nicaraguans rejected, and both sides agreed to arbitration. But before that could happen, the Legitimist government dissolved with the creation of the provisional government. The peace agreement also gave Walker the authority to negotiate a settlement with the transit company, and he subsequently deputized French to press the claim on behalf of the new government.[16]

Accessory Transit rejected French's demand to negotiate a settlement, arguing that the matter had been delegated for arbitration; French threatened to revoke the arbitrators' appointment. "The company then told the colonel to get any accountant he wished and proceed to the examination of their books, and they would pay whatever was found due." French initially agreed but then dismissed the idea, "since his government forcibly took a bag of gold from the company's lake steamer, amounting to twenty-thousand dollars," and so Accessory Transit "could not be indebted much, if at all, to the state." French then got to what seemed to be the more important part of his mission for Walker: he proposed that Accessory Transit carry "Nicaraguan colonists"—as opposed to the through passengers for California. The colonists' passage would be charged to the Nicaraguan government at a cost of $20 a head, with these charges to be factored into later negotiations over exactly how much each side owed the other. The company's agents saw that as an easy resolution and agreed to the deal, "provided they were not organized military bands, and did not propose to go" intending "to enlist as soldiers." Accessory Transit got its assurance (as worthless as it was), and Walker had a no-cost conduit for men—and also munitions, some of which French arranged to buy through shipper and goods merchant George Law, to whom Scott had introduced him. Coupled with Nicaragua's new decree of free land for emigrants, the free passage made the country even more alluring for those with tough prospects in the United States. Over the next couple of months, some one thousand emigrants would ride Accessory Transit's ships to Nicaragua.[17]

Scott lodged himself in the St. Nicholas Hotel, a relatively new thousand-room luxury hotel on Broadway at Spring Street, which the *New York Daily Times* described at its opening in 1853 as a "magnificent establishment . . . the Hotel par excellence of our day." So Scott was traveling in a style fitting for someone earning $10,000 a year (more than $230,000 in current dollars)—and whose expenses were likely covered by Accessory Transit.[18]

Given Scott's role as the transit company's agent in Nicaragua, people interested in emigrating often gravitated to him for advice. A "major or colonel Hall of Brooklyn called on me to go over across the way" from his hotel to a meeting room at the rear of a cigar store "and explain to some of his friends the condition of Nicaragua." It was a recruiting meeting, one of a series in Manhattan, New Orleans, and San Francisco led by Hall—though Williamson made several appearances as well. The men they were soliciting were to steam for Nicaragua aboard the *Northern Light* when it made its return run on December 24. The recruiters also posted small, ambiguous, and misleading ads in the local newspapers: "Wanted—Ten or fifteen young men to go a short distance out of the city. Single men preferred. Apply at No. 347 Broadway, corner of Leonard Street, Room No. 12, between the hours of 10 and 4. Passage paid." Presumably, those who responded to the ad were then told that the real plan was to join Walker in Nicaragua.[19]

Walker himself reached out to old friends urging them to either join him or recommend others to do so. He wrote to his childhood friend John Lindsley on November 26, asking jokingly if he had forgotten him and recalling their long friendship. "If you have any memory of our past studies and friendship do not fail to induce someone skilled in geology and botany to come to this country. . . . This government needs scientific men; and I will see that they do not starve if they come here." There's no indication that Lindsley replied. But Walker's two younger brothers, Norvell and James, eventually joined him in Nicaragua.[20]

With all the talk and news articles about men itching to join Walker, and the diplomatic protests from Central America, President Pierce issued a proclamation on December 8 warning Americans against joining the filibuster movement in Nicaragua. Attorney General Caleb Cushing followed it up with a circular to the US attorneys in each port city, writing that the president "desires you to take measures to detect and defeat, so far as it may be lawfully done, all such enterprises, to bring the parties guilty to punishment, and to detain any vessel fitted out to carry on the undertaking." Special notices went to San Francisco, New Orleans, and New York, where reports of pending departures were rampant.[21]

As the *Northern Light* prepared to set sail, several anonymous letters reached John McKeon, the US attorney in Manhattan, that men and weapons were being loaded onto the ship, destined to aid Walker. McKeon issued an arrest warrant for French, which created a thorny legal issue, since he'd entered the country with a letter of diplomatic appointment from the Nicaraguan president. Rather than wrestle with whether that gave French immunity from prosecution, Pierce passed along through Cushing the order that French should be arrested and then told he could go free if he promised not to engage in any further efforts to recruit men for Walker and "shall depart from the country within a reasonable time." McKeon also leaned on Joseph White, Vanderbilt's longtime fixer. He visited White at home on the evening of December 22, asking White to ensure that filibusters wouldn't be aboard the *Northern Light* when it made its return trip to Nicaragua two days later. White denied that the Accessory Transit Company was aiding the filibusters. McKeon then put his demand in writing and had it published in several New York newspapers on December 23, as a public warning to both White and the men who might seek to slip out to Nicaragua.[22]

White responded with his own scolding public letter, arguing that the company had every right to conduct business and Americans had every right to travel:

> If the aim and object of your letter is to prevent armed or unarmed men from going to Nicaragua, with a military design, whether enlisted here or to be enlisted there, you may count on the full, free, and hearty cooperation of the Transit Company. Such men, with such designs, shall not go in our ships, with our knowledge. But, to prevent all misunderstanding, I am constrained to say, that we will convey every person to Nicaragua who may apply and pay for his passage, although he may purpose to go under and by invitation of any colonization decree by the government, no matter by who administered, so long as it is the only government of that state.

In other words, the ships would carry to Nicaragua anyone who didn't volunteer that he was heading south to fight.[23]

McKeon responded by seizing the *Northern Light*. About two o'clock in the afternoon on December 24—about an hour before the posted sailing time—federal marshals boarded the ship. White also came aboard separately (it's unclear why; it may have been part of the pre-sailing routine), and Captain Edward Tinklepaugh, who had been getting clearance papers from the custom house, arrived a short time later. Some 250 men were aboard; rather than carrying tickets, they had buttons identifying them as settlers destined for Nicaragua, so clearly they were not regular passengers. "Those on board were miserably clad, and gave palpable indications of destitution, if not desperation," a *New York Daily Times* reporter noted. "One would readily see that they were adventurers and not passengers." Regardless, White refused to accept the government's authority to stop the ship from departing; the lead marshal produced a cable from Washington empowering any of the naval ships in the port to bar any suspected filibustering expeditions from leaving, and a second set of warrants to search the ship for men and weapons bound for Nicaragua. A scuffle ensued, and one of the men went over the rail into the North River, but he was quickly dragged out of the water. Several men sought to cut the ship loose so it could sail but were thwarted.

White returned to his office. Word of the showdown spread, and some one thousand people swarmed the wharf, making it difficult for McKeon, accompanied by a handful of police officers, to reach the ship himself. Just before three o'clock, he appeared at the wharf end of the plank and called out to Tinklepaugh that the *Northern Light* was not to leave. "The captain told him that the steamer would go in five minutes, it being five minutes to 3 o'clock." As Tinklepaugh spoke, he pulled out a large golden chronometer as though to check the time, drawing a huge cheer and laughter from those on deck and on the wharf. McKeon repeated his demand, and clambered atop a piling so as to be better heard, drawing insults and threats from the crowd: "Tumble him into the duck [river]" and "Smash his coconut." McKeon climbed down, surrounded himself with his bodyguards, and marched to the Accessory Transit office and repeated his order to White, who similarly rejected it. From there, McKeon went to the US barge office and ordered that a revenue cutter be dispatched to cut off the *Northern Light*, and that word be sent to the navy yard in Brooklyn for more ships.

The *Northern Light* pulled out sometime after three o'clock. The revenue cutter caught up with her near Ellis Island and signaled Tinklepaugh to stop the ship. The captain ignored the signal, and the *Northern Light* steamed on; the revenue cutter fired two cannon shots across her bow. An hour later, the *Northern Light* was at anchor in the river near the pier from which she had departed. The ship was searched the next day. More than one hundred men without proper passage through Nicaragua were put ashore, and six men were arrested. But no weapons were discovered beyond the personal arms of the passengers. A little after midnight on December 28, the *Northern Light* finally put to sea. Despite McKeon's efforts, scores of Walker recruits remained on board, including Louis Schlessinger, a Swiss mercenary of dubious skill and uncertain experience.

The US government's inability to stem the flow of men was not McKeon's failure alone. The *Daniel Webster* had set sail from New Orleans for Greytown on December 11 with armed recruits. The *Uncle Sam* and the *Cortes* similarly brought men "all armed with muskets and pistols, and generally with a few boxes of ammunition and provisions" on every trip from San Francisco to San Juan del Sur. In fact, over the course of sixteen months, Walker would receive several thousand recruits. Not all would be accepted—many failed physical exams after they arrived. Not all would stay. And many would die of cholera and tropical illnesses. But Walker was building a private army of American citizens, and they intended to convert Nicaragua into an Anglo-American country.[24]

Walker was also about to make another enemy.

––––––––––––––

Cornelius Vanderbilt had involved himself in Nicaragua because he wanted to build a canal, the kind of grand accomplishment that would cement his place in history. But when the British banks declined to invest because of the cost involved in digging deep canals and dredging parts of Lake Nicaragua, Vanderbilt had given up on the canal and focused on the "temporary" transit system. Following a complicated behind-the-scenes power struggle with other board members and investors, Vanderbilt had sold his oceangoing steamships to Accessory Transit in December 1852 (the year before Walker went to Baja) for $1.35 million, nearly all of it in cash, but agreed to continue acting as the company's booking agent in return for 20 percent of each ticket sold and 2.5 percent of gross receipts. Vanderbilt also kept his shares in Accessory Transit, bought up some more, and forced out his former partner and now boardroom rival Joseph White. Vanderbilt, who had previously resigned his board seat, returned and added two allies, including Charles Morgan, who had made his own (lesser) fortune investing in shipping. That was also when Vanderbilt and the board hired Cornelius Garrison as the firm's business agent in San Francisco. With the company—as well as his other assets—now in reliable hands, Vanderbilt set off on May 20, 1853, with most of his family for a grand tour of Europe aboard his new private 270-foot steam-powered yacht, the *North Star*.[25]

But the hands weren't as reliable as Vanderbilt thought. While he was away, White wormed his way into the confidence of Morgan, who began buying up shares of Accessory Transit stock. On July 18, a board election replaced the absent Vanderbilt with White; the company ended Vanderbilt's contract as the booking agent and named Morgan as its new president. Vanderbilt learned of the coup in September when he returned from his trip. Irate at the double-cross, Vanderbilt began to destroy the company. In January 1854, he opened a rival line to California via Panama at passage prices undercutting the Nicaragua route. The following May, he opened a steamship line in the Gulf of Mexico to attack Morgan's shipping business serving Texas and New Orleans.

By August, Vanderbilt had brought his rivals to their knees, and they negotiated a settlement, with Vanderbilt selling his ocean ships to Morgan. But Vanderbilt kept his shares of Accessory Transit stock. A year later (and coincidentally just after Walker executed Corral in Granada), Vanderbilt again began quietly buying up stock to make a play for control of Accessory Transit.[26]

By the end of January 1856, Vanderbilt was back as president of the company, which through side negotiations among Vanderbilt, William H. Aspinwall, and others gave the firm an effective monopoly on transit through both Nicaragua and Panama. And Vanderbilt vowed that the lines would not be used to ferry recruits or weapons to Walker and his filibusters, whom he vehemently opposed. He broke the agreement French had reached with White to charge to Nicaragua the $20 fare for each emigrant and "refused . . . to take any passengers, on any account whose fares were not prepaid, unless they went unarmed and avowed a peaceable intent."[27]

But Vanderbilt would soon discover that shutting down Walker's pipeline was not so easy. While he was busy with his boardroom and stock intrigues, a more threatening betrayal came together. After the provisional government was established, Walker's lawyer friends Crittenden and Randolph studied the Accessory Transit charter and its history of payments to the Nicaraguan government—or lack thereof—and concluded that by failing to build the canal and reneging on cash payments, the company had voided its charter. The two men met with Garrison at his San Francisco office in November 1855 to try "to make some arrangement . . . in reference to the transportation of men to Nicaragua." Crittenden told Garrison that the new government would likely revoke the charter and "that a new charter would be granted to some one. I told him that such a result was absolutely inevitable." Garrison complained that revoking the charter "would be an act of wrong" against the company, but Crittenden shrugged it off and then planted a seed in Garrison's head. "It was proposed to him that he should himself take a grant of a similar franchise."[28]

In December, as Vanderbilt was putting the final pieces in place for his deal to seize control of Accessory Transit in New York, Randolph, MacDonald, and Garrison's son, William R. Garrison, arrived in Granada. Randolph made his case to Walker that Accessory Transit's charter was void and that President Rivas's government should grant a new charter to someone else. Namely, them. The elder Garrison, as part of the new transit charter, promised to advance passage to anyone from San Francisco willing to join Walker's army.

"It was necessary to get at once a number of persons capable of bearing arms into the State; and none were more urgent in this policy, or more anxious when the steamer arrived to hear how many passengers were for Nicaragua, than the Provisional President and the members of his cabinet," Walker wrote later. "Internal order as well as freedom from foreign invasion depended, in their eyes, entirely on the rapid arrival of some hundreds of Americans. It will thus appear that the agreement of Crittenden with Garrison was the means, and at that time, the only means, for carrying out the policy vital to the Rivas administration."[29]

But that was a pretext, which Walker made abundantly clear when he made this agreement on the sly. The ends to be served were not those of President Rivas and the government but his own. "True, neither the President nor the cabinet knew of the means whereby their objects were accomplished; and it was in fact highly necessary to the success of the measures that they should be known by as few persons as possible." In other words, Walker would protect the transit route by seizing it from the rich and powerful Vanderbilt and plac-ing it in the hands of friends. Walker and Randolph agreed to terms, drafted the new charter, and sent MacDonald back to San Francisco with a copy for Cornelius Garrison to review. Garrison's son took a copy to New York for a secret meeting with Morgan, who had already once tried to steal control of the transit route from Vanderbilt, and who had resigned from the company's board when Vanderbilt took over. MacDonald and the younger Garrison returned to Granada to report that the principals on both coasts were in—they would accept the new charter under Randolph's name. They began making plans to launch their own steamships from San Francisco and New York to Nicara-gua, angling to maximize their revenues and presuming that once Vanderbilt learned he'd lost the charter, his ships would no longer call at Greytown and San Juan del Sur.

Randolph drew up the revocation of the original charter and the agreement for the new one for Walker to present to President Rivas and Fermin Ferrer, whom Rivas had promoted from minister of public credit to minister general. It was an easy sell. Both the Legitimists and the Liberals chafed under the Accessory Transit charter, in part over the failed payments and in part because the deal did not lead to the economic growth the country had anticipated. Since the route opened, Americans and white Europeans had settled along it and opened up little restaurants, hotels, and other support businesses from San Juan del Sur to Greytown. With the vast majority of passengers quickly passing through the isthmus, few spent money at Nicaraguan-run businesses. So the country had opened itself up as a pipeline for travel and transport of California riches but received little profit from it. After making some minor changes in the new charter, Rivas signed the revocation on February 18 and granted the new charter to "Randolph and his associates" the next day, but neither was announced until after the regular departures of the steamships for New York and San Francisco, which carried private messages to Garrison and Morgan that the deal was done.[30]

By the time Vanderbilt and the rest of the Accessory Transit board learned of the collapse of the main leg of their transit system, it was a fait accom-pli. In fact, by the time they received word, the provisional government had already seized their property in the country, from wharves to tools to ships to the teacups aboard them—worth altogether nearly $1 million—to settle the outstanding debt that Walker believed was owed. The government appointed Joseph Scott, the Accessory Transit agent, as the receiver to take inventory and operate the system. And it announced that it would turn the assets over to the new holders of the Nicaragua charter, for which that new owner eventually paid $425,000—a literal steal.[31]

But Walker was also sending a message to the US government and to American capitalists. "The speculators and politicians of the United States will ultimately open their eyes to the existence of an order of things" different from before, wrote *El Nicaraguense*, the government's bilingual propaganda sheet. "The speculations of men are not allowed to interfere with any of [the government's] plans of improvement and advance. Messrs. Aspinwall and Vanderbilt may therefore reconcile themselves to a considerable loss, for they have met an obstacle that cannot be surmounted by money, nor outwitted by negotiations."[32]

Vanderbilt, true to his nature, would not take the loss lightly.

12 | THE OPPOSITION FORMS

AS WALKER WORKED to keep American fighters flowing into Nicaragua, he also had to navigate the country's relationships with the other Central American countries. He was aware of the anger and suspicion that had prompted the ministers' bitter letters to Marcy, the US secretary of state, and he made some effort to defuse them. Máximo Jerez, Nicaragua's new minister of relations, sent letters in early November 1855 to the neighboring governments telling them that his country had "a sincere desire to cultivate the relations of harmony and paternity which are so necessary with the supreme government" of each of its neighbors. He enclosed a copy of the October 23 treaty that created the provisional government, offering it as evidence that the new leaders were the legitimate government of Nicaragua. El Salvador, which had a Liberal-aligned government, replied promptly and warmly. But no responses came from Costa Rica to the south or Honduras and Guatemala to the north, all of which were "governed by the adherents of the old servile or aristocratic party" aligned with the Legitimists.[1]

In fact, Nicaragua's neighbors were preparing for war, something Walker anticipated. He weighed that possibility during a meeting with José Trinidad Cabañas, the former Liberal president of Honduras, who had been driven from power by Legitimist rivals and fled into exile in El Salvador two weeks before Nicaraguans signed their peace treaty. When he learned of the new unity government in Nicaragua, Cabañas wrangled an invitation, and on December 3 he sat down with Rivas, Walker, and other top officials in León and asked for their help in winning back control of Honduras. Cabañas had been a solid supporter of Castellón before the Liberal leader's death, and he was hoping to draw on the bank of goodwill. His request had Jerez's support, but not that of Rivas or Walker, who thought the risk to the new government too great. Walker specifically considered the likelihood that Nicaragua's neighbors were plotting an attack, writing later:

> It was easy to perceive that sooner or later there was to be a struggle of force between the American policy of the Nicaraguan cabinet and the other governments by which it was surrounded. But it was expedient and proper to make the enemies of the Americans strike the first blow. To have sent troops to Honduras, even with the design of reestablishing Cabañas, would have afforded a pretext for the declaration that the Americans of Nicaragua were aggressive in their nature. It was only necessary for the Americans to wait in order to have their enemies move, and it would have been unwise to hasten the struggle by seeking to restore a man, however worthy, who had just been driven from his own State.[2]

The outlook didn't improve when the US government rejected Parker French's credentials as ambassador. Walker believed that the lack of US recognition fed the idea among Nicaragua's neighbors that the provisional government was illegitimate, which also "furnished them with an excuse for withholding diplomatic intercourse" and "encouraged them to take active and decided measures against the Rivas government."[3]

On January 17, 1856, Walker wrote to President Juan Mora of Costa Rica, seeking to mollify the head of the country and army closest to the transit route—and thus the biggest threat to Walker's lifeline. People "entirely mistake my character if they suppose that I harbor hostile intentions towards Central America," Walker wrote, in what was clearly a lie. "I have come to Nicaragua for the purpose of maintaining it in good order, and supporting the government. Believe me when I say this, that I shall never deviate from my genuine intentions. It is certain that my plans and my conduct have been maliciously interpreted." He ended by saying he sought "peace and good accord" with the nations of Central America.[4]

Mora was not persuaded. On February 4, Walker sent a diplomatic delegation—Colonel Louis Schlessinger, Captain Adolphus Sutter, and Nicaraguan

Manuel Arguello, a Legitimist—to deliver a message to the Costa Rican president that the Rivas government sought a peaceful relationship. Mora abruptly ordered the Americans out of the country but granted Arguello's wish to remain as a refugee from Walker.

Two weeks later, Costa Rica declared war, not against the Nicaraguan government but against "freebooters who have taken possession of the towns of Nicaragua." The goal, Mora declared, was to "drive the common enemy away from Nicaragua and to co-operate with the allied governments in sustaining the absolute independence of Central America and the integrity of its territories." Anyone who aligned with the filibusters or gave them material support would be treated as military enemies. Americans who laid down their arms "shall be pardoned" but "all the filibusters taken with arms in hand will be subject to all the rigors of the law, which in this case is death." It would be a war of extermination.[5]

Rather than wait for Mora to attack, the Nicaraguan government declared war, too, and on March 16 Walker sent Schlessinger and a force of 240 men—most of them new arrivals from New Orleans—to San Juan del Sur and from there to the Costa Rican border, where they were to invade the westernmost province of Guanacaste, which in places was only a couple of miles from the shore of Lake Nicaragua. The strategy was for Schlessinger to occupy the Costa Rican side of the border to serve as a buffer between Mora's army and the transit route. But the lack of experience of Schlessinger and his troops manifested itself even before they left, with disorganized, undisciplined drills and a failure to recognize that they were about to take on an experienced army rather than some ragtag band of villagers. Once they entered Costa Rica and bivouacked at the village of Salinas, Schlessinger sent his surgeon back to Granada with a packet of messages and reports for Walker. It might have made sense to Schlessinger to dispatch a messenger whose role didn't involve firing a weapon, but according to Walker "such ignorance of duty" in the selection of the messenger "revealed the weakness of the commander who had permitted his only surgeon to leave at a time when he might any day engage the enemy."[6]

On the evening of March 20, the Americans camped at a ranchero at a town called Santa Rosa, where Schlessinger deployed a light line of sentries. The next morning a detachment of soldiers rode out to pick up what information they could about Mora's movements and to try to enlist guides to help navigate the unfamiliar terrain. Their departure made the camp an inviting target, and in the midafternoon Mora attacked. Schlessinger was nowhere to be found, and the ill-trained men fired a few defensive shots but then, to a man, fled with no discipline, plan, or destination. Most were captured and after a hasty proceeding summarily executed. The wounded were run through with bayonets. Those who escaped slowly made their way back to Virgin Bay "by squads rather than by companies, some without hats and shoes, and some even without arms. In their flight many had been torn by the thorns through which they had been forced, and it was days and even weeks before straggling men of the expedition ceased to arrive." The undertaking was an unmitigated disaster, and Walker worried about "what effect the rout at Santa Rosa might have on the native Nicaraguans, or how far it might shake their confidence in the ability of the Americans to protect the State from its enemies." He also worried about the effect the rout would have on the morale of his own men. As Schlessinger's surviving fighters crept back, the rest of the force—including Walker's brother, James—launched into a days-long drunken binge. To try to regain some control, Walker made a show of publicly reprimanding his brother, stripping him of his captaincy.[7]

Mora, with a force of five hundred men and the aid of Legitimist refugee Manuel Arguello, entered Nicaragua. Walker made the tactical decision to move his base to Rivas—closer to the transit route, the control of which was never far from Walker's mind. To lose it, he believed, would spell disaster.

That disaster was nearer to hand than he knew. As Walker moved to Rivas, Cornelius Vanderbilt's son-in-law, James M. Cross, was aboard a northbound Pacific Mail steamer from Panama on a special mission on Vanderbilt's behalf. Word had reached New York that the Nicaraguan government had canceled Accessory Transit's charter and seized its river and lake boats, prompting a panicked sell-off that caused the company's shares to lose a third of their value. The board gave Vanderbilt carte blanche to do whatever he thought necessary to deal with the crisis. He almost immediately stopped sending the ships in his Atlantic fleet to Nicaragua, and made it Cross's secret mission to carry word to San Francisco to halt the Pacific port calls, too.

On the way to the West Coast, the steamer crossed paths with the Accessory Transit steamer *Cortes*, which was already en route to Nicaragua. Cross hailed the ship, transferred over, and consulted on the sly with the captain, a man named Collins. When the *Cortes* reached San Juan del Sur, Collins moored a distance offshore near two smaller Accessory Transit coaling boats. The passengers remained aboard—with the exception of William Garrison, who coincidentally was among the travelers. Garrison took a small launch to shore.

About a hundred of Walker's men waited at San Juan del Sur with orders to seize the coal ships and, if Captain Collins refused to pay $20 a head to land his through passengers, to commandeer the *Cortes*, as well. When four officers boarded the ship with Walker's demand, Collins greeted them cordially and invited them below to discuss the issue, where he opened up wine and champagne and arranged for a buffet. While the officers drank and dined, Collins quietly ordered that the mooring cables be slipped, and the *Cortes*, with the two coaling boats trailing behind, drifted out on the ebb tide without firing her engines or turning the paddlewheel.

By the time Walker's men discovered they'd been duped, they were at sea, far from the reach of the hundred soldiers and at the mercy of Collins, Cross, and the armed crew. Cross directed Collins to take the ship to Panama, where he made arrangements for the passengers to continue on to New York. It's unclear what became of Walker's four officers. But the bit of subterfuge was the first manifestation of Vanderbilt's counterattack.[8]

By cutting off all Accessory Transit voyages to Nicaragua, Vanderbilt's intention was to preserve assets. He was afraid Walker would seize his oceangoing ships as he had the river and lake steamers. But it also had the effect of all but stopping the flow of men and arms to Nicaragua until Cornelius Garrison and Charles Morgan could establish their own transit lines, which would take at least six weeks. "Thus one motive for holding fast to the Transit [road] was, for the moment, taken away." Still, Walker had about 850 armed men, and another 500 Americans in the country who he thought could be counted on to fight if needed. He hoped it would be enough to hold Nicaragua until the new ships could arrive.[9]

Rumors swirled that Honduras and Guatemala had reached an agreement to join forces and invade in an effort to drive out Walker. The news sent a wave of fear through the city of Rivas, sparking "a general stampede. . . . Trading women were gathering up their wares and lugging off their tables, door after door was closing upon the streets, and all the avenues leading out of town were lined with laden mules and women bending under bundles, as if fleeing from the wrath to come." The fear coursed through Walker's troops as well. Despite suffering from some unexplained painful facial swelling that had incapacitated him for several says (likely a severely abscessed tooth), Walker ordered the men to be assembled in front of his quarters facing the main square, where he delivered a lengthy address seeking to shore up their spirits. He recapped what they had done so far and what they had lost, extolling the valor of the dead, especially. But he also sought to impress upon them his sense of a grander purpose in the expedition, and incongruously tried to persuade the men that they, the white northerners, were being targeted by the Central Americans because of their race.

"We are engaged in no ordinary war," he began. "A powerful combination surrounds us on every side. A hatred to our race has united adverse states and reconciled the most hostile and repugnant factions. The object of this league is to expel us from the land with which we have identified our lives. But through your fortitude and courage the effort is destined to defeat."[10]

Walker reminded the men that he and his first contingent of fighters had been invited as settlers, and that they and the later arrivals had fought against Nicaragua's aristocracy on behalf of a constitutionally constructed government. In the process, he said, no one could accuse the Americans of committing any acts of injustice—a preposterous claim by Walker given all the threats, executions, confiscations, and depredations committed by the interlopers.

"Notwithstanding all the sacrifices we have made, all the dangers we have encountered—sacrifices not only of our blood in battle but of our lives to the pestilence—bear witness the graveyard at Granada!—are we to be driven from this country merely because we were not born upon the soil?" The men shouted back in a cascading chorus, "Never! Never!" "No, soldiers," Walker continued, "the destiny of this region and the interests of humanity are confided to our care. We have come here as the advance guard of American civilization, and

I know your hearts respond to mine when I declare that sooner than retire before accomplishing our duty, we will spill the last drop of our blood and perish to the last man!"

The men cheered, and basked in the warmth of self-satisfaction for a time, but the reality of their predicament far outweighed a few overwrought words from Walker. With the transit road of little significance for the next few weeks, and Mora's Costa Rican forces moving in from the south, Walker decided to move his men back to Granada. They marched to Virgin Bay and boarded the *San Carlos* on April 6, then steamed eastward to Fort San Carlos and down the San Juan River as far as the Toro Rapids. The circuitous route obscured Walker's movements from Legitimist spies on the south shore of the lake, and he and his men arrived unnoticed back in Granada on the morning of April 8.

The day before, the Costa Rican forces had moved in to San Juan del Sur, Rivas, and Virgin Bay. In the first two places, the soldiers sought to portray themselves as on the side of the Nicaraguans against the Americans, and both towns were taken without violence. Virgin Bay, predominantly a port for the transit route—still operating under Joseph Scott as best it could in a war zone—and filled with American workers, businesspeople, and transit customers, was a different matter. To the Costa Ricans, they were all interlopers. Charles Mahoney, a thirty-three-year-old engineer with the transit operation, was standing with other employees and some travelers outside the company's offices when the uniformed Costa Rican troops appeared, some on foot, a few on horseback. Without warning and on a single command, the soldiers opened fire, mowing down dozens of people. Nine died, all but one instantly; none of the killed or wounded carried or displayed weapons. "The force then broke open the doors of the [office], broke open trunks, and robbed the dead persons and others of money and valuables, watches and jewelry." As a final act, they torched the company's nearly completed twenty-foot-wide wooden wharf that ran sixteen hundred feet along the lake's edge, burning it to the water line.[11]

Wheeler, the US envoy to Nicaragua, complained to Mora about "such infamous conduct" as had taken place at Virgin Bay. Mora delivered his reply to the US secretary of state, informing Marcy through his envoy in Washington, Luis Molina, that the "piratical usurpation of Nicaragua" and "the lawless conduct of citizens or inhabitants of the United States . . . is a flagrant act of aggression against each and all of the" Central American countries, especially given Walker's "well-known purpose of establishing, throughout the country, the supremacy of another race." In other words, the United States could complain all it wanted, but Costa Rica, in an alliance with its neighboring countries, would accomplish what the US government had not. They would stop Walker.[12]

Three days after the slaughter at Virgin Bay, Walker decided to attack Mora at Rivas. He and his men marched south from Granada for about twenty-five miles—"slow and toilsome, owing to the heat of the day and to the long stretches of dry and dusty road without any shade"—and camped that night on the bank of the Río Gil González, about eight miles north of Rivas. During their stay, a man "found skulking near the river" was brought before Walker. "At first he denied all knowledge of the enemy at Rivas, but a rope thrown around his neck and cast over a limb of the nearest tree brought him the use of his memory, and he gave an accurate and detailed account of the several points at which the Costa Ricans were posted." He also detailed in which buildings Mora and other principal officers were housed, mentioned that the ammunition was stored across the plaza from Mora's quarters, and offered the locations of two pieces of artillery. "Unfortunately for himself, he let out the fact that he had been sent to gather news of the Americans, and hence was punished as a spy." Since Walker had ordered his men to camp in as near silence as possible, the man was likely hanged rather than shot.[13]

In the dark of early morning, the Americans broke camp and took aim at Rivas—particularly at the building quartering Mora, whom Walker wanted to capture rather than kill. One detachment split off to circle the town and enter from the south, a second to attack from the north. A third detachment was to reach the eastern edge of the town and hold for further orders, and a fourth group primarily consisting of Nicaraguan Liberals was held in reserve just north of Rivas. They swept into the heart of the city a little after 8:00 AM, catching the Costa Rican soldiers by surprise, and seized the main plaza. But Mora's men quickly recovered, reached defensive positions in buildings, and began pouring bullets into the exposed American brigades, forcing them in turn to shelter inside buildings and on rooftops and towers surrounding the plaza.

Walker tries to capture Mora at Rivas. *Frank Leslie's Illustrated Newspaper,*
April 18, 1857

Walker's men began the attack filled with energy, purpose, and hubristic faith in their superior fighting skills. But Walker's fixation on capturing Mora had led him to make a grave mistake. By driving quickly to the heart of the city, Walker had inadvertently let the Costa Ricans surround them. They exchanged gunfire for most of the day, and the Americans began losing heart as comrades fell, either dead or wounded. After the initial euphoria of seizing the plaza, "it was impossible to get any portion of the force to renew the attack with the vigor which marked its commencement."

As dusk approached, the Costa Rican soldiers began igniting the buildings in which some of the Americans were holed up, adding a sense of panic to the low morale. Walker decided to retreat. Once the sun set, he ordered the men to gather at a cathedral at the edge of the plaza, the healthy carrying the wounded. "The surgeons examined the wounded, and those declared mortally hurt were left in the church near the altar, while the others were provided with horses for the march. It was past midnight when all arrangements were completed, and the command slowly and silently" slipped out of Rivas. They didn't stop until they reached the Río Gil González.

It was an embarrassment. Fifty-eight of Walker's men, including ten officers, were dead, and sixty-two were wounded, a dozen of them officers. Another dozen men were missing, including one of Walker's brothers. Norvell Walker had fallen asleep in a tower and at daybreak discovered he had been abandoned, but he managed to escape unnoticed. Also missing were Garrison confidant C. J. MacDonald—who had become a Walker true believer—and the troop's guide, a US-born but longtime Nicaraguan doctor named J. L. Cole (no relation to Byron Cole). They surfaced ten days later in Granada saying they became separated from the main force and hid with a farm family for a week. Arriving back in Granada, Walker and the other survivors learned that Schlessinger, who had led the ruinous foray into Costa Rica, had deserted. Walker convened a court-martial in absentia, which ordered Schlessinger shot if captured.[14]

Walker's men had more success fighting off attacks by Costa Rican troops along the San Juan River and elsewhere, but the early defeat of Schlessinger's men and the failure to roust the Costa Ricans from Rivas stood as significant military failures. Those embarrassments now became compounded by an enemy even harder to combat. Cholera again swept through Granada, and the American troops, who had been relatively unscathed in earlier outbreaks, fell like flies, including several officers, further decimating the leadership ranks of an increasingly ragtag army. Walker decided to move again, this time from plague-ridden Granada to Virgin Bay, hoping a new environment might arrest the spread of the disease. (His younger brother James would fall ill and die on May 15 at Masaya, northwest of Granada.)[15]

On April 21, Walker received his first good news in weeks: a ship had finally arrived from New York with about two hundred volunteers under General Collier C. Hornsby. And further word came that Mora, facing political turmoil over his invasion of Nicaragua, had turned the troops over to his brother-in-law General José Maria Cañas and returned home. Cholera also ravaged the Costa Rican army, and Cañas abandoned Rivas and led the troops back to Costa Rica in hopes of keeping more of his men from dying. Not understanding the nature of the disease or how it spreads, Cañas, instead of saving his men, may have infected his country. More than ten thousand Costa Ricans, about 10 percent of the population, died in the following months.[16]

As the disease raged through Central America and Walker rebuilt the American Phalanx, the war ebbed. But Walker faced political problems at home. Despite the previous year's peace treaty, Nicaraguan Legitimists began organizing in the western part of the country, emboldened, no doubt, by the decision by Honduras and Guatemala to also move against Walker. Walker sent detachments of soldiers to the countryside to track down suspected Legitimist organizers and supporters, and those suspected of collaborating with the Costa Rican army. Francisco Ugarte, a brother-in-law to Dr. J. L. Cole, was among those apprehended. Accused of "ferreting out wounded Americans after the battle" at Rivas "and turning them over to the enemy to be shot," Ugarte was arrested and brought to Granada, where he offered Walker $20,000 for his freedom. Walker rejected the bribe, and after a hasty trial and over the pleas of Ugarte's wife and daughters, Walker hanged him.[17]

On May 20, Edmund Randolph, who had been bedridden by illness in León, sent word to Walker that something was wrong in the Liberals' home city, but he was too ill to figure out what exactly was happening. Among the issues: neighboring El Salvador, which initially warmly greeted Rivas's provisional government, had gone cold. On May 7, it sent President Rivas a letter declaring that the presence of Walker and his men in Nicaragua threatened the stability and freedom of the entire region. Rivas didn't respond. El Salvador's concerns dovetailed with news that Guatemala was planning an invasion. Also, Walker's men intercepted a courier carrying a letter from President Rivas to President Mora of Costa Rica, "stating that [he] desired to send a commissioner to treat for peace." Walker knew nothing of the overture and had not been part of any discussions on whether the provisional government should seek a negotiated end to the war. Walker kept the letter and detained the courier, ensuring that Mora wouldn't see it. But he also made plans for a trip to León.[18]

Walker arrived June 4 with a detachment of two hundred men. He found Rivas and Jerez showing clear signs of stress: "The face of Jerez had a cloud over it, and he appeared anxious and nervous; nor did Rivas seem as much at ease in the presence of Walker as he had formerly been." Rivas told Walker that the Salvadoran government had demanded that Rivas reduce the American footprint to no more than two hundred soldiers. Walker rejected the idea, arguing he would only accede if the government was ready to pay off the men who had come to join him—something Walker knew it could not afford to do.

But it worried Walker that Rivas thought reducing the American force was a reasonable accommodation.

Walker pressed Rivas to call a national election to transition the country from a provisional government to an established one. But his real motive was to replace Rivas as president; Walker believed Rivas's fears of invasion meant he "could not be relied on to face the coalition preparing against Nicaragua." Walker's preferred replacement was the more accommodating Fermin Ferrer, the provisional government's minister general. And he thought it prudent to have the election called "while the State was comparatively quiet." Rivas balked but eventually acquiesced, and on June 10 he called for the election to be held over three days culminating on Sunday, June 29.

Walker returned to Granada, but a couple of days later rumors swirled through León that the Americans were about to kidnap President Rivas and stage a coup. Walker, in fact, had contemplated just that if Rivas had refused to call an election. The prospect inflamed the Liberals, and Rivas and Jerez fled León for Chinandega. On June 25, Rivas made the rupture with the Americans official. He declared Walker a usurper, dismissed him from the army (an order with no sting, since Walker *was* the army), offered passports and safe conduct out of the country to any Americans who deserted, and urged his fellow Nicaraguans to take up arms with the neighboring states to push the Americans out.

Walker in turn declared Rivas a traitor, appointed Ferrer as the new interim president, and held the presidential election as scheduled. Given the instability across Nicaragua and Rivas's break with the filibusters, the vote was light, mostly conducted around Granada, and of questionable integrity, with reports claiming that some of Walker's soldiers cast as many as twenty ballots. To no one's surprise, the victor was William Walker himself.

Walker was sworn in on July 12 in a ceremony preceded by a parade and followed by a banquet and an endless series of toasts. In the span of a little more than a year, Walker—a former doctor, former lawyer, and former newspaper editor who only two months earlier had turned thirty-two years old—had progressed from mercenary to the presidency of his own country. At least for as long as he could hold on to it.

Washington couldn't keep up with the changes in Nicaragua. After rejecting the American-born Parker French as the Nicaraguan ambassador, President Pierce accepted native Nicaraguan and Catholic priest Augustine Vigil as the representative and on May 15, 1856, told Congress that the United States recognized Rivas as the president of the new government of Nicaragua. In this, Pierce overruled Marcy, his secretary of state, who considered Rivas to be a mere puppet of Walker, "a pirate and an assassin." (Marcy had suggested at a cabinet meeting that the US Navy blockade both coasts of Nicaragua to keep more recruits from reaching the isthmus, but the idea failed to gain traction, primarily because it would be viewed as an act of war.) Pierce justified his decision by citing the government's long-standing policy of not delving into how a nation's government came into being. "These matters we leave to the people and public authorities of the particular country to determine; and their determination, whether it be by positive action or by ascertained acquiescence, is to us a sufficient warranty of the legitimacy of the new government." Back when French arrived in Washington, the authority of the Rivas government had been perceived as sketchy, primarily because of the presence of Walker and his men—of whom French was one. But now, Pierce wrote, the Rivas government seemed to have stabilized and pacified the country; the nation had acquiesced to his leadership, and Vigil, as a native son, was qualified to represent his country in Washington.[19]

To say that Nicaraguans had accepted the Rivas government was a willful misreading. Pierce's decision was rooted in other political realities. A cautious man by nature, Pierce had foundered as a national leader, and with the Democrats meeting in June to nominate a candidate for the November election, he had reason to doubt that the party would put him up for reelection. His support in the North had eroded when he signed the Kansas-Nebraska Act of 1854, which allowed residents of those territories to determine whether to adopt slavery, effectively ending the geographical divisions between slave and free states established by the Missouri Compromise. The question of which path Kansans would choose sparked a miniature civil war in the territory just as Walker was cementing his control over Nicaragua. As the Phalanx was battling the Costa Rican army, abolitionist John Brown and his sons were fighting pro-slavery forces in what became known as "Bleeding Kansas." The situation was grim, but by recognizing the Walker government, Pierce might win enough support from southern Democrats to counter his diminished support in the North. (It didn't work; the president lost the nomination to his former ambassador to Great Britain, James Buchanan.)

Pierce had transportation issues to consider, too. Initially, the president had paid little attention when the Accessory Transit Company lost control of the Nicaraguan transit route. Vanderbilt himself had visited Secretary of State Marcy seeking the government's intervention, but the administration turned a deaf ear. After all, Vanderbilt's steamboats had ferried the vast majority of the filibusters to Nicaragua in the first place, subverting Pierce's efforts to curtail the practice. Vanderbilt had helped make this particular bed, and Pierce was content to let him lie in it—until upheavals in Panama jeopardized the alternate Central American route to California. The Panamanian transit route had recently been racked by riots, with violent mobs damaging property and killing several Americans. That at least temporarily made the Nicaraguan route all the more important, and it was now in the hands of the Rivas-Walker government. The United States could do little to resolve the seizure of the Accessory Transit Company's property, Pierce told Congress, "without resumption of diplomatic intercourse with the Government of Nicaragua."[20]

But Pierce's useful fiction that the people of Nicaragua had acquiesced to the new government could not survive once Rivas defected and Walker assumed the presidency. Augustine Vigil found himself shunned by his fellow Central American emissaries and fellow priests, and left Washington after six weeks. He turned his duties over to John P. Heiss, a former Nashville newspaper editor (a competitor to Walker's uncles). Marcy had dispatched Heiss to Nicaragua in February as a diplomatic courier, but Heiss quickly became enamored with Walker's ambitions and returned to Washington in June as a naturalized Nicaraguan and interim ambassador. As with French, Pierce refused to receive him, even as a temporary fill-in. And in August, Vigil's permanent replacement, Appleton Oaksmith, a native of North Carolina and a Walker man, was similarly rejected, ending the official US recognition of Walker's government. Nonetheless, Heiss and Oaksmith squabbled over who was the formal representative of Nicaragua, an odd point of contention since Pierce no longer recognized the government that sent them.[21]

Walker did have friends and supporters in Congress—primarily southern pro-slavery Democrats but also Californians. One such ally was Senator

John B. Weller, a lawyer in San Francisco during Walker's time there. When some members of Congress denounced Walker's confiscation of the Accessory Transit assets, Weller had risen to defend him. Walker responded with a letter, which Weller read from the floor of the Senate after declaring that "there is no man whose character has been more shamefully misrepresented in this country. . . . I have known him for several years on the Pacific Coast as a quiet, unobtrusive, and intelligent gentleman of uncommon energy and decided character." Walker went to Nicaragua by invitation, Weller said, "actuated by a high and honorable ambition—a patriotic desire to aid in establishing free institution in Nicaragua, and ultimately confederate, in a peaceable manner, the Central American States into one great republic." Weller criticized Pierce for not giving the Rivas-Walker government full recognition. But few people seemed to recognize the larger implications of the plan Weller was describing— that Walker's goal was to establish a unified Central American government.[22]

In his letter to Weller, Walker sought to play off smoldering anti-British sentiments over both American and British interests in Central America. Walker's men had seized a letter sent by the British consul to the British government that "shows that England is furnishing arms to our enemies; and, at the same time, the whole British West India squadron is sent" to Greytown as a show of force against the presence of Americans in Nicaragua. He also pointed out that Costa Rica had not declared war against Nicaragua but against "the American forces in the service of Nicaragua," and vowed to kill all armed Americans they capture. Then he put a romantic veneer on his efforts:

> In such a war as the one they are now waging against us there can be but one result. They may destroy my whole force—a circumstance I deem almost impossible—they may kill every American now in Nicaragua—but the seed is sown, and not all the force of Spanish America can prevent the fruit from coming to maturity. The more savage the nature of the war they wage against us, the more certain the result, the more terrible the consequences. I may not live to see the end, but I feel that my countrymen will not permit the result to be doubtful. I know that the honor and the interests of the great country which, despite of the foreign service I am engaged in, I still love to call my own, are involved in the present struggle. That honor must be preserved inviolate, and those interests must be jealously maintained.

Though Walker wrote of honor and commitment, he was hemorrhaging troops through desertion. Many men slipped off alone, but on at least two occasions, entire units disappeared. In July, a notice in *El Nicaraguense* offered a thirty-dollar reward for the arrest of each of six deserters, two of them from a unit commanded by Walker's brother Norvell. In August, Captain Andrew J. Turley, who had arrived in June with a couple dozen men (mostly fellow Mississippians), was dispatched from Managua to Tipitapa to run down a rumor of a large number of enemy troops gathering nearby. Instead, Turley led his men on a pillaging rampage through Nicaraguan villages, seemingly heading eastward to Bluefields or Greytown, intending to return to the United States all the richer for their thievery. In Chontales, just east of Lake Nicaragua, they robbed a settlement of mostly French miners, who quickly organized themselves into a mix of a posse and a local army and went after Turley and his men. The Americans, running low on ammunition, surrendered; the miners massacred them.[23]

As Walker's army shrank, he took the first steps toward establishing a navy. In June, the *San José*, a schooner sailing under an American flag, moored at San Juan del Sur, and Walker promptly seized it, arguing that it was actually a Costa Rican vessel fraudulently claiming US protection. Wheeler, the US representative in Nicaragua, refused to intercede on behalf of the ship's captain, and Walker assigned Callendar I. Fayssoux—a New Orleans adventurer, naval veteran of the Mexican-American War, and Cuban filibuster under Narciso López—to refit the ship as the *Granada*. Fayssoux armed it with two six-pound cannons and set about converting some of Walker's soldiers into sailors.

By late July the *Granada* was cruising off San Juan del Sur, inspecting ships as Fayssoux deemed necessary. On July 27 it captured a bungo, or small boat, that Fayssoux found suspicious, and the next day it seized a larger ship whose passengers included Mariano Salazar. Salazar was a former member of President Rivas's government (as a commissar, he was involved in self-dealing that led Walker to imprison him for several days). Among those who spread the false rumors in León about the Walker coup, Salazar had joined President Rivas in Chinandega when he denounced Walker. Salazar was also the owner of the ship Fayssoux had seized. Fayssoux sent him under guard to Granada, where Walker met briefly with him and accused him of treason. A little before

5:00 PM on August 3—about seven hours after his brief talk with Walker— Salazar, wearing a blue jacket and coarse brown pants, was led to a chair in the central plaza facing twelve riflemen, then shot before a large crowd of his countrymen. Similar purges happened around the country in places under Walker's control, including in Masaya, where four men were convicted of "treasonable practices"—trying to persuade some of the American soldiers to desert. They too were killed by firing squad in the main square.[24]

These public executions were intended to convey a political message and to intimidate. It didn't work. Salazar was a popular figure with an extended family, and his execution without trial simply because he was a political rival jolted the countryside. "The murder, for so it was called, of a man so universally esteemed as Salazar, excited the wrath of the entire native population, and estranged them from Walker's cause," the *New York Times* noted. So now Walker had bitter enemies not only in Vanderbilt and among the neighboring nations, but within the country he so precociously and precariously led.[25]

Walker was behaving more like a dictator than a president, with no legislature or judiciary beyond the military tribunals he sometimes hastily assembled to provide the illusion of justice before he had someone executed. Walker had also issued a series of edicts that further eroded his support among the Nicaraguan people. One announced the seizure of properties owned by "enemies of the State"—Legitimists and turncoat Liberals—and established a commission to appraise the properties and auction them off, at a minimum price of two-thirds the appraised value. Cash or military scrip would be acceptable payment, a policy designed to both bring in much-needed dollars and remove debt by redeeming the military scrip, which carried a 7 percent interest rate. Walker listed the confiscated properties in *El Nicaraguense* two months before their scheduled auctions, providing plenty of time for the news to reach the United States and for Americans, in turn, to reach Nicaragua and place bids. More than 150 properties, from homes in Rivas to sprawling cattle ranches, were listed for a January 1, 1857, auction, with a minimum value of more than $800,000.[26]

The policy angered not only those whose lands were seized but also those who feared an expansion of the practice. Some of Walker's own men were displeased as well. John H. Marshall had joined the force from San Francisco in May 1856 and was immediately assigned to help oversee the seized Accessory Transit assets. In late July, he went to Walker's headquarters to seek permission to return to the United States. Instead, "I found that I had been appointed auditor general of war (which is about the same as a judge advocate general in the United States) and also one of the commissioners to take possession of all the property in the state subject to confiscation [and] to hear and adjudicate all claims against said property." It would be a lot of work, Marshall wrote to his father, and "I did not feel willing or scarcely at liberty to decline these appointments." So he put off returning home.[27]

Walker also ordered that all legal documents be prepared in English and Spanish, and that all real estate holdings be registered with the new government to preserve the rights of ownership. This created a system the Nicaraguans didn't understand, one that set a date for compliance after which others could claim any unregistered land. Walker was bald in explaining his reasoning: "The general tendency of these several decrees was the same; they were intended to place a large portion of the land of the country in the hands of the white race." He also issued an order against vagrancy, which simultaneously removed idle men from the village streets and provided a cheap pool of labor for the new owners of the plantations.[28]

But regardless of his other goals, what Walker really needed was cash. His government's current sources of income were customs duties, a 10 percent tariff on gold and silver coins and jewelry leaving the country, and fees for retail shops to operate; it also sold monopolies for the sale of cattle and the production of *aguardiente*, a liquor distilled from sugar cane. But that didn't bring in enough revenue to run an army, especially one full of mercenaries facing off against three neighboring nations and the backroom machinations of Cornelius Vanderbilt, one of the richest men in the world.

And conventional sources of investment shut Walker out. He had sent a representative to the United States—Domingo de Goicouria, a Cuban independence advocate who had brought a contingent of 250 Cuban fighters to join Walker—to gin up interest in the sale of $2 million worth of Nicaraguan government bonds, secured by confiscated land. The first and obvious stop was New Orleans, followed by New York, but there were few takers. The moneymen in New Orleans might have been sympathetic to the cause, but they weren't about to engage in what was clearly a gamble. And in New York, no one was willing to bet against—or cross—Vanderbilt. Goicouria, who knew the mogul, made a unilateral decision to see if the tycoon might be interested in buying back the transit rights, which drew a rebuke from Walker. The rebuke turned into a quarrel, which turned nasty, and unfortunate for Walker.[29]

Selling the bonds was only Goicouria's first mission. Walker had also appointed him as his envoy to Great Britain, and the plan was for Goicouria to continue on to London. But when Pierce rescinded his recognition of Walker's government, Goicouria decided it made no sense to seek recognition from the English after the Americans had turned their backs on their fellow countrymen. Goicouria wrote Walker to tell him of his decision, making suggestions about how a new Nicaraguan government should be constituted and passing along rumors that Edmund Randolph, Walker's longtime friend, stood to reap a fortune from the new transit charter. Walker responded that he wondered whether Goicouria's allegiances were to Vanderbilt ahead of Nicaragua and said if Goicouria wouldn't go to London, Walker would name a new envoy in his place. Goicouria retaliated by publishing excerpts from his letters with Walker in the *New York Herald*.

The published excerpts included Walker's instructions to Goicouria on what promises he should secure from Great Britain. First and foremost: an agreement by the British to drop its protectorate of the Miskito Kingdom and cede Greytown to Walker's government as a necessary port from which to build a naval presence in the Caribbean. Walker noted that he was sending the Cuban Goicouria instead of an American as part of a message to the British that the future of Nicaragua was not as a US satellite or annexed state:

> You [as a Cuban] can make the British cabinet see that we are not engaged in any scheme for annexation. You can make them see that the only way to cut the expanding and expansive democracy of the North, is by the powerful and compact Southern federation, based on military principles.[30]

Until that letter came to light, the prevailing belief among Walker's supporters in both the United States and Nicaragua—including his top advisers and aides—was that Walker's ultimate goal was to prepare Nicaragua to be annexed by the United States as part of the Manifest Destiny movement.

Few had understood what Senator Weller said about Walker's plans during his speech to Congress, or knew the details Walker had shared with Charles Doubleday during their walks on the beach. But now the whole country realized that Walker's ambition was highly personal. He intended to be the leader of an independent, military-controlled state composed of the isthmus nations of Central America, Cuba, and perhaps even Mexico. Rather than seeking to expand the United States, he dreamed of building a new nation that would control trade and transit across the isthmus, and live in the fragile balance of power between the United States and Great Britain.

It was a dream of empire.

13 | RACE, SLAVERY, AND WALKER'S EMPIRE

AS A YOUNG JOURNALIST, Walker had avoided embracing slavery too directly or too stridently, but now that he was president of Nicaragua, his words and actions were those of a racist through and through. His 1860 memoir of the war in Nicaragua contained a lengthy discourse on slavery and his belief that Anglo-Saxons were the superior race. His contempt for Nicaraguans—"half-castes who cause . . . disorder"—was palpable, even as he absorbed amenable locals into his government and, for a time, his military. He held Africans in even lower regard, and saw their enslavement as something of a divine intervention, and a mechanism by which Europeans—whites—were destined to create wealth.[1]

Africa, he wrote, was "for more than five thousand years a mere waif on the waters of the world, fulfilling no part in its destinies, and aiding in no manner the progress of general civilization." It took the European discovery of the Americas, he claimed, to provide a function for Africans as

> a useful auxiliary in subduing the new continent to the uses and purposes of civilization. The white man took the negro from his native wastes, and teaching him the arts of life, bestowed on him the ineffable blessings of a true religion. . . . Africa is permitted to lie idle until America is discovered, in order that she may conduce to the formation of a new society in the New World.

And African slavery was crucial to his vision for Nicaragua:

200

> The introduction of negro-slavery into Nicaragua would furnish a supply of constant and reliable labor requisite for the cultivation of tropical products. With the negro-slave as his companion, the white man would become fixed to the soil; and they together would destroy the power of the mixed race which is the bane of the country.[2]

Walker first put these views into action on September 22, 1856, issuing an edict rescinding an 1838 Nicaraguan law that banned slavery. "The wisdom or folly of this decree," he later explained, "involves the wisdom or folly of the American movement in Nicaragua." Walker reasoned that reintroducing slavery to the country would make his government bonds more attractive to southern investors, a strategy he adopted after former US senator and former minister to Spain Pierre Soulé visited Nicaragua in August.

Soulé, a native of France who had moved to New Orleans in the 1840s, was a vocal backer of Walker's Nicaraguan escapade. In June 1855, he had joined Parker French in New Orleans for a public presentation seeking financial support for Walker, and his visit to the country was a significant moment for Walker. The US government might not recognize his presidency, but here a popular and charismatic political figure was making a formal visit. Soulé was still actively trying to raise money for Walker, and the purpose of his visit was to obtain unspecified changes in a government decree authorizing the sale of $500,000 in twenty-year Nicaraguan bonds at 6 percent interest, secured by one million acres of public land. Soulé impressed upon Walker that he would have an easier time selling the bonds in Louisiana if Nicaragua reinstituted slavery to ensure cheap labor to work the large estates, thus making them more profitable. As if to reinforce the point, Soulé paid $50,000 for a cacao plantation seized from a Legitimist family.[3]

Northern newspapers took the September decree as prima facie evidence that Walker was acting not on his own but at the behest of pro-slavery southerners, and that reinstituting slavery in Nicaragua had been the goal all along. But those arguments feel self-serving. Walker had given no intimation that he was part of any organized effort to expand slavery. Most of his early financial support had come from selling bonds in San Francisco, and most of Walker's recruits were northerners unlikely to be driven to such adventure for the sake of slavery. "The real underlying purpose of Walker's going to Nicaragua, in my opinion, was empire in the tropics, with Walker as the central figure," one recruit wrote later. "Of this I never had any doubt."[4]

But Walker saw slavery as crucial to the future of his empire, not just for financial reasons but also, somewhat counterintuitively, because he believed that reinstituting slavery in Nicaragua would help ensure against annexation by the United States. The northern states would oppose adding more slave territory to the union, and while slavery would "bind the Southern States to Nicaragua," it also would make the new nation an economic rival, which would preclude the slave states from approving annexation. Of particular concern would be the increased demand for slaves themselves, which would drive up the price in slave markets. At the same time, Walker foresaw a United States in which slavery ultimately would be banned. If that were to happen, those who saw no immorality in forced, racially based servitude would need some-place to continue the practice. Walker's Central American empire would be an attractive option. Or so he thought.

American immigrants would be able to bring their slaves with them as they bought up ranchland and farms confiscated from Walker's Nicaraguan enemies, but where would Americans who *didn't* own slaves obtain them in a place where no slave market existed? Walker intended to meet that demand by reviving the practice of kidnapping or buying Africans in their homeland and sailing them in chains to Nicaragua—the Atlantic slave trade that had all but ended a half century earlier. The odds of Walker being able to pull off his repugnant plans were, to say the least, long, but that was the future he envisioned.

The Nicaraguans, of course, had a different view of the future, as did their neighboring countries. Ten days before Walker's decree on slavery, Nicaragua's Legitimist and Liberal leaders—enemies and rivals for generations—tossed aside their mutual enmity and joined cause against Walker and his American regime. All told, the Central American allies—non-Walker Nicaragua, Costa Rica, Honduras, Guatemala, and El Salvador—put together a force of more than six thousand men, most of them conscripted. By comparison, at its peak, Walker's American Phalanx totaled about fifteen hundred men, all willing and, at least at first, enthusiastic volunteers.

The Phalanx was a motley and ever-shifting crew, with an average age of twenty-six years and average height of just under five feet eight inches, according to Walker's January–April 1857 muster rolls of 1,072 soldiers (not including about 250 officers). More than half were of light complexion and hair. Of the 674 men whose birth states were recorded, 174 had been born in New York and 77 in Louisiana, but they were drawn from across the country, and many from Europe, as well. New Orleans, the closest US port, recorded 473 recruits, and 189 signed up in California (most likely in San Francisco) and 172 in New York. About a tenth of the muster roll had enlisted in Nicaragua—men in transit who decided to stay, or those who came to Nicaragua on their own and enlisted upon arrival.[5]

Despite Walker's pretensions of running a highly organized army—there were eight companies under the First Infantry, three companies of rangers, the First Rifles and Second Rifles, two artillery units, and an Ordnance Corps—it was a gaggle of adventurers with no set uniform for the rank and file and inconsistent dress for the officers. Only 31 men listed "soldier" as their occupation before joining Walker, while 124 had been clerks, 106 laborers, and 89 farmers. Discipline was imaginary, with men spending idle hours getting drunk. Many went into battle that way. A full 195 men on the muster roll were described as having deserted, and at least 137 had been killed—a count that does not include officers and only covers the first four months of 1857.

It was, by and large, a force constantly in flux as scores of (usually) green recruits arrived on a sporadic basis, while existing fighters were siphoned off through fatal illness, battle deaths, incapacitating wounds, and desertion. Those with fighting experience in the Mexican-American War or other filibuster movements tended to serve well. Those who signed on for adventure, or who were coerced into service after arriving in search of land, made for unreliable fighters.[6]

Walker concentrated his forces in Granada but also posted them along the San Juan River, at Virgin Bay, on the transit road to San Juan del Sur, and at Rivas and Masaya. Despite glowing reports in US newspapers trumpeting Walker's success and broad support among the people, his position was precarious, his support all but nonexistent, and he controlled—loosely—about twenty-five hundred square miles of the fifty-thousand-square-mile country. By late summer 1856, only a month or so into his presidency, his hold on the territory was becoming ever more tenuous as the troops of the Allies, as Walker called the forces marshalling against him, began encircling him.

The Allies were much more disciplined and tenacious fighters than Walker and his men anticipated. In late August, Walker sent out a squadron of about forty men on a reconnaissance mission under a Lieutenant Colonel McDonald to try to find a Nicaraguan force that had ambushed and killed a local rancher loyal to Walker, and a handful of Americans who were driving a herd of (likely stolen) cattle destined to feed Walker's men. McDonald heard from local residents that some of the Nicaraguan soldiers were at a hacienda at San Jacinto, near Tipitapa. The adobe building and a nearby small cane house sat in the middle of a wooden corral atop a small rise, and with no trees or shrubs of notable size nearby, it commanded a clear view of anyone approaching and other than a few fence posts offered little in the way of defense for attackers. McDonald opted for an early morning attack, and shortly after dawn he led his men in a rapid approach up the slight rise, hoping to catch whoever was there by surprise.

Surprise was lost. As they neared, a Nicaraguan force of about seventy men opened fire from behind the thick adobe walls, killing a captain and wounding several other men and forcing McDonald into a hasty retreat. Rather than regroup and attack the far larger and better-positioned force, McDonald returned to Granada and reported the failure to Walker. The presence of the Nicaraguan soldiers in an area upon which Walker relied for food was "an inconvenience to the commissariat," but Walker was uncertain of the wisdom of trying to dislodge soldiers from such a well-defended outpost. Yet as word of the attack spread, some of Walker's men—and some who had left his service but remained in Granada—took McDonald's loss as an affront, believing that he had given up too easily. They volunteered to return and rout the Nicaraguans. "Seeing the enthusiasm of some officers and citizens, and desirous of ascertaining more exactly the strength of the enemy beyond Tipitapa," President Walker agreed. But "not without reluctance, as he doubted its success."[7]

About sixty-five men under the command of Walker's old friend Byron Cole—who served as a quartermaster and had limited battle experience—left Granada late on September 12, arriving at the hacienda around 5:00 AM on September 14. Cole divided his men into three groups and laid out a plan for each to attack simultaneously from different directions, hoping to get to the corral posts, from which they could then continue the attack with some protection.

For some reason, the men opted to rely on revolvers rather than rifles (perhaps hoping six-shot cylinders would allow them to fire more bullets more quickly).

At a signal, the Americans rushed the adobe in a shouting horde, with Cole's contingent—to their misfortune—nearing the corral ahead of the other two groups. Deadly gunfire poured from the windows and rifle slots cut into the adobe walls and the cane house. Within seconds, Cole's squadron was shredded and Cole killed. The other two waves of attackers fared slightly better, but the adobe was unwinnable without a cannon to blast through the walls. Still, the Americans kept shooting, at one point moving up to the closest part of the corral, which some of the enemy forces were using for their own protection. One Nicaraguan soldier, a young man named Andrés Castro, found both his guns jammed as an officer named McNeal moved to the other side of the fence. So he picked up a rock and threw it, striking McNeal in the head, killing him, then skittered, wounded himself, for the safety of the adobe. (The feat would earn Castro considerable fame among his countrymen; he remains a national hero.)

The Americans continued fighting for four hours until the Nicaraguans came up with the creative idea of letting loose their penned-up horses, sending them galloping from the back of the property toward the corral. The Americans, hearing the thundering hooves, feared a cavalry of Nicaraguan reinforcements was arriving. They retreated in a panic, a second defeat in as many tries at taking a single hacienda. Eleven of Walker's men were killed, ten were wounded, and three others—including Charles Callahan, a New Orleans journalist who exchanged pen for sword—were unaccounted for and presumed dead in the brush. Even *El Nicaraguense*, Walker's propaganda sheet, had trouble putting a positive spin on it, reduced to describing the attackers as heroes for "the courage, we might say, excess of daring, displayed by this small and undisciplined party."[8]

A few days after the San Jacinto fiasco, Walker noted that another two hundred men had arrived from New York City:

> A very large proportion of them were Europeans of the poorest class, mostly Germans who cared more for the contents of their haversacks than of their cartridge-boxes. . . . The promise of free quarters and rations seemed to have carried the most of them to Nicaragua; and the idea of performing duty could scarcely have entered their minds when they left the United States.

They began "to desert in numbers" shortly after Walker arranged them into companies, both disrupting his attempt to keep his troops organized and instilling yet more lawlessness and avariciousness among the non-Nicaraguan population. Walker had better luck with another contingent of 170 men who arrived in early October, also from New York, along with two twelve-pound howitzers and four hundred Minié rifles.[9]

As Walker tried to build out his force, the Central Americans were also adding troops—in larger numbers, with better discipline and more determination. President Rivas and the Liberals at León had put Ramón Belloso, a Salvadoran general, in charge of their army, which soon included a battalion of Legitimists at Matagalpa led by General Tomás Martínez—it was his men who had routed the Americans at San Jacinto. That victory emboldened Belloso to march from León with a large force (Walker estimated eighteen hundred men) about seventy miles southeastward to Managua, which was about twenty-five miles from Granada itself. Some of Walker's men sought to slow them with a campaign of harassing rifle fire, but they were outnumbered. As the Americans fell back, Belloso moved on to Masaya, about ten miles from Granada, where he and Martínez merged forces, bringing the total to about twenty-three hundred men. Walker's men at Tipitapa, fearing they would be cut off, abandoned that outpost and returned to Granada.

Walker later claimed that he had allowed the Belloso and Martínez forces to merge as a strategic move. "A war against scattered guerillas was more exhausting to the Americans than a contest with the enemy gathered in masses. The Allies were less formidable when united than when acting in detached bodies at several distant points." But the reality was he couldn't have done much about it, and his real strategy seems to have been to fortify Granada with as many men as he could in anticipation of a full-scale attack.

Walker's control of territory continued to slip away—even the contingent he had left at Rivas had been driven out. On October 11, he sallied from Granada with eight hundred men and his two howitzers, which had been jerry-rigged to insufficient carriages, in hopes of retaking Masaya. His men made headway, blowing holes through buildings with explosives until they reached the central plaza, ringed with houses holding Belloso's men. But the attack was another strategic blunder. A courier reached Walker with news that after he left Granada, the Allies had overwhelmed the two hundred men he left to guard the city and now occupied the main part of the town. As the Allies swept through, they executed several Americans with deep roots to the city whom they presumed to be with Walker, including two Protestant ministers and a leather trader from Ireland, none of whom were filibusters.

Walker quickly abandoned Masaya, returned to Granada, and drove out the Allies. The fighting was followed by a triple execution. Belloso's men had captured a Cuban aide to Walker (F. A. Laine, one of the men Domingo de Goicouria had brought to the expedition), and shot him. When word reached Walker, he ordered two captured Guatemalan officers similarly executed. But between the two battles, Walker lost twenty-five men with another eighty-five wounded, a waste of valuable troops with nothing to show for it, which further eroded trust in his capabilities as a military leader.

Details of these battles couldn't reach the States until weeks later, so there was a disconnect between the expectations of newly arriving troops and the reality of Walker's situation. A few days after the ill-conceived Masaya foray, Walker received Charles F. Henningsen, a Belgian mercenary and adventurer who had fought in the Carlist wars in Spain and been forced out of Russia for supporting a Hungarian independence movement. Walker, impressed with his background, put him in charge of two companies of artillerymen—rather grandly named, given the lack of cannons—and one company of sappers, men assigned to both repair damaged infrastructure and to blow it up as needed.

Charles F. Henningsen. *Harper's Weekly, May 23, 1857*

Walker was looking for some victories, if for no other reason than to bolster the men's spirits. But they were hard to come by. On November 11, he attacked Costa Rican forces holding the transit road, managing to drive them off and reopen the vital transit route. Walker returned to Granada but deployed more than two hundred men to Virgin Bay to protect the road and lake harbor. A few days later Walker decided to attack both Masaya and Rivas, but fearing that the moves left Granada vulnerable, he abandoned both attempts and returned.

The problem, Walker came to realize, was that his base in Granada, while an attractive defensive position, was a poor strategic position. He still believed that the only chance he stood of holding on to power was by controlling the traffic along the river, lake, and transit road. Without that lifeline to the United States, he would lose a war of attrition. So, on November 18 he decided to abandon Granada. Using two steamships, he had the sick and wounded evacuated to Ometepe Island and himself and his own men to Virgin Bay. He ordered Henningsen and more than four hundred men to destroy Granada and join him at Virgin Bay when they were done. Then they would march to Rivas and establish a new base of operations closer to the transit route.

Unleashed, Henningsen's men began looting whatever they could find and drinking deeply of caches of wine and *aguardiente* they rooted out of abandoned homes. Drunkenness slowed their execution of the order to destroy the city, and they were further slowed by another outbreak of cholera. Granada, despite being occupied by the Americans, was not sealed off. In fact, the Americans were pushing the Granadans out of the city so they could burn it. (They forced many onto steamboats and deposited them elsewhere on the lakeshore.) Word quickly reached Belloso that Walker had thinned his forces in the city and that those remaining behind were drunk and inattentive. Two days after Walker steamed away, Belloso had Granada surrounded with about fifteen hundred men, with the lake Henningsen's only escape route—though the attackers had a clear firing line to the wharf.[10]

Henningsen ordered the houses around the plaza and cathedral burned to the ground, and directed the sappers to add barricades to the cathedral. But the men were too drunk to do the work; Henningsen dismissed the captain in charge, and slowly the barricades were established. While Henningsen led a squadron of rifles out of the city center to try to drive back Belloso's fighters, some of the Allied forces swept into the plaza and massacred about twenty American sappers trying to reinforce the cathedral, forcing Henningsen to return to the plaza and recapture the building. What should have been a relatively simple act of destruction turned into a siege that dragged on for more than two weeks, with Henningsen and his men—now down to two hundred able to fight—staving off the Allies as they burned the city. They eventually were forced to take sanctuary inside the cathedral while arraying men to protect the route to the lakefront.

General José Víctor Zavala, commanding the Guatemalan forces attacking Granada, knew that Henningsen had been receiving occasional supplies via ship through the wharf complex, but he couldn't tell how many men guarded the facility so held off attacking it. A Venezuelan whom Walker had liberated from prison when he first took Granada had been fighting along with the forces ever since and was among the men at the wharf. He defected, alerted Zavala that the twenty-seven men were vulnerable to a rear attack by water. Zavala moved in with overwhelming force, routing the small garrison and sealing off Henningsen from the lake and his crucial supplies. Trapped in the cathedral and a string of small huts, his men quickly ran low on ammunition and food amid the putrefying corpses of their comrades. More fighters were stricken with cholera and other diseases, and some of them died; remarkably, however, enough of them recovered to bolster the ranks of men able to fight. Still, the predicament was dire.

Concerned over the lack of contact with Henningsen, Walker boarded *La Virgen* bound for Granada. After stopping briefly off Ometepe to investigate an attack by native tribesmen on the sick and wounded (leading Walker to order the island evacuated), *La Virgen* drew within view of Granada on December 9, where Walker saw Henningsen's men in control of several huts near the beach. Content that the destruction was proceeding, albeit slowly, Walker—oblivious to the trouble Henningsen was in—returned to Virgin Bay. The effect on Henningsen's increasingly desperate men was profound. They thought the arrival of the ship meant help had arrived; when it steamed away, many of them concluded that Walker had been defeated, and they slipped away from the fight and disappeared into the jungle.

Walker returned to Virgin Bay to find that Samuel A. Lockridge, a Texas adventurer, had arrived with 235 recruits from New Orleans. A short time later, a courier arrived with details from Henningsen on the trouble they were in, and Walker quickly dispatched 120 of the new men to Granada aboard *La Virgen*. The captain cruised far out in the lake past the city then angled in and ferried the men by launch to the same beach north of Granada that Walker had used for his initial successful attack. The soldiers encountered steady fire as they moved through the early morning darkness and then sunrise along the lakefront, essentially shooting their way through the Allied forces to reach Henningsen at the cathedral. Belloso, uncertain of what the new arrivals meant, ordered his men to fall back. As they left, they ignited a lakeside fort they had occupied, one of the few buildings still standing. Henningsen read the smoke accurately as a sign that the attackers were gone; the trapped Americas moved quickly to the fort and signaled *La Virgen* to send launches to rescue them. The last of the men reached the ship at around 2:00 AM on December 14, and *La Virgen* steamed away.

Of the 419 men under Henningsen's command when Walker ordered him to destroy Granada, 120 died of cholera or other diseases, 40 deserted, 110 were killed or wounded so badly they could no longer fight, and 2 were missing and presumed to have been captured by the Allies. The force that came to rescue them suffered 14 killed and 30 wounded. All for the sake of burning down a city.

"As to the justice of the act, few can question it; for its inhabitants owed life and property to the Americans in the service of Nicaragua, and yet they joined the enemies who strove to drive their protectors from Central America," Walker wrote later. "They served the enemies of Nicaragua in the most criminal manner; for they acted as spies on the Americans, who had defended their interests, and sent notice of all their movements to the Allies. By the laws of war, the town had forfeited its existence; and the policy of destroying it was as manifest as the justice of the measure."

As a last symbolic act, Henningsen erected a sign on the shore that read, HERE WAS GRANADA, as though the destruction was a victory of some sort. In fact, it was a barbarous act committed in the face of defeat.

Since President Pierce had cut off diplomatic relations with Walker's government, Cornelius Vanderbilt was having no luck convincing him to intervene to recover the Accessory Transit Company ships the Phalanx had seized. But Vanderbilt had never been one to wait for the actions of others. He cryptically testified in an October 1856 trial involving Accessory Transit that "I am endeavoring to protect the property. . . . I am devoting my own means to bring the matter out right." The steps he was taking would play a critical role in the fate of Walker and his nascent empire.[11]

Earlier that month, Vanderbilt had summoned Sylvanus M. Spencer to his office for a private meeting. Spencer, born around 1824, grew up as "one of the roughs" in New York's tough Thirteenth Ward. When he was eleven or twelve years old "to the great gratification of the old ladies of his vicinity, and quiet people generally, he utterly vanished." Like many young boys of the time, he took to the sea, and by 1855 he had worked himself up to a position as a mate on Howland & Aspinwall's clipper ship *Sea Witch*, one of the top ships of the day, which had sailed from Hong Kong to New York in a record seventy-four days. When the *Sea Witch* was thirteen hundred miles southeast of Rio de Janeiro in June 1855, Spencer, who had the midnight to four o'clock watch, reported that he had discovered the captain, with whom he had quarreled just hours before, battered and semiconscious in his sleeping berth. The captain died twelve hours later. Spencer's fuse was short and his temper violent, and as the man who discovered the dying captain, he became the leading suspect. Once the *Sea Witch* reached Rio, the American consul there conducted a brief investigation and ordered Spencer arrested. He was returned to New York for trial on charges of committing murder on the high seas. With no witnesses to the attack, Spencer was acquitted in late December, but no other captain would hire him. So Spencer made his way to Nicaragua, where Joseph Scott, the Accessory Transit agent, hired him, first as a stevedore and then eventually as a mate on a riverboat. Some time after Walker seized the transit line, Spencer quit and returned to New York.[12]

It's unclear exactly what Vanderbilt said to Spencer in that October 1856 meeting, or even how Vanderbilt came to know Spencer other than by reputation. It could be that Spencer reported to Vanderbilt once he returned from Nicaragua—Vanderbilt likely would have been quite keen to hear details from an employee on the seizure of his ships. Regardless, a few days after the meeting, Spencer boarded the *Cahawba*, a 250-foot-long paddle steamer that made a regular circuit among New York, Havana, Mobile, and New Orleans, carrying Vanderbilt-signed documents designating him as the mogul's agent. Spencer left the ship at Havana, then traveled onward to Aspinwall, the Panama transit route port, and continued westward overland to San José, Costa Rica, where he met with President Juan Mora and relayed a proposal from Vanderbilt. If Mora would provide the men, Spencer—whose time working for Accessory Transit gave him intimate knowledge of the fleet and waterways—would seize the river and lake vessels and move them out of Walker's reach, thus cutting off crucial supplies of men, arms, and other supplies to Mora's enemy. And Vanderbilt would provide up to $40,000 to pay for it. Since the deal would cost him nothing and could hasten the end of the war, Mora agreed.[13]

Spencer set out from San José on December 10 with 120 Costa Rican soldiers. They traveled northward across the Tilaran Mountains in near-constant rain, hacking their way through the jungle until they reached the San Carlos River, where they carved bungoes from tree trunks and lashed smaller logs together with vines to create rafts. The makeshift flotilla drifted downstream to the confluence with the San Juan River, then continued down the larger waterway. One of the river steamers, with several of Walker's officers aboard, passed by the rafts but failed to recognize the threat. As Spencer and his men neared the mouth of the Sarapiquí River, a place called Hipp's Point, they beached their rafts and quietly hacked their way to the rear of a remote encampment of Walker's men under command of Colonel P. R. Thompson. With the jungle at the camp's back, Thompson hadn't bothered to post sentries. Spencer sent a scout shinnying up a tree, from which he could see about forty soldiers eating dinner, their rifles not noticeable nearby. The Costa Rican soldiers crept up in a pincer formation and at the signal of a single gunshot swept screaming into the camp, shooting and bayoneting as they ran. About thirty of Walker's men either were slain or drowned trying to escape; ten were taken prisoner, including Thompson, who suffered a severe gash in the attack. Spencer left a detachment to hold the camp and rafted through the darkness with the bulk of his forces, down the San Juan to Greytown. By shortly after daybreak, he had seized all four Accessory Transit boats at the port, replacing Walker's Nicaraguan flag with the Costa Rican flag. "He said he meant to take them up the river, and keep them out of the way of the filibusters."[14]

There were no US navy ships in the area, so the US commercial agent at the port, Cottrell, asked the captain of a British warship anchored off the harbor to protect American interests, including the Accessory Transit ships, from the Costa Rican soldiers. The captain landed a squadron of marines to secure the property of Americans living in Greytown but declined to involve himself in what he saw as a corporate dispute over ownership of the river steamers. The men holding the ships might be Costa Rican soldiers, but they were under the command of Spencer, who carried documents from Vanderbilt authorizing his actions. And with Costa Rica and Walker at war, the ships were fair game and beyond the interests of Great Britain to interfere with. So Spencer steamed the vessels up the San Juan, easily seizing the rest of the river fleet at Castillo and beyond by simply boarding them with the armed Costa Ricans and announcing that no one would be hurt so long as no one acted against the seizure. Spencer promised to get the passengers to Greytown, where they could steam back to the United States, but those who spoke against him would be detained as prisoners of war. None objected.

Meanwhile, the Costa Rican president's brother, General José Joaquín Mora, had trailed Spencer's expedition across the mountains, and arrived at the San Carlos River with about eight hundred Costa Rican soldiers. A second reserve battalion of three hundred men followed a few days behind. Spencer sent boats to fetch them, and they soon were all moving up the San Juan, posting units at critical junctures to maintain control of the transit route. Spencer and Mora then steamed upriver to Lake Nicaragua, where Spencer hailed the unsuspecting captain of *La Virgen*. Since no word had reached the lake of the loss of the riverboats, Spencer was able to board with an armed force and take control without firing a shot that could have alerted the rest of Walker's men.

At Castillo, Spencer had seized the fort and the *Ogden*, the largest of the river steamers, which had two field artillery pieces strapped to its deck. The only prizes left were the largest of the lake steamers, the *San Carlos*, and Fort San Carlos itself, guarded by a force of twenty-six of Walker's men, ten of whom were too ill to fight. Spencer and Mora landed 250 soldiers some 150 yards down the river, around a bend from the stone fortress, then steamed the *Ogden* within sight of it. Spencer had not changed the flags on the ship, and once the *Ogden* came within view, he had the captain give

Walker's signal—two short blasts of the steam whistle. The commander of the fort, a Captain Kruger, replied with a single cannon blast, which Spencer answered with a single short steam-whistle toot, confirming that all was well.

A short time later, Kruger and six men boarded the steamer and were instantly captured by hidden Costa Rican soldiers. Spencer told Kruger he now possessed all of the river ships and controlled the river all they way to Greytown, and demanded that Kruger surrender the fort. Kruger refused, and Spencer gave him an ultimatum: he had two minutes to agree, after which the ship would open up its cannons on the fort as the Costa Rican troops moved in from the riverbank. Kruger capitulated, sending an order to his men to surrender. The Costa Rican soldiers marched into the fort as the last of Walker's men boarded *La Virgen* as Spencer's prisoners. A short time later, stripped of their weapons, they were dispatched down the river in bungoes.

The *San Carlos* itself remained free. The boat left Virgin Bay on January 2 with about 135 passengers, most from San Francisco heading to New York City, though some were trying to join Walker's force. The steamer entered the river beneath the walls of the fort and continued around a bend searching for the *Ogden*, which was supposed to take the passengers on the next leg. When the ships came into view of each other, Spencer hailed the *San Carlos*'s captain, told him that he controlled the rest of the river and lake fleet, the river itself, and the fort under whose cannon the *San Carlos* was now floating. Spencer demanded the surrender of the ship, promising that all aboard who did not resist would be granted safe passage to Greytown. The captain refused, and Spencer had the *Ogden* turned broadside, its cannons clearly visible in the deck. The *San Carlos* surrendered. Spencer boarded the ship and read a pledge from General Mora that all would be passed freely down the river, and that any of Walker's men who gave up their arms would be given free passage to leave the territory.

As Spencer completed his seamless seizure of the river transit system, a fresh shipload of Walker recruits arrived at Greytown on the *Texas* under the command of Lockridge. Walker's brother Norvell was reported among Lockridge's men, though it's unclear whether he had also taken part in the recruiting trip or was based at Greytown. As the oceangoing ship arrived,

Lockridge spotted in the harbor one of Spencer's riverboats with about fifty Costa Rican soldiers aboard. The filibusters hurriedly broke open the cases holding guns and ammunition and tried to arrange themselves into companies, but disorganization and ill discipline delayed them for so long that the enemy boat built up a head of steam and chugged on up the river.

Lockridge ordered a group of eight men to board a small yawl and follow the boat until a larger force could be assembled, and a couple of miles up the river they hid within clear view of the Costa Ricans, who were cutting and loading wood for the boiler. Outgunned, they sent word back to Greytown that the ship was anchored and assailable, but incompetence prevented a second group from managing to move up the river against the current, and the riverboat steamed off unbothered by the new filibusters.

With Spencer and the Costa Rican soldiers controlling the river, there was no way for the recruits to advance, and no boat to advance in. Lockridge managed to buy a dilapidated steamer, and as he oversaw its repair he tried to drill his men. But they were desperate characters in a desperate place. In fact, Greytown—a backwater port in the best of times—was quickly running low on food and other supplies, since the settlement's main trade route was up the river. And there was no room in the collection of palm-roofed huts for Walker's stranded men to find housing.

"We were compelled to go up about a mile near the woods and make preparations for camping in an old marsh," one officer, A. C. Allen, an adventurer from New Orleans, recorded in his diary. "It has been raining all day and I am told it rains continuously for six months in the year." The first night's dinner was a stew made of the leftovers they had brought from the *Texas*, served up—apparently unheated—in a barrel. Allen added:

> Tonight, is my first night in this expedition of sleeping on the ground. And as it is raining and I am ringing [*sic*] wet, I expect to have an exquisite time of it. I understand we will be compelled to remain on this beautiful and romantic spot, until we can gather, manufacture, steal, or capture a steamboat. And as they are a scarce commodity in this neighborhood, I guess it will be a sweet little time before we get off. This place looks gloomy, everybody looks gloomy and I feel very unromantic.[15]

They built makeshift lean-tos to try to shield themselves from the worst of the elements, but the quarters barely sufficed:

> It is raining and the water is pouring through the roof of our house in delightful & refreshing streams. And as the best thing we can do, we are laying with all the old wet coats & blankets rolled around us we can find, drawed up, shivering, listening to one another, cuss & grunt, grinning and bearing it. With not a dry gun in camp uncertain at what moment the enemy may pounce on us; and commence a general slaughter. And positively sustain that all our luggage, trunks &c are getting gloriously soaked. One thing is certain; I won't have very pleasant dreams to night.[16]

Camp thievery was a constant, as were disputes over issues both little—Allen slept in a group bed and insisted on wearing his boots—and large, including attempted desertions. One soldier charged into the sea screaming for a British launch to rescue him; he was captured, returned to camp, and bound with ropes. Two others were shot at as they tried to pass a sentry. And the filibusters had trouble with British officers wandering into the camp and offering their opinions on how bad off Walker was and what deaths likely awaited the men should they eventually move up the river.

At one point, Captain Cockburn of the British ship the *Cossack* arrived with a contingent of men and an order from the commander of the British ships in the harbor. Lockridge was to have his men present themselves to Cockburn to ascertain whether any of them were British subjects. Outgunned by the cannon-laden ships, Lockridge acquiesced. Once the men had assembled, Cockburn relayed a message from the British commander explaining that Walker stood no chance of success against the arrayed forces of Costa Rica, El Salvador, Honduras, and Guatemala, not to mention the opposition of most of Nicaragua. He offered protection and passage to the United States for anyone who wished to desert. About twenty men did so, nearly 10 percent of the force walking off under the hateful gaze of those who felt they were being abandoned.[17]

Charles Doubleday, Walker's intimate aide who had left in disillusionment after Walker privately detailed his dream of empire, arrived on a separate ship a couple of days after Lockridge. He had closely followed developments in the newspapers, including the military losses and mounting Central American opposition. "The crisis had arrived for me," Doubleday wrote later. "I could read of [Walker's] successes and those of my countrymen without regretting that I was not with them. When the story of hardships, reverses, the opposition of overwhelming numbers, came to be chronicled, I could only feel that my place was with them." He too suffered through the conditions at Greytown, and shared the British captain's view of the likely outcome. Yet he felt compelled to be there, an indicator that beyond the avaricious ambitions of many adventurers who joined Walker, some were true believers in the man himself.[18]

On February 4, the steamship *Texas* arrived once again from New Orleans carrying Colonel Henry Theodore Titus and about eighty men who had recently fought on the side of slavery in the Bleeding Kansas battles. There Titus had achieved, as Walker put it, "a sort of newspaper notoriety, thus making his name familiar as the leader of the 'border ruffians.'" When the new arrivals met up with already-stranded filibusters, Lockridge had Titus keep his men in a separate battalion. Both commanders' egos far exceeded their competence, and a jealous rivalry arose, with each pursuing different strategies and giving conflicting orders on issues such as the maintenance of the camp. The winter rains continued with a depressing constancy, and the lack of discipline, the disunity, the persistent fevers and other diseases, and the standing invitation by the British for protection led to yet more desertions. But the Costa Ricans were having trouble too, particularly with the ravages of cholera.[19]

Despite the disorder and lack of a seaworthy ship, a squadron of Lockridge's men under Captain Chatham Roberdeau Wheat managed to move up the east bank of the San Juan River—primarily by hacking their way through the jungle—and, using a small cannon, laid siege to the Costa Rican forces at the mouth of the Sarapiquí River, the first step in taking back control of the river transit route. A second group of Walker's soldiers, under Doubleday's command, then arrived on the west side of the river before sunrise and hid in a clearing strewn with logs that had been cut but unused by the Costa Ricans to add to their fortifications. As the sun rose, the attackers opened fire from behind the logs while Wheat resumed his shelling.

"The firing for about an hour was really very sharp, and the casualties frequent on our side, for whenever a head or arm was exposed in the act of firing, the rain of bullets was pretty sure to find it," Doubleday wrote. The double attack worked, though, and soon the sound of gunfire from the fort became sporadic, and Doubleday and his men charged "by fording the shallow river a little above, surprised . . . that we encountered so little opposition to our advance from an enemy who had replied so well to our fire from behind the logs. On entering the fort the thing was explained by the large number of dead we found." The Americans buried their dead comrades, but Lockridge, in what he saw as a message to the British who had warned them of failure, had the dead Costa Rican soldiers' bodies tossed in the San Juan to float down to Greytown.

After the filibusters had control of the Sarapiquí, Lockridge's newly repaired steamer *Rescue* arrived with Colonel Titus and his men. Lockridge agreed to let them proceed up the San Juan to try to take the fort at Castillo. On February 14, the *Rescue* neared the fort; soldiers assigned to river-edge batteries and to the *J. N. Scott* steamship tied up at the wharf fled for the protection of the main fort. Titus issued an ultimatum: surrender or the fort would be shelled and taken. The colonel didn't know that the commander of the fort, an Englishman named Cauty, had only a couple dozen healthy men to rely on. Oddly, Cauty replied with an offer of a twenty-four-hour truce, at the end of which, if no Costa Rican reinforcements had arrived, he would surrender the fort. Odder still, Titus accepted. Before the twenty-four hours were up, a massive contingent of Costa Rican soldiers landed on the bank just north of the fort; seeing the flood of fresh men, Titus retreated with the recaptured *Scott*, and a few days later left the country. Lockridge set up a new camp on an island a few miles below Castillo, but the humiliation led to more desertions. Those assigned to night watch duty took advantage of the lack of supervision to fashion rafts, "and men and officers floated down the river to Greytown, leaving the camp unguarded."[20]

Unable to seize the fort at Castillo, and thwarted in a separate attempt to push the Costa Rican forces from a high point from which he could have taken a second try at Castillo, Lockridge gave up. Walker had told him that if he could not reestablish the river transit he should cut his way to the lake and then make his way to Rivas. Lockridge decided instead to take the *Scott* to Greytown, land at Aspinwall, cross through Panama to the Pacific, sail to San Juan del Sur, then march to Rivas. Only one hundred of the remaining men agreed to go; the rest intended to head home once they reached Greytown.

The *Rescue* and the *Scott* steamed down the river and, uncertain whether the filibusters still held the point at the mouth of the Sarapiquí, the *Scott* pulled to the bank about a mile north and dispatched a reconnaissance squad down the riverbank. Doubleday and scores of other soldiers remained aboard the *Scott*, along with weapons, gunpowder, and ammunition that had made the ship a floating arsenal.

"I was watching them as they wound in and out among the trees, my elbow resting on the window-sill of the pilot-house on the upper deck of the *Scott*, when suddenly I felt myself hurled into the air with terrific force," Doubleday wrote. The ship's boiler had exploded "tearing the entire front of the boat into fragments." Doubleday "plunged into the steam and scalding water" where the boiler had stood "from which, half stupefied, I managed to raise myself, but was utterly unable to take a single step away from the dangerous proximity of steam and fire. Flames were springing up in all directions, and the agonizing wail from the charred and bruised victims of the catastrophe arose on the air, some begging to be shot and put out of their intense pain."

Explosion of the *J. N. Scott*. Frank Leslie's Illustrated Newspaper, May 2, 1857

Amid the confusion, several men quickly realized the second immediate danger: the store of gunpowder, covered by now burning sheets of canvas. Acting quickly, two officers commanded uninjured men to pull away the flaming cloth, which they succeeded in doing, and then turned to the victims. Several men reached Doubleday, "lifting me tenderly over the wreck. At my urgent request they laid me in the cool water of the river, for my sufferings from the boiling water and the steam were intolerable." A doctor quickly assessed that while badly burned, Doubleday had suffered no other serious injuries, and Doubleday ordered him to move on to others worse off. At least twenty men died in the blast itself, and scores more were injured.

The survivors were moved aboard the *Rescue*—a fitting name for the moment—and carried to Greytown, where nearly all accepted a British offer to take them to Panama, where they could book passage to return to the United States. Walker's brother, Norvell, was among the takers. He fell ill on the ship between Aspinwall and Havana, though he seemed to recover a bit after transferring to the *Empire City* for the trip to New Orleans. The first morning he was able to leave his berth and walk the deck for a bit, raising hopes among his colleagues that he would recover, but then he quickly deteriorated and died around sunset that evening. "Every effort was made to have his body embalmed in ice" until the ship reached New Orleans, but the ship's captain "would not consent, and we were compelled to bury his body at sea." It's unknown when and how Walker learned of the death of his brother, the second to perish in service to his cause. While Walker noted their presence in the country in his memoir of the war, he didn't mention either of their deaths.[21]

While nearly all the men with Lockridge fled Greytown, Doubleday decided to stay rather than risk sea travel with such bad burns. A German family long in residence in the town took him in, and with the help of regular visits from the British naval doctor, Doubleday recovered, though his body remained scarred. By then, with Sylvanus Spencer and the Costa Rican soldiers maintaining tight control of the river transit, Doubleday had no avenue for reaching Walker beyond the arduous trip through Panama. And Doubleday could clearly see there was little left to fight for, so he too boarded a northbound ship for home, leaving Walker to his fate.

As Walker's forces shrank, the Allies' continued to grow. Walker directed his men to turn Rivas into a fortress that could, if necessary, be defended by a relatively small number of men. Charles Henningsen and his men burned huts at the edge of the village and "cut away the thick tropical undergrowth which might conceal and protect an attacking foe." The destruction of the huts also reduced living space for the Phalanx, and Henningsen ordered many of his men to move into a church. In the middle of streets leading to the central plaza, Walker's men built low walls of adobe with open passages on the sides, backed by artillery pieces. Other men, augmented by conscripted locals with machetes, began hacking a five-mile path through the jungle to Virgin Bay, to give them access to the lake without having to fight their way down the transit road.

While all this was going on, Walker awaited the arrival of the *San Carlos* with more men and arms. But when it failed to show up on the scheduled day, and then the next, Walker began to worry that it wouldn't arrive at all, that something unexpected and catastrophic had befallen it. He sent a small boat with eight men to Fort San Carlos to see what they could learn of the steamers, but the men fell right into the hands of General Mora's troops and failed to return, exacerbating Walker's consternation. Eventually he learned of Spencer's takeover of the boats and transit system. There would be no reinforcements.[22]

Mora, who had taken full command after Spencer seized the fleet, now controlled the river and lake, the knowledge of which "diminished greatly the spirits and confidence of the troops at Rivas." Nicaraguan and Guatemalan forces, augmented by Salvadorans and Hondurans, moved into villages around Rivas, including San Jorge, fortifying each into a redoubt once they had control. Walker sent reconnaissance missions out to test the range and scope of the Allies, and to try to push them out of some of the settlements, hoping to disrupt what he correctly presumed was an effort to entrap the filibusters. "The rapidity with which Central American troops throw up barricades is almost incredible, and long practice has made them more expert at such work than even a Parisian mob," Walker wrote. While some of his men's raids succeeded with annoying guerrilla-style tactics, most met overwhelming attacks of gunfire, forcing their retreat and further eroding the confidence of Walker's men. In one attack on San Jorge, which Walker saw as key to confounding Mora's plans to trap him, "several of the [Phalanx] officers had taken too much liquor during the morning, and did not apprehend clearly the purport of the orders they received." Henningsen and another commander named Sanders disliked each other, which also affected the planning and will of the attackers. After a daylong effort, the Americans gave up and fell back to Rivas, with eighty dead or wounded and nothing gained.[23]

In an effort to display to the men that all was not lost, Walker marched a large portion of his force to San Juan del Sur to greet the *Orizaba*, expected from San Francisco. The port remained in Walker's control largely because of Callendar Fayssoux's presence in the harbor on the *Granada*, with her cannons. But because of its proximity to Costa Rica—about fifteen miles—it was a tempting location from which to desert, so Walker posted some of his most loyal men as sentries to keep the others from sneaking off. One such unit stumbled across a man "dressed in General Walker's blue-shirt-and-cotton-breeches uniform," the mark of an officer, who was heading south toward the border but who, "seeing our party, with startled look, he turned, and went in the direction of San Juan." He was caught and escorted back. Walker ordered him executed before the entire detachment, and a few hours later the man was deposited in a chair at the edge of the ocean and shot by a firing squad, all but one shot missing him—intentionally so, as most members of the squad did not want to kill him. He fell back into the water "where he lay struggling, and stained the waves red with his blood." The sergeant leading the execution waded into the gentle surf, put a gun to the man's head, and fired. "This exhibition, which in another army were calculated to strengthen just authority, here only aroused indignation and disgust," one of Walker's men later confessed. "There was no tie of honor or honesty to keep any man with us who wished to escape, and this deed seemed to us without decent sanction." That night, eleven more men disappeared.[24]

The *Orizaba* arrived February 1 carrying another forty recruits, and Walker led the newly expanded force down the transit road to Virgin Bay, where they hoped to surprise one of the steamers. *La Virgen* drew near the port but the captain, sensing something was amiss, steamed off, and the Phalanx returned to Rivas. On February 3, Walker led another sortie to San Jorge but, despite catching the Allies by surprise, faced withering gunfire from behind the barricades, Walker losing yet more soldiers and officers. He fell back once again to Rivas.

All the while, Walker was waiting for Lockridge to regain control of the San Juan River and the steamships. And all the while more of his men, seeing their comrades shot down and their territory circumscribed, deserted, some singly, some in groups. Rumors that a group of forty men had slipped away after the failed attack on San Jorge emboldened yet others amid talk of a possible coup to replace Walker with Henningsen or some other officer who was perceived to have the necessary experience. But so few men retained any faith in Walker's ambitions—most came for adventure and a little land, not to be killed in service to Walker's dream of empire—that desertion was the top choice.

The morning after the latest San Jorge fiasco, David Deaderick set off with his unit under orders to forage for feed for the Phalanx's animals. Instead, the commander of the unit led them a few miles down the southern road, then called a halt and announced that they were going to Costa Rica and then home, per an agreement reached the previous day. Deaderick and a couple of other men said they knew nothing of the agreement and would return to Rivas. But revolvers came out and the unit continued on, later publishing a letter in Costa Rican newspapers (reprinted in the New York papers) disavowing Walker and the Nicaraguan campaign.

The letter reads as though it was written after negotiations with the Costa Rican government, or maybe *by* the Costa Rican government, as it echoes General Mora's offer of free and safe passage to deserters but also raises the possibility of remaining and settling in Costa Rica. It recounts a warm welcome by the Costa Ricans and contrasts it with the emigrants' experiences on arriving in Nicaragua:

> How many of you are there who were induced to come to the country as peaceable emigrants (Some bringing wives and children). How were you received when you arrived in Nicaragua? Were you assigned land by the colonization office? Were you furnished with seeds and agricultural implements and facilitated in taking possession of and commencing the cultivation of your 250 acres (or more) of land? You cry along with us, No! and we respond what you full well know; you were handed a musket or rifle at your introduction to Nicaragua, and told you were enrolled in some company to fight for the land you were to have, and to fight for it, too, against the natural and rightful owners of it; but above all, you were to fight to advance the mad ambition of a man so devoid of

natural sympathies and the sentiments which ennoble human nature that he would feel no compunction of conscience in destroying a world did he but think he would reign King, even over its desolation.[25]

Mora also found a way to sneak pamphlets to the edges of Rivas that similarly promised free passage to those who quit the fight. It seemed to have some effect. Walker noted that his morning report of February 6 listed twenty desertions over the previous twenty-four hours; two days later, the daily roster listed six more desertions.

The USS *St. Mary's*, a 149-foot-long three-masted sloop of war with 22 guns and 162 men, arrived at the San Juan del Sur harbor on February 6. Captain Charles H. Davis sent word to Walker that he'd like to visit Rivas, and Walker sent a squadron to San Juan del Sur to escort him and some of his men. They arrived on February 18, and while Davis's men wandered through the fortified town, Davis politely engaged with Walker, persuading him to release some small boats he had confiscated from an American ship, the *Narragansett*, for use on Lake Nicaragua. Walker asked Davis to raise the issue of the transit steamers with General Mora. Like the *Narragansett*, Cornelius Garrison and Charles Morgan couldn't operate their transit company without their boats, which were now held by Costa Rican forces. Davis agreed. He already planned to visit Allied commanders in San Jorge to determine whether any of the crews on the steamers were Americans being held against their will (much as the British had done with the filibuster force at Greytown). It's unclear whether Davis actually raised the question of the steamers once he got to San Jorge; regardless, Mora would have been foolish to give them up.

Recruits and some munitions continued to trickle through San Juan del Sur, sent along by Cornelius Garrison in San Francisco. The fresh blood enabled Walker to conduct a series of attacks against the Allies' fortified villages, but little came of the efforts beyond losing more men and further eroding morale. A report from February 24 offers a snapshot of Walker's army. Of 2,288 men who had signed up with Walker, 685 men (109 of them officers) had been killed by disease or in action. Another 37 had formally resigned, while 293, including 9 officers, had just walked away. Walker himself had run off another 206 men whom he deemed unworthy of fighting for him, and 141 men simply were unaccounted for—some suspected deserters or prisoners of war, though about half were presumed dead, their bodies lost in the jungle or at the bottom of the lake. That left Walker at that moment with 926 officers and men. And with the San Juan River under the Allies' control, Walker was cut off from two of his most productive sources of recruits, ships steaming in from New Orleans and New York City.[26]

The Allies, meanwhile, were using the river and lake that Walker so desperately needed to move their own men and munitions into Virgin Bay, San Jorge, and elsewhere, strengthening the forces with which Mora intended to overwhelm Walker. Colonel Titus, the commander who had fled the country after failing to capture the fort at Castillo, returned to Rivas with a wholly fabricated story of the fight for the San Juan River. Defeat was never mentioned. It wasn't until other reports arrived days later that Walker learned that the efforts to retake the river had failed. He still did not know that Lockridge had ignored his suggestion to cut his way through the jungle to the lake and was planning to cross through Panama to reach San Juan del Sur.

In late March, Mora and the Allies began pressing Walker with a three-pronged attack. Walker and his dwindling forces managed from behind adobe barricades to keep the attackers at bay, though the artillerymen had been forced to melt found metal to create ammunition. The attack settled into a siege. Walker was able to slip couriers through the cordon to maintain contact with Fayssoux, but he couldn't get fresh food. "It became necessary for the commissary to have two quartermaster's oxen killed; and these, with a slight mixture of mule meat, furnished the rations for the next morning. The mule meat was eaten by the troops as beef; and in two or three days none but horse or mule flesh was issued as the meat ration." Yet the horses and mules were crucial transport over the rough roads and countryside, so Walker was feeding his men the flesh of the animals they might need to escape.[27]

The attack continued in a remarkably desultory fashion. It seemed Mora was content to keep Walker and his men pinned down in Rivas and starve them out. A twenty-four-pound cannon was brought within range, and it shelled the city on a regular basis. Rifles and muskets delivered more pinpointed attacks, felling the filibusters one by one, and Walker lost yet more to "the shameful desertion which most affected the spirits and the strength of the defenders of Rivas." All along Walker had been dismissive of the Europeans among his troops, blaming them for most of the early desertions, but he noted now that "the fatal infection [had] spread among the Americans." In fact, they had been slipping off all along. And the pace accelerated as Rivas began running low on horses and mules to eat. A courier arrived on horseback; the animal was shot and butchered. Walker maintained faith that Lockridge would somehow restore the transit line and reinforcements would arrive from the lake, and he determined to hold on to Rivas as long as they had provisions. He feared Lockridge would succeed only to find that Walker had failed and Rivas had fallen.

Captain Davis followed the collapse of Walker's empire from the USS *St. Mary's*, and on April 23 he sent one of his officers, a Lieutenant Huston, to the Allies headquarters, and then on to Rivas with an offer from Davis: the captain was willing to deploy a squadron of his marines to escort any remaining women and children out of Rivas. It was a precursor to a negotiated surrender. Huston and a corporal serving as an aide arrived at Walker's stronghold. Walker received Huston and ordered that the corporal not speak to his men about conditions outside Rivas. But while Huston and Walker talked, so too did the corporal, telling the men that the Allies had control of San Juan del Sur and the rest of the countryside. They spent the night, and the next morning escorted the women and children who wished to leave. Walker gave Huston a message for Davis that he "considered his position at Rivas impregnable to the force at the disposal of the enemy so long as his provisions lasted," and that if the provisions ran out before Lockridge could join him from the lake, he would abandon Rivas for San Juan del Sur.[28]

The Allies were indeed in San Juan del Sur. Fayssoux contemplated shelling the port to drive them out, but Davis was there to protect US interests, and many businesses at the port were owned by Americans. So if the *Granada* shelled the port, Davis would likely shell the *Granada*. The two captains agreed to a truce, which let the Allies firm up their control on shore. Couriers reached Fayssoux offering to buy the *Granada*—he viewed them as attempted bribes— and Davis worked on Fayssoux as well, inviting him to a meeting with one of the Allied commanders aboard the *St. Mary's*, where the commander offered his thanks for the kind treatment Fayssoux had afforded some of the native forces he had taken prisoner. In another meeting, the Allies asked Fayssoux what he wanted in return for quitting the war and turning over the ship; he refused to respond. Barricades began to go up onshore, and Fayssoux told Davis that if he did not persuade the Allies to remove them, he would shell the city. Construction ceased.

Davis felt the conditions were right to persuade Walker to abandon Nicaragua. He sent a message to Rivas on April 30 offering safe passage to Panama for all of Walker's men. Walker found the offer "offensive," replied that the offer was vague, and invited Davis to Rivas to discuss it. Davis declined, telling Walker the offer was clear: "Abandon the enterprise and leave the country" under Davis's protection, or wait for the Allies to destroy Rivas. Walker countered with an offer for Davis to meet with two of his aides at the Allies' headquarters, if safe passage was assured. Davis procured the guarantee from the Allies and met with Henningsen and another officer at the Allies' encampment at Cuatro Esquinas, just a half mile from Rivas—the close proximity indicating how tightly hemmed in the Americans were.[29]

Davis was blunt. His only objective was to limit further bloodshed. He had negotiated permission with Mora for the filibusters to leave under Davis's protection and the protection of the US flag. Lockridge, he informed them, was no longer in the country and would not be steaming to their rescue from the San Juan River. No more steamers would land men or supplies at San Juan del Sur. Depleted rations and desertions left Walker without enough resources to save their own lives, let alone scratch out a military victory against such an overwhelming force as the one arrayed against them.

Henningsen replied that there remained plenty of fight in the force, and that he knew Walker wouldn't agree to abandon Rivas without better confirmation of the fate of Lockridge than Davis's word. They could still fight their way through Mora's siege and reach San Juan del Sur and the *Granada*. Davis, though, said that he would not allow the ship to leave the harbor—the *St. Mary's* could sink her with one broadside—and that he was under orders to seize her before he was compelled to leave San Juan del Sur in a few days' time. In other words, it was now or never for Walker to quit and avoid annihilation.

Henningsen tentatively accepted on Walker's behalf and returned to Rivas with the terms written out. They conferred, Henningsen detailing the tone and substance of his talk with Davis. Walker agreed to surrender to the US forces— notably not to Mora and the Allies—and to abandon Nicaragua. Davis and a contingent of marines, along with General Zavala of the Allies, traveled to Rivas and at 5:00 PM joined with Walker to address the full remaining filibuster force in the ravaged city's main plaza. Walker read the agreement to his men—they already knew what was transpiring—and assigned to Henningsen the task of turning over the city to Davis's protection. There were, the records noted, 173 men wounded or sick or attending to the wounded and sick, 102 Allied prisoners, 148 healthy officers and soldiers, 86 armed citizens working for the filibusters (in what capacities was unclear), and 40 Nicaraguans who had remained as part of Walker's fighting force.

As Henningsen dealt with the mundane details of surrender, Walker and sixteen officers mounted horses provided by the Allies and rode off under guard and protection to San Juan del Sur, where the defeated president of the Republic of Nicaragua boarded the *St. Mary's*. A dispute over the fate of the *Granada* sputtered on over the next day. Davis went ashore on unrelated business and ordered a Lieutenant Maury to seize the ship. Maury boarded it and demanded the surrender; Fayssoux refused. Maury returned to the *St. Mary's* and demanded that Walker order Fayssoux to give up the ship. Walker said he would not issue such an order except under a show of force. Tired of the games, Maury ordered the twenty-two-gun warship positioned broadside facing the two-gun *Granada*.

So it was that Walker, with his pretension to military position and then the presidency, tendered his capitulation to a lieutenant in the US Navy.

14 | WALKER RETURNS TO NEW ORLEANS

AN OLD FRENCH FORT, La Balize, guarded the mouth of the Mississippi River, though by the 1850s it was less a fort than a stopping point from which river pilots boarded oceangoing ships to guide them through the ever-shifting sandbars to New Orleans, some seventy-five miles up the river. The outpost also had a telegraph machine, and when the *Empire City* stopped on May 27, 1857, to gather its pilot, a wire sent to New Orleans delivered the news that not only had the grand side-paddle steamer arrived at the end of its regular New York City–Havana–New Orleans run, but William Walker and his top officers were aboard.

Word whipped through the city and a crowd began gathering at the wharf, watching with building excitement as the ship finally chugged into view around the bend in the river. According to a report in the next day's *New Orleans Delta*, the onlookers cheered when the ship fired a cannon salute as it passed Canal Street, and a return "salute from the guns of the Washington Artillery then commenced and sent its echoes over the waters, and above the din of the busy city, and to the hearts of the hero and his comrades, welcoming them as brave warriors should be welcomed, by the thundering and martial roar of cannon." New Orleans, which had offered so much support in money and men, was happy to have its adopted son home.[1]

As men lashed the *Empire City* to the wharf, so many people clambered to get near that the captain had to warn them away—especially those who sought to leap aboard from the tops of pilings. It took effort to clear enough space for the gangway, finally allowing the throng to move from wharf to deck.

They chanted Walker's name until he emerged, waving his hat and nodding to acknowledge the welcoming cheers. He struggled through well-wishers to the bottom of the gangway, where two large men hoisted him on their shoulders and led an impromptu parade to a carriage some forty yards away. Walker disappeared inside and the horses clattered off, carrying the conquered hero to the grand and pillar-fronted St. Charles Hotel, where another crowd had gathered, forming yet another throng to wade through to get inside.

A short time later Walker appeared on the second-floor portico overlooking St. Charles Street, where cheers again rose up in an excited rush. Walker's soft voice didn't extend far out into the mass, and his supporters and the merely curious strained to catch the words of his "short soldier-like speech," thanking the people of New Orleans for their support. He went back inside, but more clamor from those in the hotel's grand rotunda compelled another speech, with Walker climbing atop a table to be seen.

"In his calm, earnest manner, and with manly eloquence, he said it was a proud consolation, after months and years of trial, to experience the approbation that was given to the causes he advocated," the *New Orleans Delta* wrote. "It was a triumph greater than arms could ever win. With such manifestations, it was impossible that the cause of Nicaragua could fail, no matter who were its enemies; no matter how much they labored; no matter how much they willed. The enemy, he said, would yet be put beneath our feet."

Walker didn't mention what the venture had cost in lives. The best estimate comes from Charles Henningsen, who held on to records that counted 2,518 men as having enlisted in Walker's army, from the first men who sailed with him from San Francisco to the last recruits who slipped into Rivas before Walker surrendered. Of those, battles and disease killed about 1,000, an astoundingly high 40 percent. No wonder some 700 men deserted. Ill discipline led Walker to kick out 250 of the recruits. Counting the 320 men with Walker when he surrendered, that left about 250 men unaccounted for, likely among the dead and the deserted. So altogether, Walker had under his command when the war ended only 13 percent of the men who had joined him, and two-thirds of the rest had died or run off. It's hard to see exactly what his supporters found to cheer about.[2]

Walker still considered himself to be president of Nicaragua, and he made no bones about intending to return to his rightful office. After spending a few days in New Orleans, he traveled by steamer up the Mississippi River to Memphis, and then to Louisville, Kentucky, where he visited his sister, Alice Richardson, his sole surviving sibling, then made his way east by train to Washington, DC, where he met privately on June 12 with President Buchanan. Walker said later that he informed Buchanan that he planned to go back to Nicaragua, but they also apparently talked about Walker's departure from Rivas. A couple of days later, Walker sent a written report to Buchanan condemning Captain Davis's interference in Nicaragua. He argued that the Allies arrayed against him were faltering, and he would have withstood the siege had Davis not intervened (though in his later memoir Walker made clear that Davis had not threatened him into leaving, that he took the escape route willingly). He zeroed in on Davis's seizure of the *Granada*, which Walker contended was illegal. It was an odd complaint to levy, since Walker had confiscated the ship in the first place, and Davis had in all likelihood saved the lives of Walker and his men by doing likewise. But Davis's authority to take the ship was vague at best.[3]

Walker then traveled by train to Perth Amboy, New Jersey, across the Arthur Kill from the southern tip of Staten Island. His arrival on June 16 had been not only expected but planned for by a special committee and subcommittees designated to handle various honors and celebrations. While falling short of the breadth and passion of his embrace at New Orleans, the reception was still tremendously warm. A small group that included Nicaragua campaign veterans Henningsen and Chatham Roberdeau Wheat traveled by steamer to meet the train at Perth Amboy, then brought Walker back with them to New York City. At pier 1 on the North River, a one-hundred-gun salute from the Battery heralded their arrival. Thousands swarmed the wharf, cheering as Walker appeared hatless on the deck and bowed slightly to acknowledge the applause. As in New Orleans, when Walker tried to move from the ship to a carriage, the crowd swept him up and carried him along.[4]

As Walker's carriage fought through the crowds to a reception at the park across the street from city hall, a light rainfall developed into a heavy, steady downpour, but the weather did little to thin the crowd. Walker, standing beneath a large umbrella, briefly offered a defense of his actions in Nicaragua and thanked New York for its support—an apt acknowledgment, given that a large portion of his force had signed up there. He then hurried away to the St. Nicholas Hotel, only to learn that no one had reserved a room for him. After some inquiries, Walker sped off in the carriage to the Lafarge House hotel, entering through a private door and slipping up to his room unnoticed, finally finding a point of calm in the storm-racked city.

Coincidentally, Walker arrived in New York just a few days before the last of his men were repatriated aboard a US warship. When Walker quit Rivas, he and his officers traveled home quickly, first via US warship to Panama, then across the isthmus to regular passenger ships. But the ailing men he had left behind, and the women and children who had been escorted out of Rivas under Captain Davis's protection, found themselves stranded in Panama. Penniless and ill—many stricken by a measles outbreak—they were refused passage by captains of the commercial ships serving Aspinwall. So Commodore Hiram Paulding, commander of the US Navy's Home Squadron, eventually loaded them aboard his flagship, the *Wabash*, and steamed north, arriving in New York City on June 28. Four had died en route, leaving 138 refugees from the debacle.

Walker's warm welcome began to fade as he continued to publicly criticize Davis, and as the condition of the men aboard the *Wabash* became widely known. Reporters for the *Herald* and the *Daily Times* visited the ship after the healthy had already gone ashore, leaving behind ninety-two men—the sick, the wounded, and those with no place yet to go. The men's condition was shockingly bad. "Many of them are scarcely able to move; some have lost their legs, others arms, others again have great festers, swollen wounds, gangrene, etc." Rags barely covered emaciated bodies, their skin tanned "parchment brown . . . large feverish eyes protruded over hollow spaces that once were cheeks." When the fighters first boarded, the naval officers said, many of the men had wounds that had never been treated, and their bodies were "incased with dirt and covered with vermin." Lice writhed on them, and they were forced to shave their heads. The sailors, fearing the spread, bathed themselves in rum as a repellant. For all their agonies, the filibusters retained faith in Walker's dream of making Nicaragua a new America, but "were unanimous against Walker's competency." They refused to let the reporter use their names—because, they said, Walker had promised them money to travel to their homes in New Orleans and elsewhere in the South, and they feared crossing him.[5]

It's unclear whether Walker ever made good on the promise of travel money for his men. He was not one to look backward or worry about debts. In New York, he focused on the future, as he tried to raise money and stoke interest in a fresh campaign. He held meetings with George Law, the shipping magnate, as well as supporters and some of his fellow filibusters. After a few days, Walker took a steamer to Charleston, South Carolina, then traveled by coach to Nashville, where he spent a few days visiting family and friends, though he stayed at the City Hotel. No records survive describing the tenor of that homecoming, but with the deaths of his two brothers in Nicaragua, he surely had much to discuss with his father. On July 8, the statehouse opened for a public presentation by Walker, in which he recapped his exploits and made clear again that he felt a moral responsibility to return to Nicaragua, describing himself as a naturalized Nicaraguan citizen. "Too much good blood has been shed upon that soil to permit it to remain under the control of the degenerate race who had lorded over it for centuries," Walker said. "That blood will rise. Those thousand lives have not merely to be avenged, but the object for which they were lost must be, and I hope speedily, accomplished."[6]

Walker, with Callendar Fayssoux, returned to New Orleans and then embarked on regular trips around the South, speaking to large groups and raising cash from small ones. When he first went to Nicaragua, he had gone somewhat quietly, with a contract to bring settlers with him and a wink-and-a-nod agreement that they would fight for the Liberal cause. Now he openly argued that he would return to Nicaragua on a different mission: the furtherance of slavery. He didn't mention his aspirations for personal empire but couched his ambitions in terms of the nobility of the white race—left to their own devices, the inferior races of Central America would never be able to take full advantage of the natural resources of the territory. In one letter published in a Mobile, Alabama, newspaper, apparently a response to criticism of his goals, he wrote that the South needed him to succeed in Nicaragua if the South itself was to prosper:

> It involves the question of whether you will permit yourselves to be hemmed in on the south, as you already are in the north and on the west—whether you will remain quiet and idle while impassable barriers are being built on the only side left open for your superabundant energy and enterprise. If the South is desirous of imitating

the gloomy grandeur of the Eschylian Prometheus, she has but to lie supine a little while longer, and force and power will bind her to the rock, and the vulture will descend to tear the liver from her body. In her agony and grief she may console herself with the idea that she suffers a willing sacrifice.[7]

Walker's plans, unsurprisingly, caught the attention of President Mora in Costa Rica and other Central American political leaders who had hoped they were done with him. In September, they sent a joint letter via their ministers in Washington informing Secretary of State Lewis Cass that they were aware of Walker's efforts to raise men and money for another expedition, possibly as soon as mid-September. The emissaries had remarkable detail—the plan was to sail to Bocas del Toro in Panama, pick up arms there, and then land at Greytown. They noted that while the United States might not be able to prevent the filibusters from leaving, they asked that it "direct that a vessel of war of the United States shall prevent the debarkation of these aggressors in Bocas del Toro, and give formal orders to the US vessel that may be stationed at San Juan del Sur to repel, also, the landing of the expedition along that coast, and to turn them back to the United States as violators of their laws and as disturbers of the peace and security of friendly nations." President Buchanan directed Cass to send a notice to nineteen US attorneys, fifteen marshals, and eleven port collectors warning of the likely departure of filibusters, and asked them to ensure that no one left the country in violation of the Neutrality Act.[8]

Walker wrote to Cass that he had no intention of violating any US laws, emphatically stating that "I deny the charge with scorn and indignation." Further, the protest by Costa Rica and Guatemala was inappropriate, Walker argued, because they had no cause to make demands on behalf of Nicaragua. "The people of Nicaragua have not consented to the military authority at present exercised over them by the agents of Costa Rica and Guatemala," he wrote, adding that he hoped the United States "will, by its conduct, assert and vindicate the independence of its sister republic, the sovereign State of Nicaragua." Of which, he maintained, he was president.[9]

Antonio Irisarri, the Guatemalan and El Salvadoran minister in Washington, had added Nicaragua to his portfolio at the request of the provisional government that took over once Walker left the country. He read Walker's letter in the newspapers and responded with venom in another letter to Cass:

Truly astonishing is the impudence with which this adventurer, expelled from Nicaragua by her forces and those of all the Central Americans, attempts to constitute himself the champion of Nicaragua. The man, whose course in that country was an exclusive one of assassination of the defenders of that country—the burner of whole villages, the spoiler of national property, the trampler on all rights, the plunderer of churches, the leader of the foreign stipendiaries which he gathered under his own banner—alone could have alleged his right of citizenship in Nicaragua, and thereby held as dunces all men else on earth.

Irisarri complained that the filibusters "with miserable cunning, can baffle the laws of the United States" and warned that if they landed in Nicaragua again, they would be killed.[10]

Buchanan and Cass did not want Walker to return to Nicaragua any more than the Central Americans did. The American Atlantic and Pacific Ship Canal Company, with the support of the US government, had recently signed a contract with the new Nicaraguan government to restart the transit route across the isthmus. But if Walker returned to Nicaragua, the company wouldn't send ships or other assets for fear that Walker would just confiscate them as he had with Vanderbilt's fleet. Buchanan also had designs on Cuba, and since the 1830s had advocated that the United States find a way to buy it from Spain. But Walker's movements in Nicaragua unsettled the entire region and complicated these negotiations. Buchanan and Cass feared, too, that another expedition by Walker—or any other American filibuster, for that matter—would weigh on relations with Great Britain, since neither country was supposed to establish new possessions in Central America under the Clayton-Bulwer Treaty. Even though Walker wasn't acting for the United States and wasn't sanctioned by it, there was significant public speculation that Walker was working with tacit support from the administration. The administration could deny it all they wanted, but their stance was severely compromised by a letter Cass had written the previous summer, before becoming secretary of state, in which he praised Walker's efforts in Nicaragua.[11]

On November 11, 1857, the port collector in New Orleans had Walker arrested under the Neutrality Act. Walker posted a $2,000 bond, and the next day he slipped off aboard a US mail boat for Mobile. It was no secret that

Walker intended to use the steamship *Fashion* for the trip to Nicaragua, and the federal authorities detained it at New Orleans for an inspection. But a port official reported that he found only "270 lawful emigrants" and no signs of military equipment, so the ship was cleared. History does not record whether the inspector truly missed or simply pretended not to see the guns and munitions hidden in the bottoms of crates filled with farming equipment. But the *Fashion* left that night, arrived in Mobile two days later to pick up Walker and a few men traveling with him, and turned south to Greytown.[12]

Walker's second invasion of Nicaragua was on.

The *Fashion* landed the first group of men under a Colonel Anderson a dozen miles southeast of Greytown at the mouth of the Colorado River, a short offshoot of the San Juan River. Their mission was to ascend the Colorado to where it sluiced away from the San Juan, about thirteen miles downriver from Sarapiquí, and fortify the juncture to take control of the river. They also were to stop any vessels from traveling upriver from Greytown, and thus prevent anyone from the port from getting word to the Nicaraguans and Costa Ricans along the transit route that Walker had returned.[13]

The *Fashion* continued on to Greytown, anchoring offshore at around 2:00 PM on November 24. Walker had hoped to land his men that night, under cover of darkness, but tropical squalls, strong seas, and a dangerous swell forced him to wait until daybreak. The USS *Saratoga*, a twenty-two-gun sloop of war, was anchored in the harbor, and its captain, Frederick Chatard, became suspicious when he saw the *Fashion* steam to the edge of the harbor and then pull away to anchor.

Just after daybreak, the *Fashion* weighed anchor and steamed into the harbor. As it passed the *Saratoga*, Chatard was "entirely lulled when . . . not more than fifteen or twenty men appeared on her deck." Walker had ordered most of the men to remain out of sight below. The ship steamed up to the old Accessory Transit Company wharf on the Punta Arenas side of the harbor. Joseph Scott was still operating the river and lake fleet, while the Costa Rican government controlled the river and southern portion of the lake. Before Chatard could intervene, Walker and about 150 men streamed from ship to shore. Chatard sent some men to inspect the ship and its manifest, and they returned with word that the papers certified the *Fashion* as legally cleared to depart the United States. Though Chatard knew that the landing party was Walker and his men, he decided that he lacked the authority to act, despite clear communications from Washington that naval vessels should do whatever was in their power to keep Walker and any other filibustering expeditions from landing. (Chatard would later be relieved of his command over his inaction.)[14]

As for Scott, he objected to Walker's presence and ordered him off the property. On this matter he had Chatard's backing; the captain told Walker in a brief conversation aboard the *Saratoga* that he considered the grounds to fall under US protection. So the filibusters took over some houses outside the Accessory Transit property and began building large sheds to shelter the rest of the men, under the direction of several officers who were survivors of the first expedition, including Fayssoux, Thomas Henry, and Collier Hornsby.

"He has hoisted his flag above and below Scott's grounds," Chatard reported to his commander, Hiram Paulding, aboard the *Wabash*. "The soil he is on is not under my jurisdiction; but I have given him to understand, very plainly, that any outrage by him on American property at that place or at Greytown will call from me immediate punishment, which I would not hesitate to inflict, because that would be a clear case."

Walker, true to form, fired off a letter to Paulding complaining about Chatard's impertinence in backing Scott's claims to the property and fleet. Walker argued that he, in fact, as president of Nicaragua, had appointed Scott to oversee the Accessory Transit assets, and the Nicaraguan government had not sold them or signed them over (ignoring the control of the region by Costa Rica). Walker pointed out that he had informed Buchanan that he intended to return to Nicaragua, yet the government still cleared *Fashion* to leave the country for Greytown, an implicit approval. It was a spurious argument that fell on deaf ears.[15]

Walker's arrival at Greytown angered and scared the villagers, most of them expatriate Americans, Britons, and other foreigners. One of them, an American merchant named Samuel Wood, who for a time had led the municipal government, begged Paulding for protection. He detailed his losses from Walker's first foray to Nicaragua.

Walker . . . plundered us of our goods, destroyed our houses in Nicaragua, and put my son in prison, and a sentinel at our door. . . . Sir, we are American merchants here, father and son, and were doing a large and extensive business, and had two stores in the city of San Juan, a store and goods at Virgin Bay, and a hotel in Granada city, and one at Castillo Rapids, with a large amount of furniture and provisions, which was burnt at both the places by Walker.

Whether the plea made a difference is unclear, for Paulding was already on his way to Greytown.[16]

Walker ordered Colonel Anderson to advance to the Castillo Rapids and try to steal a river steamer. The men spent two days cutting through the jungle and fording creeks before they reached the fort overlooking the rapids. In the dark morning hours, four men sneaked aboard the tethered steamer *Morgan* and cut her loose, letting the current carry her quietly away from the wharf and a distance down the river before they fired the boiler, finally gaining the attention of the Costa Rican forces. Another team stole aboard the *Ogden* above the rapids and fired up the boiler to send her down the rapids.

Cannon fire erupted from the fort, and Anderson, with a couple dozen men, responded with a direct attack on the stronghold. The battle cry "Walker!" went up as the *Ogden* chugged into view, and the small Costa Rican squadron, fearing they would be annihilated, abandoned the fort. With control of the lower portion of the San Juan complete, Anderson sent the *Morgan* to Greytown with some prisoners and men to report in with Walker and then return with whatever additional troops Walker might want to send upriver.

As Anderson worked, Chatard harassed Walker's encampment, sending a Lieutenant Cilley and two men to visit a store near the camp. One of Walker's sentries ordered the sailors to leave and not return without the exiled president's permission; they refused. Walker's men threatened the sailors, warning that if they returned they would be fired upon. After receiving Cilley's report, Chatard wrote to Walker that "if you were to dare to touch one of my officers, I would feel justified to retaliate in the extreme, and would not hesitate to do so." Then Chatard sent another detachment on several small boats, one bearing a howitzer, to conduct live-fire practice on targets at the very edge of the camp, outraging Walker. He once again took to his pen and filed a complaint with Paulding accusing Chatard of unprofessionalism and open provocation of the president of a nation with which the United States was not at war.[17]

Paulding responded on December 6, when he anchored the *Wabash*, a forty-two-gun, three-hundred-foot-long warship, off Greytown. His letter was direct, dismissive, and contemptuous:

> Your letter of November 30 was received at Aspinwall and sent with my despatches to the government. That of December 2 came to my hands yesterday. These letters surprised me with their tone of audacity and falsification of facts. Your rude discourtesy in speaking of Captain Chatard, of the *Saratoga*, I pass without comment. The mistake he made was in not driving you from the Point Arenas when you landed there in defiance of his guns. In occupying the Point Arenas, and assuming it to be the head quarters of the army of Nicaragua, and you its commander-in-chief, you and your associates being lawless adventurers, you deceive no one by the absurdity. Lieutenant Cilley, of the *Saratoga*, informs me that he was in uniform, and you say he was in plain clothes, when you threatened to shoot him. Whilst you use such threats, it may be of some importance for you to know, that if any person belonging to my command shall receive injury from your lawless violence, the penalty to you shall be a tribute to humanity.
>
> Now, sir, you and your followers are here in violation of the laws of the United States, and greatly to its dishonor; making war upon a people with whom we are at peace; and for the sake of humanity, public and private justice, as well as what is due to the honor and integrity of the government of the United States, I command you, and the people associated here with you, to surrender your arms without delay, and embark in such vessels as I may provide for that purpose.[18]

The next day, aboard the *Wabash*, the *Saratoga*, and the four-gun *Fulton*, which had joined the other US warships, some three hundred sailors and marines transferred in rolling seas to launches and headed for the harbor. They towed barges bearing howitzers, which they anchored and then trained on the filibusters' camp. The vast bulk of the force landed ashore and immediately fell into two lines of attackers on the right and at the rear of the camp, leaving the only escape the open ocean—where Paulding had ordered the *Saratoga*, bristling with cannons, broadside to the shore and the camp. A Captain Engle then approached the camp and asked to meet with Walker, to whom he delivered Paulding's scathing letter demanding he lay down his arms.[19]

For the second time in a span of seven months, Walker surrendered.

By landing in Nicaragua and arresting an American on foreign soil, Paulding had overstepped his authority. But given that he'd been ordered to intervene to stop American filibusters, these actions seemed prudent. He had indeed stopped Walker, and quite dramatically. In the filibuster's actions prior to his surrender, "there was an impertinence that offended me and I commanded his instant embarkation," Paulding later wrote to his wife. Once aboard the *Wabash*, Walker, "this lion-hearted devil, who had so often destroyed the lives of other men, came to me, humbled himself, and wept like a child." One senses that Paulding was exaggerating to his wife; crying seems far out of character for someone generally described as reserved and controlled. Nevertheless, Paulding came to view Walker as "a smart fellow" who "requires a sharp fellow to deal with him." Walker also told Paulding "that he considered he was acting with the knowledge and approbation of the President, and that he never would have embarked in the enterprise but from this belief." Paulding found that notion absurd, but it's consistent with other comments Walker made on the subject—suggesting that the filibuster may have genuinely believed he had Buchanan's tacit support after his White House meeting. A sitting president would not grant a meeting to someone whom he considered to have violated the Neutrality Act, Walker argued, yet Buchanan had received Walker. It's certainly plausible that Buchanan, who had a reputation for being noncommittal and hard to read, left Walker with a false impression of where the president stood.[20]

Paulding, meanwhile, was confident that he had acted in accordance with his orders, but he recognized the problem he'd caused by sending men ashore to arrest Walker. "I have taken strong measures in forcing him from a neutral territory," he wrote to his wife. "It may make me President or cost me my commission." Still, "I am sure I have done right." But Walker's supporters in Congress and elsewhere were just as sure he had done wrong. Meetings were held across the South in which Paulding was excoriated and local resolutions were adopted condemning the commodore's actions. Members of Congress introduced measures calling for Paulding's censure, and some demanded—echoing Walker's own statement to reporters upon his arrival in New York—that the US government return Walker and his men to Nicaragua.

The Senate demanded a report from Buchanan on Walker's arrest and forced repatriation, including copies of communications and orders among Paulding, his lower-level commanders, and higher-ups in Washington. Buchanan complied, and simultaneously condemned and lauded Paulding. The commandant "committed a grave error . . . in the sincere conviction that he was promoting the interest, and vindicating the honor of his country." Besides, Buchanan noted, Paulding had done no harm to Nicaragua—and in fact had "relieved her from a dreaded invasion." Yet Buchanan still relieved Paulding of his command. The commodore retired to his home in Huntington, on New York's Long Island, where he spent the next few years fighting off lawsuits by some of the men he had arrested and removed from Nicaragua.[21]

Despite his ignominious second removal from Nicaragua by US naval ships, Walker maintained that he was still the country's rightful president. He continued to travel and give speeches on his cause, raising yet more money and building interest in another movement. He also directly attacked Buchanan, arguing in a January 25, 1858, speech in Mobile that the only reason Buchanan had targeted Walker's filibuster was because the president's friends were backing a rival isthmus transit route through Mexico. Newspapers around the country either quoted from Walker's speech or reprinted it in its entirety, sparking yet another round of political furor over US policy toward Walker and Nicaragua.[22]

Yet there was a sense of a turning tide. Southern expansionists still backed him, but his double failure (triple if one included his invasion of Mexico) raised serious questions about his abilities, and his obvious personal ambitions were beginning to leave many cold. A Memphis *Eagle and Enquirer* correspondent wrote from New Orleans:

> It looks strange to hear men talking about the spread of Republican institutions, calling Walker the pioneer of those blessed institutions, when not long since, he declared himself . . . to be in favor of a strong military government in Nicaragua, and the reasons for it were to counteract the great Northern Republic [the United States]. But Walker's day is done. He cannot again be galvanized into life. . . . Time was

when greatness was almost within his grasp; yet by a series of mismanagement, he lost the splendid opportunity, and must now be content that he is placed upon a level with mediocrity, having lost that halo of greatness—the halo of success.[23]

Walker went from Mobile to Nashville, where at the invitation of childhood friends such as John Lindsley, he gave a speech on February 20 at the Odd Fellows Hall. While he was visiting his hometown, a federal grand jury in New Orleans indicted him and several fellow filibusters on charges of violating the Neutrality Act over the return trip to Nicaragua. Walker appeared in court in New Orleans on March 3 with his lawyer and supporter Pierre Soulé, and he was released on $4,000 bail—a bit of a surprise, since he had jumped bail just a few months before to return to Nicaragua. The trial began June 1 and lasted only two days. Walker and the defendants claimed that they couldn't be guilty of violating the Neutrality Act because they were Nicaraguan citizens and, in the case of Walker, the elected president of the republic against which he allegedly was plotting. The judge instructed the jury that Walker was not in fact president, but the jurors deadlocked, with ten of the twelve voting to acquit. Walker demanded a retrial, preferring exoneration to a no-verdict, but the government, seeing the handwriting on the jury room wall, dropped the charges.[24]

Walker stayed in New Orleans, where he continued plotting from a boarding house at 119 Exchange Place, an alley off Canal Street three blocks from the river. Meanwhile, the diplomatic landscape was shifting across the Caribbean and Central America, reflecting the uncertainties he had helped create. The Buchanan administration had backed the attempt by the Atlantic and Pacific Ship Canal Company—now owned by Joseph White, who had bought up the worthless shares—to restart the Nicaraguan transit route, but it had collapsed after only a few runs. The route's value was now uncertain; it was closed for long enough after Sylvanus Spencer's Costa Rican raiders seized the ferries that business had shifted to the Panama route. Even as the total number of people crossing the isthmus was decreasing as the gold rush tapered off, the passenger flow through Panama jumped from 15,412 in 1855, the year before Walker first arrived in Nicaragua, to 20,596 in 1858. President Buchanan still wanted to reach an agreement with the Nicaraguan government for a new transit contract that would ultimately include a canal. But Walker's invasions and the Nicaraguans' perceptions that he had Buchanan's support soured the new government of President Tomás Martínez on any deals with the Americans.[25]

Cornelius Garrison and Charles Morgan, to whom Walker had granted the transit route charter after revoking it from Vanderbilt, eventually wrangled a fresh contract from Costa Rica, thereby recovering the fleet and assets Spencer had seized. But the route itself was still in limbo, technically Nicaraguan but no longer in their control. Buchanan, skeptical of Garrison and Morgan because of their connections with Walker, persuaded President Mora to void that contract, and Vanderbilt, who still asserted that he owned the fleet, began working back channels with a Costa Rican general to seize physical control of the transit route, much as he had done with Spencer. Word of that effort leaked back to Buchanan in Washington, who then refused to back any Vanderbilt play on the isthmus and sought a new contract with Nicaragua for Joseph White, Vanderbilt's former partner and agent. Buchanan pledged to use the US military to protect American interests along the route.

To the Nicaraguans, this scenario felt like a territorial grab. So they gave a new contract, held jointly with Costa Rica, to a Frenchman named Felix Belly, a move that outraged pretty much everybody else. But Belly failed to draw the investors he needed to make it work, so the advantage swung back to the wily Vanderbilt. Instead of jockeying for his own contract, however, Vanderbilt decided to play a different game. Earlier he had made a secret deal with the operators of the Panama route to not compete for Panama business in return for a $40,000 monthly payment. Now he renegotiated, promising to stay away from the Nicaragua route as well for a total of $56,000 per month. When that became known, the public and political backlash was considerable, and the Panama route owners—who were receiving $900,000 a year from the US government to carry mail—dropped the anticompetition contract with Vanderbilt. By this point, with the Nicaraguan charter still up in the air and Panama route holding an insurmountable advantage, the efforts to reestablish the Nicaraguan route came to an end.

Britain, meanwhile, had agreed to drop its protectorate of the Miskito Kingdom and return Greytown and the neighboring coastline to Nicaragua, and to cede to Honduras the Bay Islands off the country's Caribbean coast. The British had held on to them primarily to thwart US expansionism in the region, and with the Clayton-Bulwer Treaty in effect, they were no longer needed to serve that purpose. European influence in the region did not end, however, as the governments of Nicaragua and Costa Rica, distrusting the US government, then released the "Rivas Manifesto." The pact, named for the city in which it was issued, declared that the two countries were placing themselves under the protection of Great Britain, France, and Sardinia, "who have caused the independence and nationality of the Ottoman empire to be respected." Presidents Martínez of Nicaragua and Mora of Costa Rica announced that they felt the need for European protection because the US government had failed to stop Walker, and that the United States' representatives in Central America (they likely had John Wheeler in mind) "have been the accomplices and auxiliaries of the invaders, acting as masters . . . and openly menaced Central America with an inevitable annexation."[26]

Against that backdrop, Walker kept trying to return. On December 6, a schooner named *Susan* slipped out of Mobile with two of Walker's men aboard: Charles Doubleday and Colonel Anderson, who had held the San Juan River during Walker's last foray in Nicaragua. (Walker was to follow on a different ship.) A few nights later, Doubleday subsequently recalled, a watchman failed to note white foam in the sea off Belize and the *Susan* ran onto a coral reef "with such force as to break in the middle, where the sharp coral protruded through her bottom, holding her fast, a fortunate circumstance for us, as, if she had gone over the narrow reef, she would have sunk instantly in the deep sea. The sudden arrest of motion sent one of the masts overboard, and the large rent in her bottom caused her to fill with water almost instantly." Doubleday was in his berth when the *Susan* grounded, and he had to wade through waist-deep water over an angled floor and scramble up a ladder to reach the deck. Men wielded axes to cut free the broken mast, which helped stabilize the wreck, but the constant battering of the waves made the position precarious. The captain sent off a mate and two men in a small launch in the direction of Belize, hoping to alert rescuers of the *Susan*'s fate.[27]

For three days the men waited, seeing two ships appear in the distance then move on, before a small boat bearing fishermen from an island about ten miles distant spotted the wreck and began ferrying the men in groups to their village. Eight days later, a passing British warship, the *Basilisk*, was hailed and steered to a mooring near the island. The castaways discovered that the mate and his two colleagues were aboard—they had reached a port in Belize where the *Basilisk* was at anchor and had gone with her to rescue the men. When they discovered the empty wreck on the reef, they began searching for survivors until they encountered the fishing boat. The captain learned from the initial contact that the *Susan* was taking filibusters to Nicaragua but "chose to view us as shipwrecked people only" and offered to return the men to Mobile.

Thus ended yet another Walker effort.

Walker continued to press, but the US government pressed back. He concocted a ruse under which men would ostensibly sail for Panama en route to California but instead peel off for Nicaragua, but it fell apart when port officials refused to let the ship leave the mainland. A second effort similarly died. Walker was running out of money, supporters, and men, and now faced the additional hurdle of trying to sneak past warships belonging to the British, who had agreed to keep filibusters from reaching Nicaragua.

So Walker returned to the field in which he had found the most success: writing. His exploits were already the stuff of legend, famous in the South and infamous in the North. S. H. Goetzel, an Austrian immigrant who in 1854 had opened a bookstore and publishing house in Mobile, advised Walker that his story, told in his own words, would sell some twenty thousand copies. Walker hunkered down and over the next several months wrote his memoir of the war in Nicaragua, finishing by March 11, 1860.[28]

Oddly, Walker composed it in the third person, referring to himself as Walker or "the author," and while the details are self-aggrandizing and some notable failures are omitted, it is a fairly straightforward if occasionally over-wrought accounting of what happened. Deaths are glorious, the enemy is always vastly inferior in spirit and skill, and casualty estimates are deflated on his side and inflated for the other. But the book puts the lie to the old observation that history gets written by the victors. Here, the vanquished leader got his say. "The author of the following narrative does not expect to attain perfect truth in all things," Walker warned in the brief introduction. "He merely asks the reader to give him credit for the desire to state facts accurately, and to reason justly about the circumstances attending the presence of the Americans in Nicaragua."[29]

As Walker wrote, he also underwent a religious conversion, though whether it was a matter of faith or opportunism is unclear. Raised Protestant but having exhibited little religious devotion after leaving Nashville, Walker now became a Roman Catholic, despite his early anti-Catholicsm and disdain for priests. No records reflect why he chose to get baptized, but there's an easy speculation: the Catholic Church played a significant role in the daily lives of the people of Nicaragua, and if Walker intended to resume his place as their president—in fact, their emperor—it would be easier to pull off if he could at least show a front of sharing their religion.

After he gave the manuscript to Goetzel, Walker traveled to Washington and then New York. Goetzel arrived there a couple of days later, planning to have the book printed both in Mobile and in New York City. Walker received letters at the address of his uncle, Caleb C. Norvell, the *New York Times*'s commercial editor, and wrote to Fayssoux that he intended to stay in New York for a week or so until the book was printed. "The publisher insists on putting an engraved likeness of the author in the book; and although it offends my sense of propriety I have to admit to it as a part of the 'humbug' of the trade."[30]

But Walker also was meeting with backers and trying to make arrangements for passage to Aspinwall for small groups of his supporters. Under his latest plan, his assembled force would move from there into Nicaragua. In mid-March he traveled to Louisville to visit his sister, and then to New Orleans, expecting to arrive around April 12. Throughout, he wrote to Fayssoux of various ways they could return to Nicaragua, and what Walker chose to believe was a desire by the people there to have his government reinstated. "On arriving here," he wrote from Louisville, "I got a letter from Granada saying that the people in Nicaragua are ripe for our return."

While Walker was gone, Unwins Elwyn, a wealthy British landowner from Ruatan, the largest of the Bay Islands, arrived in New Orleans looking for him. Fayssoux met Elwyn on Walker's behalf and heard a plea that must have quickened the adventurer's heart. The English-speaking residents of the Bay Islands feared for their future—especially their land and businesses—once Great Britain fulfilled its treaty obligations and turned over control of the island to Honduras and its president, José Santos Guardiola—Walker's early enemy from the Nicaraguan campaign. Exactly when that handover would occur was unclear—the two governments were in negotiations over the specifics of it, and over how the British citizens of the island would be treated. But many of the English speakers rejected the idea of coming under Honduran control. They wanted Walker, once the handover occurred, to serve as their protector and drive off the Hondurans, making the Bay Islands a small but independent state.

Walker returned to New Orleans in April, listened intently to Fayssoux's account of the meeting, and signed on, though he advised the Ruatan residents not to be too hasty in seeking independence. "From a distance, it seems to me they can more speedily and effectually secure their rights by other means than by declaring themselves independent of Honduras," Walker wrote in a letter to Elwyn. He added that the islanders should, once the Hondurans had control, present Guardiola with a list of demands and expectations, including "the ratification of all the titles to land you now possess" and stipulations that "no tax should be levied on the islands without the consent of the people residing on them" and that no Honduran troops be quartered on the island during times of peace. And when, as was likely, Honduras ignored or rejected the demands, then the islanders would have the foundation for an independence movement. "All I desire to say at present is in the way of caution against any rash proceeding." Walker pledged to send some of his men, who would "by their good behavior and orderly character, aid you in the difficulties you expect on the islands." And he said he would likely follow in a few weeks.[31]

Walker concocted a scheme in which a former top aide in Nicaragua, Anthony Rudler, would oversee small groups of men traveling on fruit-trade ships to take up residence on the island, and after the Honduran flag replaced the Union Jack over Ruatan, Walker would arrive with yet more men. None of those involved wanted to take on the British navy—but the Honduran army was a different matter, especially if the Americans would be defending an island.

The plans came together swiftly, and Walker worked in a trip to Mobile, where he picked up two donations totaling $180 "to pay for passage to Ruatan." He continued on to Montgomery, where "I hope to do something" before returning to New Orleans. But nothing that Walker engaged in seemed to occur in secrecy, much to his misfortune.[32]

15 | RUATAN, TRUJILLO, AND THE END OF A DARK DREAM

THE FIRST OF WALKER'S MEN arrived inconspicuously at Ruatan on April 30, 1860, ten days after Walker's letter to the would-be rebels. They found an atmosphere of uncertainty and trepidation, but also disorganization and no clear leader among those who feared the Honduran takeover. They reported they were "well-received and immediately made arrangements for their own subsistence, also for other squads of emigrants as they might arrive." They established a small colony about five miles from Coxen Hole, the island's main port (later renamed Port McDonald), and over the next six weeks "Americans made their appearance in considerable number, coming as passengers in a regular way, in the schooners engaged in the fruit trade between Ruatan and New Orleans." But the sudden influx of Americans created its own stir, and rumors ran rampant among descendants of African slaves that the Americans were planning to take over and enslave them.[1]

On May 21, the acting governor of the islands convened a public meeting at Coxen Hole and announced that the details of the handover had been settled and signed a few days before. The date of the formal change was yet to be set, but it would be "at an early date," and all British subjects currently on the islands who wished to leave would be transported and given land on another British colony in the Caribbean. Those who remained would continue to receive protection from the Crown, but they would be governed by the Hondurans.[2]

The English-speaking islanders held their own meeting immediately afterward and agreed on a set of demands to be made of their incoming national government. The list included ratification of existing property titles and the legal right to make more purchases, the right to some level of home rule on local decisions, no taxes levied without local approval, no quartering of troops in peacetime, no conscription of the British islanders or their workers, retention of English as the official language, no requirement for passports, and freedom of religion and the right to protest. Walker might have felt satisfaction that the list included some of his recommendations, and emboldened that with a single letter and the dispatch of some men he had managed to serve as more of a leader than any of the islanders. However, the list of demands he'd encouraged worried the British, who, fearing an insurrection, stationed a small garrison of troops on the island in case trouble erupted.

Walker sailed for Ruatan in June to meet with residents and with his men who were already there. Walker and about twenty-five additional filibusters arrived on the bark *John A. Taylor* on June 12. After a week or so, Walker decided to abandon the island for the time being—fearing, presumably, that his presence and the continuing arrivals of American men and guns would be too much for the new British garrison to miss. He settled on Cozumel, a two-day sail by schooner to the north off the coast of Mexico, as the best spot to organize the men and the mission. But they dropped hints in Coxen Hole that they were headed to the Swan Islands, about 125 miles to the northeast. Two days after they left, the sloop HMS *Icarus*, under the command of Nowell Salmon, arrived at Coxen Hole to learn that Walker had left "with two schooners and about 75 men, and several cases containing arms. They were joined by a barque outside the port."[3]

Walker's ships became separated at sea, but all arrived at Cozumel around June 23. Walker's ship "anchored off the south point of the island, upon which some few huts and a flock of goats were the only objects showing habitation visible." Upon landing, they found one native family living in the hut and no other neighbors for miles. The men set to work building shelters and moving supplies and weapons ashore. Three days later, another ship arrived with more men and munitions.[4]

Before Walker left Ruatan for Cozumel, another group of his men under the command of Anthony Rudler had boarded the *Clifton* on its regular trade run from New Orleans to Belize City and then Ruatan. The *Clifton* carried in its hold a large store of guns and ammunition in crates labeled as the *Clifton*'s usual shipments of merchandise. Walker would also need people in the United States to make sure his supply of men and weapons kept

flowing, so Callendar Fayssoux remained in New Orleans as Walker's agent and recruiter. But references to Walker's new designs on Central America began to surface in newspapers, and loose lips on Ruatan conveyed added intelligence to the authorities. So the British and Honduran governments quietly agreed to postpone the handover until they knew exactly what Walker was intending.

The *Clifton* reached British-controlled Belize on June 14, and the passengers milled about the waterfront as crates of goods were offloaded and items for the return trade were laded. But the number of men waiting to carry on to Ruatan—not usually a destination for such a crowd—aroused the suspicions of the port officials. An inspection discovered the weapons, which were confiscated, and the *Clifton* was denied permission to leave. Rudler and the men were not detained, but they had no guns and no transport to reach Ruatan, where they expected to rendezvous with Walker.

Walker had chartered the *John A. Taylor* for a month, and on June 27 most of the men at the Cozumel camp loaded themselves and the weapons aboard the ship, which set off to meet up with Rudler and his men. Walker had no inkling that the British and Honduran governments were now working together to frustrate his invasion. Cruising off Ruatan, he was surprised to see British ships at anchor, so the *Taylor* stayed at sea, but within site of the island, hoping for the rendezvous with the *Clifton*.

Rudler managed to rent another ship at Belize, the *Martha*, and skipped out to sea unnoticed by the British authorities. That the Royal Navy had confiscated Rudler's arsenal was a problem they'd have to resolve once they met their first objective—meshing the two expeditionary forces. But shortly after the *Martha* left port, the winds died away, leaving the sails listless on their masts and the ship at the mercy of the currents. The men—who were passengers, not crew—had little with which to occupy themselves. Some baited hooks and tossed them over the side, but even the fish seemed becalmed in "the slow heaving sea," as one member of the expedition wrote later.[5]

While the sun was brutally intense, at night the men spread blankets on the deck and played cards or sang songs. Slight breezes occasionally puffed up the sails and pushed the ship forward. Eventually the men could see a green mound on the hazy horizon: Ruatan, about twenty miles away. "We walked up and down the deck, cursing the wind," which seemed to do some good, for the breeze finally stiffened and "we spread all sails." The *Martha* picked up speed as the sun dropped below the horizon. "It is nearly midnight when we hear the thunder of the surf" on coral. The captain sailed parallel to the reef until he reached a gap, then nosed the ship through and into the calm waters of the harbor.

The *Martha* cast anchor near a large topsail schooner, and as the *Martha*'s launches were prepared to make for shore, a small tender approached from the schooner. They were from the *John A. Taylor*, the men announced, and Walker was aboard. Rudler and his men quickly ferried themselves to the *Taylor*, where they joined up, finally, with the main expeditionary force.

Once all were aboard, Walker led Rudler to the stern, where they spoke quietly but earnestly, Rudler no doubt reporting his litany of bad news: the confiscated weapons, gunpowder, and ammunition, which Walker could clearly see had not been transferred from the *Martha*; the impoundment of the *Clifton* by the British navy; the days becalmed at sea aboard the *Martha*; assorted deaths from disease during the voyage; and, confirming Walker's suspicions, word that the Royal Navy was very active across the southwestern portion of the Caribbean. After some time they walked back to the middle of the deck and Walker approached Thomas Henry, another of his trusted lieutenants. They spoke quietly, mouth to ear, for some time, then Walker separated.

As they talked, a canoe paddled by "a half-naked Jamaica[n]" closed in on the *John A. Taylor*. The man hauled himself aboard via a dangling rope, then passed a small note to Walker. It's unknown what was written on the note, but it was most likely a warning that the *Icarus* had arrived at Coxen Hole with a fresh detachment of British soldiers. Walker read the note by the moonlight, then ordered the captain to take the ship to sea. He held another round of hushed conversations with Rudler and Henry as the *John A. Taylor* weighed anchor and made for the bight and the open waters beyond.

The ship cruised off the thirty-six-mile-long island for the next day. Walker and Rudler made one mysterious trip by launch to Ruatan, and later a courier was welcomed aboard as Walker, Rudler, Henry, and two other lieutenants continued lengthy and sometimes heated discussions, shifting between English and Spanish but too far from the men for any to make out the words. Dolan, one of the lieutenants, finally came forward and ordered the men to fall in. They scrambled into lines on both sides of the deck, their backs to the sea.

Walker walked forward from the stern, followed by Rudler and Henry, until he stood between the two rows of men, and began talking. The initial plan, as they knew, was to help the Bay Islands assert independence from Honduras. But, Walker said, he harbored grander plans. His intent all along had been, once the Bay Islands were free, to use Ruatan as a base for a fresh incursion in Nicaragua, where he planned to reclaim his rightful place as president. For many of the men, it was the first time they learned of the scope of Walker's ambition for the Ruatan venture, though it couldn't have surprised them, given Walker's history.

The British had yet to quit the islands, Walker said, and it didn't seem as though they intended to do so, despite the treaty with Honduras. It would be foolhardy to move on Ruatan and dangerous to remain at sea in the vicinity. So the expedition was faced with a choice. They could press on toward the mainland and seize Trujillo, home to one of the strongest forts on the Honduran coast, and use that as the springboard for an invasion of Nicaragua. Or they could point the *John A. Taylor* north and return to New Orleans, where Walker would form a fresh expedition. It was up to the men.

Dolan followed with a few memories of fighting with Walker in Nicaragua and said that "he knows well what lies before us if we decide to advance." He asked the men to vote with their bodies—all those in favor of pressing on, come stand with him. Walker and Rudler moved aft, and almost as a block the men clustered around Dolan, waving their hats and shouting, "Hurrah for Honduras!"

Their destination: Fortaleza de Santa Bárbara, which had been built in the sixteenth century to defend the land in the name of the Spanish king and to repel pirates preying on ships ferrying silver and gold back to Europe. Now it was manned by the Honduran army and defended with thirty-six cannons, the largest of them capable of firing sixteen-pound balls from atop a low bluff overlooking the Caribbean. The weapons were out of date but still lethal.

Walker ordered the ship southeast for Trujillo, nearly fifty miles away. The men retrieved crates bearing their weapons from the hold. Each man received a belt and forty rounds, and a rifle from which they carefully wiped excess oil and checked to make sure the firing mechanisms worked. Once equipped, they gathered for a brief meeting under Dolan's direction. "Then we break ranks, get our blankets, and lay down on the deck" to catch what sleep they could before landfall. Because none knew how long it might be before they could sleep again.

The ship neared Trujillo in moonlight "so bright that you can read fine print," then continued eastward for about three miles. Walker ordered the ship to veer closer to shore, then anchor and lower the landing boats. Walker and ninety-one men eventually went over the side and took their places for the short pull to shore, where they disembarked in shallow water and, with little chatter, sloshed their way to the beach. Following quiet orders, they fell in and, with Henry and Dolan in the lead and Rudler and Walker, a Toledo sword in hand, covering the rear, the invaders began the sluggish march along the white sands to Trujillo.

They were a short distance from the edge of town when a single cannon shot boomed in the distance—an alarm fired after someone spotted the armed Americans and sped to the fort to alert the Honduran soldiers. Within minutes, scores of villagers armed with a mishmash of weaponry—sidearms, machetes, and sticks—moved into Trujillo's plaza to help defend the town. A small detachment of armed soldiers approached, hoping to cut the invaders down on the open space of the beach from hidden vantage points in the jungle. But their first salvo struck no one, and the Americans' return fire sent the advance unit fleeing.

Walker and his men reached Trujillo at about four thirty in the morning. They crossed the narrow Río Cristales and "marched orderly along the deserted streets of that little town"—the citizen defenders had dissipated almost as quickly as they had formed—until they came within view of the Fortaleza de Santa Bárbara, with its twelve-foot-thick walls rising eight feet above the ground, the top lined with cannons and "black with men, their muskets flashing." Walker and Henry conferred quietly, then Henry stepped before the men and asked for volunteers to join him in an audacious move—a direct, frontal assault on the fort to draw fire and give the rest of the invaders a chance to reach the main gate. Walter Stanley was among those who stepped forward, and a few minutes later they made their move, dashing out of cover at sprint speed and running yards apart to make it harder for the Hondurans to mow them down. They ran directly for the wall, and the barrage from the fort came almost immediately, a mix of rifle fire and grapeshot blasted from cannons. One bullet grazed Stanley's head, momentarily stunning him. "Three of our men fell, and as the rifle dropped from my hand, I noticed a stream of blood flowing from my right arm, which hung limp, and powerless at my side." Stanley kept running until he and the others, save one man immobilized with a shattered leg, reached relative safety—the angle from the top of the wall was too sharp for the bullets to reach them.[6]

The diversion worked. "Before the smoke has cleared, Col. Henry has led his men over us and spring on each other's shoulders they mount the walls." As the Americans began firing, the Hondurans turned and scrambled down from the cannon positions. One of Henry's men reached the main gate and opened it, and the rest of the invaders flooded into the main yard as the Hondurans disappeared through side and rear gates, leaving their firearms, clothing, and other personal possessions—a panic of a retreat. After tightening a tourniquet on his bleeding arm, Stanley followed his comrades through the main gate, entered the first building he reached, and stretched out on a cot.

As the sun rose, the sails of the *John A. Taylor* moved into view offshore. Walker helped assess the wounded as Henry issued orders to the healthy to secure the fort and maintain pickets to watch for counterattacks. But Trujillo was theirs.

The routed Honduran troops didn't run far. They remained outside Trujillo while a messenger sent word to General Mariano Alvarez, the regional military commander based at Olanchito, some fifty miles southwest of Trujillo, that the filibusters had the fort. Walker settled into the business of organizing his garrison. His first act named Colonel Henry, his trusted confidant and strategist, as commander of the fort, Dolan as adjutant general, and a filibuster named Ryan as ordnance officer. Henry established a schedule of sentries along the fort walls as Walker helped tend to the wounded. Six men had been killed in the attack on the fort, and four others were grievously wounded, including Stanley with his wounded arm and Dixon, the man with the shattered leg. Stanley wrote that Walker "cut the sleeve from my arm, washed and bandaged my wound, gave me a glass of brandy, and detailed a man to pour cold water on my arm. He examined and dressed the wounds of the others the same way, and gave us the kindest and most considerate care and attention." Walker also directed that one of the large stone buildings be emptied and converted into a hospital, where the men were arrayed on hammocks under the ceiling rafters and tile roof, which made for a comfortable resting spot for the two-foot-long and larger iguanas that overran the region.

Walker spent the next two days overseeing his men as they sorted through supplies the Hondurans had left behind and investigated the mostly deserted village, questioning the few remaining villagers and robbing and looting as they went. Walker also issued a proclamation to the Hondurans about his intent in landing at Trujillo, explaining that he was there on behalf of the residents of the Bay Islands who did not want to come under the control of Honduras. Walker recalled that five years earlier he "was invited to the Republic of Nicaragua" with a promise of "certain rights and privileges" in return for his services. "We performed the services required of us, but the existing authorities of Honduras joined a combination to drive us from Central America." He aligned himself and his followers—"naturalized Nicaraguans"—with the plight of the (mostly English) people in the Bay Islands who did not wish to fall under Honduran control, and held himself out as a well-intentioned knight who had come to defend the defenseless.[7]

To do that would mean overthrowing the Honduran government of President Guardiola, his former nemesis in Nicaragua, though Walker didn't say it in such direct language. "It becomes therefore a common object with the naturalized Nicaraguans and with the people of the Bay Islands to place in the government of Honduras those who will yield the rights lawfully acquitted in the two states." Walker wrote that his issue was not with the people of Honduras but with "the Government which stands in the way of the Interests, not only of Honduras but of a Central America. The people of Honduras may therefore, rely on all the protection they may require for their rights both of person and of Property."

But it was going to take more than the men in Fortaleza de Santa Bárbara to guarantee that. After securing the fort, Walker had sent the *Taylor* back to New Orleans with word for Fayssoux to send men and guns to join him at Trujillo, and there wasn't much he could do until they arrived. Even then, his best chance for success would be in forging an alliance with José Trinidad Cabañas, Honduras's former Liberal president, who was trying to overthrow Guardiola. Yet Walker was being presumptuous. Would Cabañas accept the alliance? When Walker controlled Nicaragua, he had refused to send troops to help Cabañas challenge Guardiola, because he feared starting a war with Nicaragua's northern neighbor. Then he had gone from invited soldier of fortune to president by undercutting his Nicaraguan hosts and executing General Ponciano Corral. So while Cabañas might be able to use Walker and his contingent of experienced invaders, he also had reason to distrust the American. To align with Walker would be to gamble with his own political future, and maybe his life.

To try to get in touch with the former president, Walker sent Henry, Dolan, and a few other men in search of a Cabañas supporter rumored to live nearby. It's unclear how long they were gone, but when they returned to the fort, Henry was drunk. Smoking a thick cigar, he staggered into the building housing the ammunition and gunpowder, where Ryan was overseeing several soldiers as they put together packets for the fast reloading of the fort's cannons. Ryan sharply ordered the drunk colonel out of the magazine. Instead, Henry pulled a bowie knife from his belt and moved toward Ryan, who pulled a pistol and, as Henry advanced, fired a single shot, blowing away most of Henry's right jaw.[8]

The gunshot drew a crowd, including Walker. He ordered his wounded friend to be carried by stretcher into the hospital ward, where he was deposited in the space next to Stanley. Walker reverted to his medical past and treated Henry's wound as best he could, but there was little to be done. "Henry lay like one dead, except for his heavy breathing," Stanley later recalled. Walker's own face had "turned gray and hopeless." Dolan arrived at the bedside and reported to Walker the details of what had happened, gleaned from interviews with Ryan and others in the munitions room. Walker's face creased as he listened, then he quietly told Dolan to have Ryan resume his duties. The blame was clear, and Ryan's actions defensible.

Walker spent the rest of the day and the night at Henry's side, the wounded man remaining unconscious. Stanley, tortured by the gunshot to his own arm, drifted in and out of sleep. "When I awoke occasionally from fitful slumber during the night, I found Walker still in the same place, never moving except to apply a wet cloth to Henry's wounded face." As the sun rose, Walker finally left the ward and assumed Henry's role as fort commander, ordering a change in the guard and other preparations to ensure the fort could be readily defended.

With a small contingent, the loss of any man is problematic. But for Walker, the loss of Henry deprived him of his most trusted adviser, a man who could be rash but who also could accurately read a situation and ably lead men in battle, and who didn't hesitate to offer ideas and analyses that challenged Walker's reading of a situation. The filibuster would also have to figure out how to delegate command for a two-pronged effort he had planned: leaving a sufficient force to hold the fort while marching the rest in search of Cabañas. That wouldn't happen though, until the reinforcements arrived. And Walker had no way of knowing that the British had intercepted the ships carrying the men and weapons he was so patiently awaiting, and so didn't realize exactly how precarious his position had become.

Salmon, the British naval captain, learned on August 11 that Walker had "taken Trujillo little or no resistance having been offered to him." He sailed three days later from Belize, anchoring the *Icarus* in Trujillo Bay on the evening of August 19. Walker watched warily from the fort. The next morning Salmon moved the *Icarus* to a closer anchorage and led a small contingent ashore to confer with William Melhado, the acting British consular agent assigned to watch out for the Crown's interests in the port city. Salmon found an odd sight. The village "was entirely deserted, with the exception of Mr. Melhado, who had kept the British flag flying." Walker occupied the fort but was "flying the Hondurian [*sic*] colors."[9]

Salmon was operating in a gray area. His orders were to protect British interests, but that required determining what exactly those interests were and whether the orders gave him enough leeway to act. Too timid or too aggressive a response could affect his career, leading perhaps to an inquiry and a letter of reprimand, or maybe to harsher penalties. Once his launch beached at Trujillo he was on foreign soil without invitation, an act over which the Hondurans could (but likely wouldn't) raise objections. But Melhado provided Salmon with the excuse he could use to move forward: the fort held $2,025 in cash and "government paper" valued at 1,390 British pounds that were the collateral for debts owed to the Crown. Securing that collateral, which the Hondurans had clearly lost control of, gave him the pretext for action.

Not that Salmon needed much in the way of assurance. At age twenty-five, he was young for the responsibilities that had been entrusted to him as a captain in the British navy. One American journalist who saw him in Honduras described him as "a burly, bluff young British officer, of a very pompous, authoritative manner." Only three years earlier Salmon had risked his life during the Siege of Lucknow in Uttar Pradesh, part of the Indian Mutiny against British rule, by climbing a tree to help direct fire against the insurgents, an act that earned him a bullet in the thigh and the Victoria Cross, which Queen Victoria had bestowed in June 1859.[10]

Calculating that a military showdown would be bloody even if one-sided, Salmon preferred to negotiate Walker's surrender. He had no doubt of his superiority in firepower, men, and experience but was concerned with the damage he would cause by shelling Trujillo. Merchants there, he estimated, held about $88,000 in goods "obtained on credit from English Merchants at

Belize." Shelling the fort and village "would place the inhabitants in a still worse position than they then held." Better to persuade Walker to quit, trading Walker's weapons for return passage to the United States.

Salmon wrote a terse letter to Walker that began with four numbered points: First, that the custom house in the fort held receipts that belonged to the British government; second, that it also held the cash and government paper guaranteeing British loans; third, that Walker's seizure of Trujillo had a significant impact on the trade of British merchants in Belize; and fourth, that Walker's presence in the region had stalled the transfer of the Bay Islands from Great Britain to Honduras, an unacceptable interference by a civilian into the diplomatic affairs of two countries. The Crown would not stand for that, Salmon insisted, warning Walker that he intended to "re-establish in Truxillo the authorities commissioned by the existing Government of Honduras." While Salmon described it as a "request," he told Walker to surrender and stipulated that the Americans' weapons, other than the officers' sidearms, would be turned over to Honduras "as a security against any further descent on their coasts."

Salmon's emissary, Lieutenant Kenwick J. L. Cox, went ashore with a military guard, delivered the letter to the fort, and waited for Walker's response, which came quickly. Walker wrote that he wasn't aware of the British interest in the custom house, and that the money and government paper wasn't there. If it had been, he would be happy to turn it over. And rather than damaging trade with British merchants in Belize, Walker said, his seizure of the village would lead to much more robust trade in the future. He defended his motives in going to Honduras as honorable:

> It would be a long story for me to tell why I claim the right to make war on the existing authorities of Honduras; suffice it to say that my presence here at this time is due entirely to the engagement which I consider I had in honor contacted with a people desirous of living in Central America, under the nominal laws and customs of the English realm. Claiming with them common interests under institutions derived from the Code of Alfred, I thought it no wrong to assist them in the maintenance of rights they had lawfully acquired.[11]

Still, Walker wasn't about to face down the *Icarus* and British troops, particularly since he had a few British subjects among his followers. He said it would be no dishonor to accede to Salmon's demand, and asked who would foot the bill for their "re-embarking" and what vessel would be used.

Salmon replied with a rebuke, telling Walker that "judging from the numerous applications made to me for protection and assistance," the Honduran people didn't want Walker's protection. "You must be quite well aware that I am authorized" to provide protection "to any friendly State that may request." And the Honduran government had requested it. Salmon said there were two ships at Trujillo through which Walker could arrange the departure for himself and his men at their own cost. He rebutted several of Walker's points while welcoming his statement that "you do not consider it any dishonor to lay down your arms at the request of a British officer." He finished the letter by asking Walker "to inform me when your arrangements for re-embarkation are complete, feeling sure you will comply, knowing what must result from a refusal."

Walker asked for a delay until morning to make the arrangements. Salmon agreed to what he saw as a reasonable request. Walker followed up the exchange by sending an emissary to discuss passage with the captains of the two ships—a ruse to make Salmon think he was going to quit Trujillo the next day. Instead, as night fell, Walker and his men prepared to run, quietly ruining the weapons and gunpowder they couldn't carry, arranging for the sick, including the doomed Colonel Henry, to be cared for by the surgeon and assistant who agreed to stay, lightly armed, in hopes that the British would get to them before the Hondurans. Around midnight, under the cover of darkness, the rest of the men formed two lines and quietly left through the fort's main gate, moved through the deserted streets of Trujillo, and disappeared into the jungle.

When Salmon reported later to his superiors that "they fairly gave me the slip," it was an embarrassing admission. Salmon had Walker in view, and within cannon range, but whether out of hubris or a lack of imagination he failed to consider that Walker would simply flee. But flee he did.

Salmon's first hint came at sunrise, when the top of the fort walls were devoid of men, and he could spot none of the movement that would suggest a fort full of soldiers awakening for the day. A scouting expedition reported back that only the doctor, his aide, and the six sick and wounded men remained. Nearly all the weapons left behind were worthless—sixty of the seventy-two rifled muskets had bent barrels. Salmon posted sentries to protect the Americans, who were now his prisoners, and sent a messenger to alert the commander of two Honduran regiments stationed outside Trujillo that the fort was theirs.

Salmon didn't immediately mount a pursuit. He sailed with the wounded prisoners to Ruatan and returned three days later to word that Walker was likely at the Río Negro. Trailed by a second schooner bearing two hundred Honduran soldiers recently arrived from Olanchito, Salmon went in pursuit. Cornering Walker was easier than he anticipated. After learning Walker was ailing and his men also ill, dispirited, and wounded after their flight from Trujillo, Salmon led a small flotilla of launches up the river until they reached the trading post.

Salmon found the filibusters in ragged shape, wounded and diseased, and in no condition to offer much resistance. Salmon was direct. His ship was anchored offshore within easy cannon distance, as was the second ship full of Honduran soldiers—more than twice the manpower that Walker had, and the Hondurans were healthy while Walker and his men were physical wrecks. Walker must surrender or be wiped out. Walker asked Salmon if he would be surrendering to a British officer, apparently fearing he might inadvertently be agreeing to surrender to the Hondurans. Salmon assured him twice that "yes, you surrender to me as a British officer."

It was the end of the expedition, Walker knew. He ordered his men to fall in, explained the terms of the surrender, and told his men to claim the protection of the American flag. The British soldiers began gathering and carrying the men's weapons to the long boats. During the night, General Alvarez and the Honduran troops steamed back to Trujillo. The next morning, Salmon had Walker's men ferried to the *Icarus*—Walker and Rudler were already aboard. It took several hours and multiple trips with the longboats, the process slowed by Salmon spending a few minutes interviewing each of the men as they reached the deck. To a man they claimed American citizenship— except for Walker, who insisted to Salmon that he was the rightful president of Nicaragua, and Rudler, who described himself as Walker's chief of staff. Walker and Rudler were kept separate from the men, who were confined to the ship's main deck under armed guard. Hammocks for the wounded and the sick swung under an awning, but the rest settled in wherever they could find space.

When they were all finally aboard, Salmon set off for Trujillo, arriving around midnight. Although Salmon had told Walker that the American was surrendering to the British navy, once they were underway he informed Walker that he and Rudler, as Nicaraguans and not Americans, would be handed over to the Honduran authorities. Walker was incensed at what he saw as his captor's duplicity. A correspondent for the *New York Herald* aboard the *Icarus* spent some time interviewing Walker, who gave the journalist copies of letters he and Salmon had exchanged, and then dictated "a brief protest against his surrender to Hondurian [*sic*] authorities. His dictation was calm and deliberate, giving me ample opportunity to write down every word before pronouncing the next." Walker refused to identify Salmon by name, referring to him only as the *Icarus*'s captain, as though by emphasizing this role his point would be more pronounced:

> I hereby protest, before the civilized world, that when I surrendered to the captain of her Majesty's steamer *Icarus*, that officer expressly received my sword and pistol, as well as the arms of Colonel Rudler, and the surrender was expressly, and in so many words, to him, as the representative of Her Britannic Majesty.
> WILLIAM WALKER.
> On board the steamer *Icarus*, September 5, 1860[12]

Once daylight was bright enough, the men were transferred to shore "and paraded in front of" Alvarez's soldiers before being imprisoned in the very fort they had held only days earlier. If there was any consolation, they were under the guard of Salmon's men, not the Honduran army.[13]

It's unclear what conversations Salmon had with Alvarez, but the general signed an agreement dated September 8 in which he turned over all seventy of Walker's surviving men and officers "subject to the conditions that they be permitted to return to the United States" if they promised not to engage in any more filibusters in Central America. While the United States government would arrange for the passage, Alvarez would retain the men's weapons. And Alvarez would also get custody of Walker and Rudler, "to be dealt with according to

Law," as well as the sloop and two senior officers that Salmon had captured at the mouth of the Río Negro as he pursued Walker. (What happened to these other two officers subsequently is unknown.) Despite the date on the agreement, Salmon had already left Honduras, sailing out the day before for Belize. He left some men behind and planned to return by September 17 to ensure that no more of Walker's followers arrived to cause trouble.

Alvarez held Walker and Rudler in small, lightless cells away from the rest of the men, and ordered them to be placed in chains while he arranged for their trial on charges of piracy and filibusterism.

Over the next few days, both men were interrogated by Norberto Martinez, commander of the Honduran forces in Trujillo, and they also wrote out statements to the court. A Briton named Mauricio White interpreted for the interview of Rudler, who claimed that Walker had dragged him into this misadventure and that he had no intention to invade Honduras. This view, he said, was backed up by additional statements from captains John V. Hoof and J. S. West. When they left the United States, they had planned to settle in Ruatan, and "as far as I knew, there was no plan to attack" Trujillo. Rudler said his personal plan was to start a fruit business on Ruatan. "General Walker never communicated to me that he had any design of attacking the port of Trujillo or any other part of Honduras. My being with the attacking party was one of those unaccountable as well as unavoidable circumstances, which was utterly beyond my control, and the result of deception" on the part of Walker. Rudler's statement was transparently false, given how inextricably involved with the plan he had been all along. He probably cooked up the story in cooperation with Walker once they learned they would be turned over to the Honduran army—an effort by Walker to protect his officer.[14]

Walker took a more direct approach in his interviews, telling Martinez that he had never intended to have much of a presence in Trujillo. Local citizens whom he wouldn't identify had invited him to Ruatan, he said, and Nicaragua had been his ultimate destination once reinforcements caught up with him. With Ruatan protected by the British, he turned to Trujillo. Walker had, he said, the support of pro-slavery forces in the United States. He carefully protected his men, arguing that he alone knew what he was planning. The men, highly trained and well disciplined, merely followed his orders. Walker declined to name sympathizers he knew in León and elsewhere in Nicaragua, because, he said, they weren't aware of his plan to return to the country. He did identify Fayssoux as his agent in New Orleans working to procure more troops and materiel, an admission that was of no consequence since Fayssoux was far outside the Hondurans' reach.

After several days of interrogations, Martinez presented to Walker and Rudler formal charges of piracy, robbery, and filibustering, which Walker refused to sign, arguing that neither he nor his men committed any crimes, let alone piracy. He wrote in his formal response that "piracy is an offense well-defined by law and consists in robbing on the high seas. The crime cannot be committed on the land, and therefore it is impossible for me to have been guilty of it when attacking the garrison of Trujillo." And rather than robbing Trujillo, he said, his presence made the town and its citizens' property safer than before he arrived. "As to 'filibuster,' the word has no legal signification, and it is therefore impossible for me to know with what I am charged when I am accused of 'filibusterism.'"[15]

Walker challenged the authorities to find an established law he had violated, and sought to put his actions within a different context. "I am ready to abide the consequences of my political acts, but it is a legal absurdity to judge me for alleged offenses either not known to the law or so defined that it was impossible for me to commit them within the limits of the state of Honduras."

Whether Walker the lawyer thought he had a real legal defense is impossible to know, but he believed himself to be the legitimate president of Nicaragua and, with a battalion of armed men, had violently seized a Honduran military fort. If his claims of a legitimate presidency are to be taken at face value, rather than committing a "political" act, Walker had waged war on a neighboring country. And if one discounted his claim that he was a president, he had at the least invaded a foreign country with the intent of installing a new government.

Either way, his fate was sealed. On September 11, Martinez sentenced Rudler to four years of hard labor and ordered Walker to be shot the next morning.

Walker spent the night in his cell with a priest, who offered prayers and conversation and the chance for confession and absolution—the benediction of last rites. The priest was still there when, shortly after sunrise and while the cool of night still lingered in the air, soldiers accompanied by a second priest arrived. Several of the soldiers entered the cell and unshackled the slightly built adventurer, then prepared him for the quarter-mile walk to an abandoned barracks. It was a Wednesday morning, a time when the streets should have been bustling with the business of the day. But all the village knew what was about to happen, so the streets were quiet except for a small gathering of people who waited patiently, expectantly, outside the fort as monkeys, parrots, and a menagerie of other tropical animals howled and squawked and twittered in the surrounding jungle.

The main gate swung open and soldiers emerged walking two abreast, their bayonets fixed, followed by the two priests on either side of Walker, who carried a crucifix in one hand and a candle in the other. Then came another double column of soldiers. As the last cleared the gate, villagers fell in behind to complete the grim parade. Through the streets they marched, the people of Trujillo filling doorways and leaning out of windows, some jeering and a few tossing insults. Walker had seen himself as a protector of the people; the people viewed him as something else entirely. A pirate. An invader. An opportunist who, given the chance, would enslave many of them.

The old barracks were little more than ruins, but a couple of thick converging walls remained to serve the morning's purpose. Soldiers led Walker into the corner. The priests murmured soft words, and Walker occasionally whispered back. Four soldiers with rifles stepped forward, stopping about twenty paces from Walker. The priests, who had done all they could, moved away.

Walker stood silent. At a command, the soldiers fired and Walker crumpled to the ground, bleeding and twitching. A second command sent another volley, Walker's body jerking as the bullets hit. Then a lone soldier stepped forward, placed his revolver a few inches from Walker's face, and pulled the trigger, a superfluous act of savagery that left no doubt that William Walker, the "gray-eyed man of destiny" whose dreams of empire had disrupted three countries and led to the deaths of thousands, was now, finally, dead.

A NOTE ABOUT SOURCES, AND ACKNOWLEDGMENTS

BY THE TIME THE HONDURAN SOLDIERS EXECUTED WALKER, the United States was already moving inexorably toward civil war. In October 1859, John Brown launched his raid on the US arsenal at Harpers Ferry, hoping to empower slaves and spark an uprising. He was caught and hanged on December 2, but his plot in some ways lit the fuse of the Civil War. In the spring of 1860, the Democrats chose Stephen Douglas as their nominee for president. Southern Democratic "fire-eaters" who found Douglas to be wishy-washy on slavery held their own convention and nominated John Breckinridge, outgoing president James Buchanan's pro-slavery vice president. The Republicans nominated Abraham Lincoln, whose moral opposition to slavery offended the slave states. By then the Whigs had collapsed, and some reconstituted themselves as the slavery-neutral Constitutional Union Party, then nominated Tennessee senator John Bell, who opposed the expansion of slavery while believing the Constitution protected the institution itself. The election campaign was in full swing at the time of Walker's execution, and the fractures in the nation were reflected in the vote totals eight weeks later: Lincoln took 40 percent of the popular vote, all in the North and West, while the pro-slavery candidates split the South. Douglas came in second in the general vote with 30 percent, but Lincoln ran away with 60 percent of the Electoral College. Six weeks after the election, before Lincoln took the oath of office, South Carolina seceded from the union, and the slide toward war became inevitable. And with that, Walker, one of the most talked-about figures of the 1850s, began to fade from history.

The filibuster era was a fascinating and pivotal time in American history, and I have intentionally avoided trying to capture its full sweep here, preferring to drill down into Walker's place in it. I also decided for the sake of focus to not include details of Henry Kinney's Nicaraguan expedition; he and about two dozen followers arrived in Greytown about a month after Walker did but never really gained traction, and many of his men eventually deserted to join Walker. Since he had minimal impact on the trajectory of Walker's takeover, I left him on the sidelines. But for those curious about the broader context of the filibuster era, and about Kinney, I recommend the work of Robert E. May, especially *Manifest Destiny's Underworld; Slavery, Race, and Conquest in the Tropics*; and *The Southern Dream of a Caribbean Empire, 1854–1861*. Walker's own book, *The War in Nicaragua*, is a must-read as well. Other significant works include Amy S. Greenberg's *Manifest Manhood and the Antebellum American Empire*. There is also a significant amount of primary material curated and posted at the website Latin American Studies, www.latinamericanstudies.org. I must note that tying down statistics on the numbers of men who joined Walker and died in his various campaigns was a vexing task involving many conflicting tallies. I gave preference to the numbers that seemed to make the most sense and were provided by people in the best position to know them.

I'm fortunate to have friends and acquaintances willing to share expertise and, as necessary, do some legwork for me in finding records in far-flung places. I owe special thanks to longtime friend Ivan Roman in Washington, DC, for translation work; Ed Plunkett, poet by night and librarian by day at Ohio State University in Columbus; John Norvell of Canandaigua, New York, who generously shared with me hard-to-find details on the Norvell family (Walker's mother's family); and Faith Barker, who aided in researching records in London. A special debt (I believe I promised him a beer) is owed to T. J. Stiles, whose *The First Tycoon: The Epic Life of Cornelius Vanderbilt* is the definitive work on Vanderbilt and the Accessory Transit Company, for steering me to a collection at the New York Public Library that offered detailed first-person takes on those events and on Walker's actions.

Pursuing Walker's life led to a range of archives and libraries. Special thanks to: Steven Smith, public service librarian and stacks manager for the Historical Society of Pennsylvania; the staff of the Tennessee State Library and Archives in Nashville; Kelley Sirko and the rest of the staff at the Metro Government

Archives of Nashville and Davidson County in the Nashville Public Library; the National Archives in Washington, DC, and College Park, Maryland; archivist Barbara Rust at the National Archives in Fort Worth, Texas, and Charles Miller at San Bruno, who were especially helpful; the Library of Congress; Patricia L. Keats at the Society of California Pioneers in San Francisco; the staff at the Bancroft Library at the University of California, Berkeley; the Louisiana Division of the New Orleans Public Library; Jim Havron at the Albert Gore Research Center, Middle Tennessee State University in Murfreesboro; and the Huntington Library in San Marino, California.

As with all these projects, special thanks go to my agent, Jane Dystel, and her literary partner Miriam Goderich. And to Jerome Pohlen and the rest of the staff at Chicago Review Press, who (fortunately) find these slices of history as interesting as I do. Thanks also to friends and neighbors, particularly Gavin and Beth Huntley-Fenner, Katherine and Drew Jacobs, Sarina Sherwin, and Paul Kiburis, and other regulars of our weekly Parkside Pub gatherings who inquired about my progress on this book more often than politeness called for. And finally, as with everything, to the lovely Margaret, who over the course of six books has been my first sounding board, first reader, first editor, first everything.

NOTES

Prologue: Trujillo, Honduras, August 21, 1860

1. Injuries detailed in "Later from Walker's Expedition," *Daily Picayune*, New Orleans, August 25, 1860.
2. Anonymous handwritten memoir of Walker's Honduras campaign, William Wyles Collection. This seems to be the basis for a first-person account attributed to Walter Stanley that is included in Jamison, *With Walker in Nicaragua*, 171.
3. Details of Walker's escape are drawn from a report by Captain Nowell Salmon in Beeler, ed., *Milne Papers*, particularly 2:89–93; *New Orleans True Delta*, September 29, 1860; and *New York Herald*, October 4, 1860.
4. Stanley (attributed), handwritten memoir. See also Jamison, *With Walker in Nicaragua*, 166–177.
5. Salmon to Samuel Morrish, September 11, 1860, in Beeler, ed., *Milne Papers*, 2:89.
6. Ibid., 91.
7. Stanley (attributed), handwritten memoir.
8. *New York Herald*, October 4, 1860.
9. Salmon to Morrish, September 11, 1860, in Beeler, ed., *Milne Papers*, 2:92.

1. Nashville

1. John E. Norvell, "How Tennessee Adventurer William Walker Became Dictator of Nicaragua in 1857," *Middle Tennessee Journal of Genealogy and History* 25, no. 4; see also Lawson, "William Walker: His Early Life."
2. See US Census data for 1820; also Lovett, *African-American History of Nashville*, 5. W. W. Clayton, *History of Davidson County, Tennessee, with Illustrations and Biographical Sketches of Some of Its Prominent Men and Pioneers* (Philadelphia: J. W. Lewis, 1880), 203.
3. Mary Norvell to William Norvell, October 12, 1822, in William Norvell Papers. I am also indebted to John E. Norvell, a retired Air Force lieutenant colonel and

descendant of Lipscomb Norvell, for generously sharing some of his research and details of Norvell family history.

4. Details on family homes found in Walker subject file, Tennessee State Library and Archives, Nashville; Jennie Thompson Howell, *Family Talk*, unpublished memoir, Tennessee State Library and Archives, reprinted in Lawson, "William Walker: His Early Life," 4.

5. John M. Bass, "William Walker," *American Historical Magazine*, July 1898, 207.

6. Wayne Cutler, ed., *Correspondence of James K. Polk*, volume 5, *1839–1841* (Nashville: Vanderbilt University Press, 1977), 700–701. Anson and Fanny Nelson, *Memorials of Sarah Childress Polk: Wife of the Eleventh President of the United States* (New York: Anson D. F. Randolph, 1892), 66.

7. Thomas, *Old Days in Nashville*, 78. Bass, "William Walker," 208.

8. Details on Walker are found in a reminiscence by classmate J. W. Bradford, "William Walker," *Daily Alta*, August 6, 1856. Descriptions of Litton drawn from classified ads he posted in Nashville newspapers, 1834–1835.

9. John Ferling, *Almost a Miracle: The American Victory in the War of Independence* (New York: Oxford University Press, 2007), 423–427. Carl P. Borick, *A Gallant Defense: The Siege of Charleston, 1780* (Charleston: University of South Carolina Press, 2003), 229.

10. "Notes of Caleb C. Norvell," unpublished, in the collection of John E. Norvell. Clayton, *History of Davidson County*, 199, 203, 321.

11. Cantrell to Moore, February 10, 1927, Walker vertical file, Texas State Library and Archives, Nashville; Bicentennial Project, Alamo DAR Chapter, O'Shavano DAR Chapter, and San Antonio de Bexar DAR Chapter, *The Alamo Heroes and Their Revolutionary Ancestors* (San Antonio: Daughters of the American Revolution, 1976), 63–64. For a succinct history of the Texas volunteers, see Robertson's Colony Records (AR.87.RT), Archives and Records Program, Texas General Land Office, Austin, www.lib.utexas.edu/taro/txglo/00059/00059-P.html; Norvell, "Tennessee Adventurer William Walker." Robert T. Walker's death is mentioned, without dates or more details, in *Masonic Record*, July 1869, 134.

12. Lawson, "William Walker: His Early Life," 8–12.

13. J. W. Bradford, "William Walker," *Daily Alta*, August 6, 1856. Geyer, *William Walker*, vol. 1, *The Crescent City*, 24, 26. Lawson, "William Walker: His Early Life."

14. Walker to Lindsley et al., November 6, 1841, in William Walker Correspondence.

15. Windrow, *John Berrien Lindsley*, 11.

16. The surviving letters are reprinted in Windrow, *John Berrien Lindsley*, appendix C. The allowance sum is from an interview with Major John M. Baldwin in Langerstedt, "Political Career of William Walker."

17. Walker to Lindsley, July 15, 1843, in William Walker Correspondence.

18. Walker to Lindsley, November 14, 1843, in William Walker Correspondence.

19. Walker to Lindsley, November 19, 1844, in William Walker Correspondence.

2. New Orleans, and Ellen

1. John L. O'Sullivan, "Annexation," *United States Democratic Review* 17, no. 85: 5.

2. Geyer, *William Walker*, vol. 1, *The Crescent City*, 13. See also individual biographical entries in Clayton, *History of Davidson County*.

3. The consulates are listed in the *New Orleans Annual and Commercial Register for 1846* (New Orleans: E. A. Michel, 1845).

4. Geyer, *William Walker*, vol. 1, *The Crescent City*, 13.

5. See individual biographical entries in Clayton, *History of Davidson County*. Lloyd Vogt, *New Orleans Houses* (Gretna, LA: Pelican, 1997), 59.

6. Walker to Lindsley, February 25, 1846, in William Walker Correspondence.

7. Walker to Lindsley, April 3, 1846, in William Walker Correspondence.

8. Eleanor Newman Hutchens, "Dating the Bibb House: Lore, Theory, and Fact," *Historic Huntsville Quarterly of Local Architecture and Preservation*, Winter/Spring 1985, 5–7. The physical description of Ellen is from "'Lost' Facts About Filibuster's Sweetheart Unearthed," *Times-Picayune*, September 26, 1937.

9. For Ellen's education, see Joyner, *From Pity to Pride*, 174–175. "Ellen Galt Martin," *Godey's Lady's Book and Magazine*, October 1858, 396–398.

10. Ellen Martin to Elizabeth Martin, April 20, July 2, and October 23, 1846, in Elizabeth S. Martin Papers.

11. Ellen Martin to Elizabeth Martin, September 20, 1847, and June 15, 1848, in Elizabeth S. Martin Papers.

12. Walker to Lindsley, April 3, 1846, in William Walker Correspondence.

13. Walker to Lindsley, June 4, 1846, in William Walker Correspondence.

14. "Venice," *Commercial Review*, January 1847, 48–56.

15. Walker to Lindsley, January 21, 1847, in William Walker Correspondence.

16. Walker to Lindsley, September 5, 1847, in William Walker Correspondence.

17. Ellen Martin to Elizabeth Martin, March 19, 1849, in the Elizabeth S. Martin Papers.

18. "Deaths," *Times-Picayune*, April 19, 1849. "Obituary," *Times-Picayune*, April 22, 1849. "Died," *Daily Delta*, reprinted in *Southern Advocate* (Huntsville, AL), May 18, 1849. (It's unknown why the Huntsville paper decided to run the obituary a month after her death.) Tombstone index, GS-271, City Archives and Special Collections, New Orleans Public Library. "'Lost' Facts About Filibuster's Sweetheart," *Times-Picayune*, says the brother died two years earlier, but a letter from

Ellen to her cousin after that date refers to her brother as alive, so it seems the article is in error as to the year of death.

19. "Died," *Daily Delta*.

3. A Journalism Career Begins

1. *Daily Crescent*, March 5 & 7, 1849; "The Lower California Republic," *Times-Picayune*, December 23, 1853.
2. Walt Whitman, *Complete Prose Works* (Philadelphia: David McKay, 1897), 196; Emory Holloway, ed., *The Uncollected Poetry and Prose of Walt Whitman* (Garden City, NY: Double, Page, 1921), 77–78.
3. *Daily Crescent*, March 7, 1849.
4. *Daily Delta*, July 28, 1856; *Intelligencer* (Vidalia, LA), March 17, 1849.
5. See Merry, *Country of Vast Designs*, chap. 18, "Wilmot's Proviso."
6. "Mr. Calhoun's Address," *Daily Crescent*, July 26, 1849.
7. "The Delta and the Canal Bank," *Daily Crescent*, July 23, 1849.
8. "The Delta Newspaper," *Daily Crescent*, July 25, 1849.
9. See Polk's diary entries for May–June 1848, in Quaife, ed., *Diary of James K. Polk*.
10. Chaffin, *Fatal Glory*, 35–37.
11. Zachary Taylor, "Proclamation 51—Warning to United States Citizens Against Participating in an Unlawful Invasion of Cuba," August 11, 1849, American Presidency Project, www.presidency.ucsb.edu/ws/index.php?pid=68061.
12. Ambrosio Jose Gonzales, *Manifesto on Cuban Affairs Addressed to the People of the United States* (New Orleans: Daily Delta, 1853).
13. "Cuban Slave-Trade," *Daily Crescent*, June 2, 1849.
14. "Canada and Cuba," *Daily Crescent*, July 30, 1849.
15. "The Round Islanders," *Daily Crescent*, September 3, 1849.
16. "Cuba Affairs," *Daily Crescent*, September 27, 1849.
17. Caldwell, *Lopez Expeditions*, 61.
18. "More About Rey," *Daily Delta*, August 21, 1849.
19. Kirsten Silva Gruesz, *Ambassadors of Culture: The Transamerican Origins of Latino Writing* (Princeton: Princeton University Press, 2002), 113, 143.
20. "Cuba and *La Patria* Newspaper," *Daily Crescent*, November 14, 1849. *Daily Crescent*, November 17, 1849.
21. "Charge of Assault," *Daily Crescent*, November 24, 1849.

4. San Francisco

1. "Valedictory," *Daily Crescent*, February 4, 1850.

2. "Celebration on the Oregon," *Daily Transcript*, July 24, 1850.

3. Geyer, *Favored of the Gods*, 24. "Arrival of the Steamer Oregon," *Daily Alta*, July 22, 1850.

4. Henry R. Wagner, *California Imprints: August 1846–June 1851* (Berkeley: privately published, 1922), 33.

5. Bancroft, *History of California*, 11:175–177.

6. Pancoast, *Quaker Forty-Niner*, 372.

7. Sherman L. Ricards and George M. Blackburn, "The Sydney Ducks: A Demographic Analysis," *Pacific Historical Review* 42, no. 1 (February 1973): 20–31; Stewart, *Committee of Vigilance*, chaps. 1–4.

8. "Murder and Robbery in the Heart of the City," *Herald*, December 31, 1850.

9. "The Public Administrator," *Herald*, January 10, 1851.

10. Alonzo Phelps, *Contemporary Biography of California's Representative Men* (San Francisco: A. L. Bancroft, 1881), 310.

11. "Another Duel," *Daily Alta*, January 17, 1851.

12. "Snaffling Public Sentiment," *Herald*, January 14, 1851.

13. "Daring Attack and Robbery," *Herald*, February 20, 1851.

14. "A Way to Stop Crime," *Herald*, February 22, 1851.

15. Stewart, *Committee of Vigilance*, chap. 4. Williams, *History of the San Francisco Committee of Vigilance*, 171–175.

16. "The Excitement in the City," *Herald*, February 24, 1851.

17. Williams, *History of the San Francisco Committee of Vigilance*, 177.

18. "Oscar T. Shuck, *History of the Bench and Bar of California* (Los Angeles: Commercial Printing House, 1901), s.v. "Levi Parsons"; "The Press a Nuisance," *Herald*, March 4, 1851.

19. Nathaniel Bennett, *Reports of Cases Argued and Determined in the Supreme Court of the State of California* (San Francisco: Marvin and Hitchcock, 1851), 539–555, and "Report of the Select Committee of the Assembly" formed to consider a demand by Walker that Parsons be impeached.

20. "Meeting on the Plaza," *Daily Alta*, March 10, 1851.

21. Records for April 21, 1851, in *Journals of the Legislature of the State of California* (San Jose: Eugene Casserly, 1851), 1644.

22. "Terrible Conflagration," *Daily Alta*, May 4, 1851

23. Louis Schlessinger, "Personal Narrative of Louis Schlessinger, of Adventures in Cuba and Ceuta," *Democratic Review*, September 1852.

24. Chaffin, *Fatal Glory*, 79.

25. Ibid., 128–139

26. Hardy, *History and Adventures of the Cuban Expedition*, 46–48.

27. "The Cuban Expedition," *New York Herald*, April 28, 1851.

28. Quisenberry, *Lopez's Expeditions to Cuba*, 108–109.

29. For a good overview of the role of the French in California and northern Mexico, see Wyllys, *The French in Sonora*.

30. See Rufus Kay Wyllys, "The French of California and Sonora," *Pacific Historical Review* 1, no. 3 (September 1932): 337–359.

31. Geyer, *Favored of the Gods*, 28–29.

32. Rufus Kay Wyllys, "The Republic of Lower California, 1853–1854," *Pacific Historical Review* 2, no. 2 (June 1933): 194.

33. T. Robinson Warren, *Dust and Foam or, Three Oceans and Two Continents; Being Ten Years' Wanderings in Mexico, South America, Sandwich islands, the East and West Indies, China, Philippines, Australia and Polynesia* (New York: Charles Scribner, 1888), 212.

34. Walker, *War in Nicaragua*, 21.

5. The Republic of Sonora Rises

1. Walker, *War in Nicaragua*, 19.

2. Scroggs, *Filibusters and Financiers*, 34.

3. Pancoast, *Quaker Forty-Niner*, 373–374.

4. "Trial of Wm. Walker for Filibustering," *Daily Alta*, October 18, 1854.

5. "Summary of News," *Daily Alta*, October 1, 1853.

6. Croffut, ed., *Fifty Years in Camp and Field: Diary of Major-General Ethan Allen Hitchcock*, 400.

7. Inventory included in court files over the seizure of the *Arrow*, US v. Brig Arrow, record group 21, no. 1224, National Archives, San Bruno, CA. Croffut, ed., *Fifty Years in Camp and Field: Diary of Major-General Ethan Allen Hitchcock*, 400.

8. "The Brig Arrow," *Daily Alta*, October 3, 1853.

9. Croffut, ed., *Fifty Years in Camp and Field: Diary of Major-General Ethan Allen Hitchcock*, 401.

10. "Departure of the Sonora Expedition," *Daily Alta*, October 18, 1853.

11. "The Testimony," *Daily Alta*, October 18, 1854.

12. Walker, *War in Nicaragua*, 22.

13. Bancroft, *History of the North Mexican States and Texas* 2:721–724. "Further from Mexico," *Daily Alta*, February 5, 1854. Anonymous, "Filibustering Expedition, from San Francisco to Lower Calif. & Sonora. Written by an Officer of Col. Walker's Expedition of 1853" (San Francisco, 1904), in Autobiographies &

Reminiscences of California Pioneers, Historical Committee of the Society of California Pioneers.

14. Walker's official Sonora proclamations are compiled in Woodward, ed., *Republic of Lower California.*

15. Anonymous, "Filibustering Expedition," 117.

16. Woodward, ed., *Republic of Lower California*, 25.

17. "Report of the Independence of the Republic of Lower California," *Daily Alta*, December 8, 1853, reprinted from the *San Diego Herald.* Anonymous, "Filibustering Expedition," 120.

18. "The Main Purpose of the Filibustering Expedition," *Daily Alta*, December 26, 1853.

19. Walker, *War in Nicaragua*, 21–22.

20. Soule, Gihon, and Nisbet, *Annals of San Francisco*, 475.

21. "Letter from Sonora," *Daily Alta*, January 3, 1854; "Later from Sonora," *Herald*, January 3, 1854.

22. Anonymous, "Filibustering Expedition," 121.

23. Ibid., 123.

24. "Address of President Walker to the People of the United States," November 30, 1853, reprinted in the *Daily Alta*, December 8, 1853.

25. Robert Cleland, trans., "Bandini's Account of William Walker's Invasion of Lower California, *Huntington Library Quarterly* 7, no. 2 (February 1944): 153–166. John K. Driscoll, *Rogue: A Biography of Civil War General Justus McKinstry* (Jefferson, NC: McFarland, 2006), 84.

26. Lawrence D. Taylor, "The Mining Boom in Baja California from 1850 to 1890 and the Emergence of Tijuana as a Border Community," *Journal of the Southwest* 43, no. 4 (Winter 2001): 463–492.

27. "Defeat of the Filibusters," December 13, 1853, and "Late from Sonora," which included a letter from Bandini, December 27, 1853, both in the *Daily Alta*; Cleland, trans., "Bandini's Account of William Walker's Invasion," 153–166; James Mitchell Clarke, "Antonio Melendrez: Nemesis of William Walker in Baja California," *California Historical Society Quarterly* 12, no. 4 (December 1933), 318–322.

28. Details of the siege are drawn from the *Daily Alta*, December 27, 1853; Cleland, trans., "Bandini's Account of William Walker's Invasion," 153–166; and Clarke, "Antonio Melendrez," 318–322; Anonymous, "Filibustering Expedition," 124; and Walker, *War in Nicaragua*, 106. The circumstances of the deaths of McKibben and McCormick are noted in the *Daily Alta*, January 10, 1854.

29. Departure of the *Caroline* in "More from Mexico," *Daily Alta*, February 5, 1854.

30. "Late from Sonora," *Daily Alta*, December 27, 1853.

31. "Topics of the Day," *Herald*, January 10, 1854.

6. The Republic of Sonora Falls

1. *Daily Alta*, December 16, 1853.

2. Hitchcock to Adjutant General Samuel Cooper, December 15, 1853, in Letters Received by the Adjutant General, 1822–1860 (main series, record group 94), Records of the Adjutant General's Office, 1762–1984, National Archives. Bell, *Reminiscences of a Ranger*, 208–210.

3. Wells, *A History of the Central American War*, 30–32.

4. J. M. Reid, "The Ensenada," *National*, June 1854.

5. *Daily Alta*, January 10, 1854.

6. Robert Cleland, trans., "Bandini's Account of William Walker's Invasion of Lower California, *Huntington Library Quarterly* 7, no. 2 (February 1944): 159–160. "Statement of Theodore Ryan," *Herald*, March 15, 1854.

7. "Letter from San Felipe," *Daily Alta*, May 6, 1854; *Daily Alta*, January 10, 1854.

8. Reid, "The Ensenada."

9. Reid, "The Ensenada"; "Sonora," *Sacramento Daily Union*, February 6, 1854, includes details from Carroll Mullone, who joined the defectors; Anonymous, "Filibustering Expedition, from San Francisco to Lower Calif. & Sonora. Written by an Officer of Col. Walker's Expedition of 1853" (San Francisco, 1904), in Autobiographies & Reminiscences of California Pioneers, Historical Committee of the Society of California Pioneers, 126.

10. "Later from Lower California," *Daily Alta*, January 30, 1854. "The Filibusters at Sonora," *Herald*, January 21, 1854.

11. Cleland, trans., "Bandini's Account of William Walker's Invasion," 160; "From Los Angeles," *Sacramento Daily Union*, February 20, 1845. "Statement of Theodore Ryan," *Herald*, March 15, 1854.

12. Letter by one of the *Portsmouth*'s men, *Herald*, February 19, 1854.

13. "Further from the Filibusters," *Herald*, reprinted in the *Sacramento Daily Union*, February 25, 1854. Wool to Adjutant General Samuel Cooper, February 28, 1854, in Letters Received by the Adjutant General.

14. "Important from Lower California," *Daily Alta*, March 15, 1854; Scroggs, *Filibusters and Financiers*, 44–45.

15. Affidavit of A. S. S. Horn, included in letter from Wool to Jefferson Davis, secretary of war, March 31, 1854, in Letters Received by the Adjutant General.

16. *Daily Alta*, March 15, 1854.

17. "Highly Important from Lower California," *Sacramento Daily Union*, March 10, 1854; "By Telegraph to the Union," *Sacramento Daily Union*, March 15, 1854. "Statement of Theodore Ryan," *Herald*, March 15, 1854.

18. Walker, *War in Nicaragua*, 22–23.

19. Letters from Wool to Jefferson Davis, secretary of war, January 7, March 1, and March 31, 1854, in Letters Received by the Adjutant General. Bancroft, *History of the North Mexican States and Texas*, 2:682.

20. "The Misfortunes of Ambitious Vanity," *Los Angeles Star*, April 22, 1854. Details of the march to Sonora are largely drawn from this account by one of Walker's deserters.

21. "Letter from San Felipe," *Daily Alta*, May 6, 1854.

22. "Breaking Up of Walker's Party," *Daily Alta*, April 26, 1854.

23. Wells, *Walker's Expedition to Nicaragua*, 38–39.

24. Cleland, trans., "Bandini's Account of William Walker's Invasion," 163–165.

25. "Arrival of the Southerner; Breaking Up the Filibusters!," *Daily Alta*, May 16, 1854.

26. The casualty count is from Wells, *Walker's Expedition to Nicaragua*, 38–39. It is incomplete—for instance, it doesn't include Crocker and Ruddach, who had wounded each other in a duel.

27. Wool to Jefferson Davis, secretary of war, March 15, 1854, in Letters Received by the Adjutant General.

7. Why Nicaragua Mattered

1. Kemble, *Panama Route*, 1.

2. For a good, concise history, see Folkman, *Nicaragua Route*.

3. "The News from Europe," *New York Herald*, October 28, 1850.

4. Richardson, *Compilation of the Messages and Papers of the Presidents*, 5:33–40.

5. Kemble, *Panama Route*, 24–25.

6. *Daily National Whig*, February 7, 1849. Kemble, *Panama Route*, 88 and appendix II. Kemble drew his estimates from newspaper and custom house reports, which were incomplete, particularly for people traveling in steerage. So the passenger estimates should be considered a minimum.

7. Details drawn from Marryat, *Mountains and Molehills*, chapter 1.

8. For details on Vanderbilt's early years and his collaboration with Gibbons, see "The Duelist," chapter 2 in Stiles, *First Tycoon*.

9. Folkman, *Nicaragua Route*, 16–18. Stiles, *First Tycoon*, 180–181.

10. The contract is reprinted in "Message of the President of the United States," May 15, 1856, in Sen. Ex. Doc. 68, 34th Cong., 1st Sess. 84–94.

11. Orville W. Childs, *Report of the Surveys and Estimates of the Costs of Constructing the Inter-Oceanic Ship Canal* (New York: William C. Bryant, 1852).

12. Folkman, *Nicaragua Route*, 35–37. Stiles, *First Tycoon*, 193. Squire, *States of Central America*, 439–440. Childs, *Report of the Surveys*, 137.

13. "Nicaragua," *New-York Daily Tribune*, September 26, 1851.

14. "Very Interesting from Nicaragua," *New York Herald*, December 20, 1852.

15. Churchill to the editors of the *New York Express*, reprinted in Great Britain Foreign Office, *Correspondence with the United States Respecting Central America* (London: Harrison and Sons, 1856), 103–104.

16. "The Affair of the Prometheus," *Southern Press*, December 20, 1851. Senator Lewis Cass speech, Cong. Globe, 32nd Cong., 1st Sess., December 16, 1851.

17. Details of the diplomatic efforts are reprinted in Great Britain Foreign Office, *Correspondence with the United States*.

18. George W. McCerran's report, in Great Britain Foreign Office, *Correspondence with the United States*, 241–243.

19. Captain John P. Hollins to Captain Thomas Wilson, March 27, 1853, and Wilson to Hollins, March 28, 1853, both in Great Britain Foreign Office, *Correspondence with the United States*, 245.

20. James M. Woods, "Expansionism as Diplomacy: The Career of Solon Borland in Central America 1853–1854," *Americas* 40, no. 3 (January 1984): 399–415.

21. Fabens to Marcy, May 15, 1854, in Great Britain Foreign Office, *British and Foreign State Papers*, 46:859–864.

22. Details drawn from Commander George N. Hollins's report to Secretary of the Navy James C. Dobbin, July 16, 1854, in Great Britain Foreign Office, *British and Foreign State Papers*, 46:885–888.

8. Walker Returns to San Francisco

1. "Arrival of the Southerner," *Daily Alta*, May 16, 1854. "The Last Act in the Sonora Burlesque," *Sacramento Daily Union*, May 18, 1854.

2. *Daily Alta*, May 6, 1854.

3. "Arrival of the Southerner," *Daily Alta*, May 16, 1854.

4. Soule, Gihon, and Nisbet, *Annals of San Francisco*, 535. Rufus K. Wyllis, *The French in Sonora (1850–1854): The Story of French Adventurers from California into Mexico* (Berkeley: University of California Press, 1911), 170–171.

5. Adolphe Boucard, *Travels of a Naturalist* (London: privately published, 1894), 42–44.

6. The indictment, jury summons, witness subpoenas, and other trial-related documents are found in US v. William Walker (1854), record group 21, box 3, National

Archives, San Bruno, CA. The record contains no transcripts, but the *Daily Alta* covered it extensively, including publishing long transcripts of testimony. Quotes here are from those articles, too numerous to list individually.

7. "William Walker an Editor," *Sacramento Daily Union*, June 5, 1854. John M. Wayland, *The Washingtons and Their Homes* (Staunton, VA: McClure, 1944), 241–242. David Morris Potter, ed., *Trail to California: The Overland Journal of Vincent Geiger and Wakeman Bryarly* (New Haven: Yale University Press, 1945), 1. Scroggs, *Filibusters and Financiers*, 84.

8. Details drawn from the preface to Wells, *Explorations and Adventures in Honduras*; and Walker, *War in Nicaragua*, 24–25.

9. Burns, *Patriarch and Folk*, 46–47.

10. Ibid., 191–192.

11. Wells, *Explorations and Adventures in Honduras*, 26.

12. Wells, *Walker's Expedition to Nicaragua*, 42. Doubleday, *Reminiscences*, 8.

13. Walker, *War in Nicaragua*, 27–28.

14. "Nicaragua Filibusterism: Why Gen. Wool Did Not Interfere with Walker's Expedition from California," *New York Times*, July 23, 1857.

15. William O. Scroggs refers to the supposed duel in his *Filibusters and Financiers*, but the details he includes seem to refer to the earlier duel.

16. Walker, *War in Nicaragua*, 32. Different accounts offer slightly different tallies for the size of Walker's initial force. His book says fifty-eight, so I've gone with that number.

17. Scroggs, *Filibusters and Financiers*, 80. *Daily Alta*, January 16, 1854.

18. Walker, *War in Nicaragua*, 30–32.

19. Wells, *Explorations and Adventures in Honduras*, 45–46.

20. Walker, *War in Nicaragua*, 32.

21. Ibid., 36.

22. John Hill Wheeler diary, June 5, 1855, in John H. Wheeler Papers. Marcoleta to Marcy, June 2, 1855, and Marcy to Marcoleta, June 5, 1855, in Sen. Ex. Doc. 68, 34th Cong., 1st Sess. 21–22 (May 15, 1856).

23. Burns, *Patriarch and Folk*, 153–159.

24. Walker, *War in Nicaragua*, 35–36.

25. Doubleday, *Reminiscences*, 104–105, 111.

26. Walker, *War in Nicaragua*, 38–41.

9. On to San Juan del Sur

1. Doubleday, *Reminiscences*, 113–120.

2. Walker, *War in Nicaragua*, 49.

3. Doubleday, *Reminiscences*, 120–121.

4. Ibid., 128.

5. Walker, *War in Nicaragua*, 53.

6. *Alta California*, reprinted in the *Sacramento Daily Union*, July 19, 1855.

7. Doubleday, *Reminiscences*, 131.

8. Doubleday described commandeering the ranch. Walker's account said they bedded down at an abandoned hut on a hilltop, with no mention of the ranch or family. Yet Walker referred to the men eating a "hearty breakfast," to which they would have had no access in the scene Walker described, since they were carrying no food.

9. Walker, *War in Nicaragua*, 63.

10. Ibid., 65.

11. Doubleday, *Reminiscences*, 152.

12. Walker, *War in Nicaragua*, 75

13. Ibid., 75, 80.

14. Bancroft, *History of Central America*, 3:331.

15. Walker, *War in Nicaragua*, 86. Doubleday, *Reminiscences*, 156.

16. Walker, *War in Nicaragua*, 87.

17. *Los Angeles Star*, November 12, 1853, and January 14, 1854. *Daily Alta*, January 19, 1855. *Sacramento Daily Union*, June 8, 1855.

18. *Daily Alta*, July 16, 1855. *Marysville Daily Herald*, September 11, 1855.

19. Walker, *War in Nicaragua*, 86–87.

20. Wells, *Walker's Expedition to Nicaragua*, 55.

21. Details of the battle are drawn mainly from Walker and Doubleday's accounts. While Walker reported three attack points by the Legitimists, Doubleday recounted only two. Walker's memoir was more detailed, written sooner after the campaign than Doubleday's, and supported by a separate account by William V. Wells written a year after the battle, so I've deferred to his version of events.

22. Walker, *War in Nicaragua*, 93. Wells, *Walker's Expedition to Nicaragua*, 56.

10. The War for Nicaragua

1. Walker's memoir says Castellón died an hour or so after the dispatch reached León, but Walker arrived in San Juan del Sur on September 5 and wrote that he immediately sent the reports to León. Castellón died on September 8. So it's unclear how much time elapsed between León learning of the victory and Castellón's death—or whether Castellón learned of the victory before his demise.

2. Reprinted in the *New York Herald*, included in scrapbooks, John H. Wheeler Papers.

3. Walker, *War in Nicaragua*, 106.

4. Since this version of events was written more than twenty-five years later, Doubleday likely embellished how detailed Walker was, intermixing his own later analysis of what Walker's plans were with the actual conversations. But the framework seems plausible, so I decided to include it. Doubleday, *Reminiscences*, 166–167.

5. Walker attributed Doubleday's departure to a rebuke Walker issued after Doubleday argued about a decision Walker had made. Both versions are somewhat self-serving, but they're not mutually exclusive. The flashpoint might have been the rebuke, but Doubleday's depiction of Walker and his ambitions lies within the Tennessean's character. Walker, *War in Nicaragua*, 107.

6. Ibid., 103.

7. Scott's descriptions are drawn from Joseph N. Scott deposition, Costa Rican Claims Convention, July 2, 1860, record group 76, National Archives, Washington, DC.

8. Walker, *War in Nicaragua*, 110.

9. Ibid., 110–111.

10. Brenizer to "brother-in-law and sister," October 27, 1855, in John Brenizer Letters, ac. no. 70-92, box M-84, Tennessee State Library and Archives, Nashville.

11. Reprinted in Sen. Ex. Doc. 68, 34th Cong., 1st Sess. 23 (May 15, 1856).

12. Walker, *War in Nicaragua*, 118.

13. Ibid., 105.

14. Ibid., 119–120.

15. Many accounts say French and Fry arrived with around sixty men, but in a deposition French said it was at least eighty-four. French deposition, Isaiah Thornton Williams Papers, box 1.

16. Scott deposition, Costa Rican Claims Convention, 25–28. Parker H. French deposition, MacDonald v. Garrison, Isaiah Thornton Williams Papers, box 42.

17. Affidavit of Captain George B. Slocum, October 23, 1855, in Sen. Ex. Doc. 68, 34th Cong., 1st Sess. 27 (May 15, 1856); Scott deposition, Costa Rican Claims Convention, 29.

18. Most accounts say the attackers were Legitimists; Scott testified that they were French, though Scott was not at the attack site—he gained his information from talking to survivors. It seems most likely it was a combined force. Scott deposition, Costa Rican Claims Convention, 34. Wells, *Walker's Expedition to Nicaragua*, 72–73. See also witness affidavits in Sen. Ex. Doc. 68, 34th Cong., 1st Sess. 25–32 (May 15, 1856).

19. Walker, *War in Nicaragua*, 123.

20. Declaration by Jose Maria Estrada, October 25, 1855, in Sen. Ex. Doc. 68, 34th Cong., 1st Sess. 143 (May 15, 1856).

21. Walker, *War in Nicaragua*, 124–125.

22. The agreement is included in Sen. Ex. Doc. 68, 34th Cong., 1st Sess. 33–34 (May 15, 1856).

11. President Walker

1. Parker H. French deposition, MacDonald v. Garrison, Isaiah Thornton Williams Papers, box 42.

2. A. P. Crittenden deposition, MacDonald v. Garrison, Isaiah Thornton Williams Papers, box 42.

3. Walker, *War in Nicaragua*, 127.

4. Ibid., 127–128. Joseph N. Scott deposition, Costa Rican Claims Convention, July 2, 1860, record group 76, 35–36, National Archives, Washington, DC. Joseph N. Scott statement, Granada, Nicaragua, October 23, 1855, in Bancroft Library, coll. no. BANC MSS Z-Z 100:174, University of California, Berkeley. Crittenden and French depositions, MacDonald v. Garrison.

5. Wells, *Walker's Expedition to Nicaragua*, 91. John Hill Wheeler diary, November 3, 1855, John H. Wheeler Papers, box 1.

6. Walker testified that he had sent the troop reduction orders. "Highly Important from Nicaragua," *New York Times*, November 29, 1855.

7. The letters were reprinted in "Highly Important from Nicaragua," *New York Times*. Interestingly, Walker's uncle, Caleb C. Norvell, was the *Times'* commercial editor at the time.

8. Walker, *War in Nicaragua*, 135–136.

9. John Hill Wheeler diary, November 8, 1855, in John H. Wheeler Papers. Wheeler, *Reminiscences and Memoirs*, 28. Walker, *War in Nicaragua*, 138–139.

10. Wheeler to Marcy, October 23 and October 30, 1855, reprinted in Sen. Ex. Doc. 68, 34th Cong., 1st Sess. 24–35 (May 15, 1856).

11. John Hill Wheeler diary, November 4, 1855, John H. Wheeler Papers, box 1.

12. Marcy to Wheeler, November 8, 1855, in Sen. Ex. Doc. 68, 34th Cong., 1st Sess. 35–36 (May 15, 1856).

13. John Hill Wheeler diary, November 10, 1855, John H. Wheeler Papers, box 1. Diplomatic statements are reprinted in Sen. Ex. Doc. 68, 34th Cong., 1st Sess. 40–45 (May 15, 1856).

14. Marcoleta to Marcy, December 8, 1855, in Sen. Ex. Doc. 68, 34th Cong., 1st Sess. 46–47 (May 15, 1856). Walker, *War in Nicaragua*, 165–166.

15. "Very Interesting from Nicaragua," *New York Daily Times*, December 13, 1855; and "District Attorney McKeon on 'Colonizing' to Nicaragua," *New York Daily Times*, December 24, 1855.

16. Vanderbilt to Marcy, March 17, 1856, in Sen. Ex. Doc. 68, 34th Cong., 1st Sess. 120–121 (May 15, 1856). W. O. Scroggs, "William Walker and the Steamship Company in Nicaragua," *American Historical Review* 10, no. 4 (July 1905): 798. Scott deposition, Costa Rican Claims Convention, 85.

17. Scroggs, "William Walker and the Steamship Company," 799.

18. "St. Nicholas Hotel," *New York Daily Times*, January 7, 1853.

19. Scott deposition, Costa Rican Claims Convention, 69, 223. "District Attorney McKeon on 'Colonizing,'" *New York Daily Times*.

20. Walker to Lindsley, November 26, 1855, in Windrow, *John Berrien Lindsley*, 192.

21. Letter from Cushing, December 8, 1855, in US Department of State, *Papers Relating to the Treaty in Washington*, vol. 1, *Geneva Arbitration* (Washington, DC: Government Printing Office, 1872), 626.

22. "District Attorney McKeon on 'Colonizing,'" *New York Daily Times*. Cushing to McKeon, December 27, 1855, in Sen. Ex. Doc. 68, 34th Cong., 1st Sess. 14 (May 15, 1856).

23. "Filibusters Arrested," *New York Daily Times*, December 25, 1855.

24. Scott deposition, Costa Rican Claims Convention, 115, 170. Scott estimated Walker received eleven thousand recruits, but that seems excessively high. He likely was referring to the total passengers from the ships, not just Walker's recruits.

25. Stiles, *First Tycoon*, 176–177, 220–221, 225. "The Vanderbilt Steam Yacht North Star," *New York Daily Times*, May 21, 1853.

26. For a succinct timeline of these events, see Michael Schreiber, "The Route Across Nicaragua 1849–1868 and Plans for a Nicaragua Canal 1886–1902," *Nicarao: The Philatelic Journal of the Nicaragua Study Group*, April 2016.

27. Vanderbilt to Marcy, March 26, 1856, in Sen. Ex. Doc. 68, 34th Cong., 1st Sess. 80–81 (May 15, 1856).

28. Crittenden deposition, MacDonald v. Garrison.

29. Walker, *War in Nicaragua*, 151–152.

30. Ibid., 155.

31. "News from Central America," *Weekly Herald* (New York City), March 15, 1856.

32. *El Nicaraguense*, February 23, 1856.

12. The Opposition Forms

1. Walker, *War in Nicaragua*, 159–160. "News from Central America," *Weekly Herald* (New York City), March 15, 1856.

2. Walker, *War in Nicaragua*, 162–163.

3. Ibid., 168.

4. Walker to Mora, January 17, 1856, reprinted in *Weekly Herald* (New York City), March 15, 1856.

5. The declaration signed by President Juan Mora is reprinted in Sen. Ex. Doc. 68, 34th Cong., 1st Sess. 134–135 (May 15, 1856). Walker, *War in Nicaragua*, 165.

6. Walker, *War in Nicaragua*, 183.

7. Ibid., 184–185. Scroggs, *Filibusters and Financiers*, 185.

8. The ruse of the *Cortes* was widely reported, including in the *Western Literary Messenger*, June 1856, 186. Joseph N. Scott deposition, Costa Rican Claims Convention, July 2, 1860, record group 76, 55–56, National Archives, Washington, DC. Walker, *War in Nicaragua*, 189.

9. Walker, *War in Nicaragua*, 189.

10. The speech was witnessed by a journalist, who likely added some of his own rhetorical flair to Walker's words. "Our Nicaragua Correspondence," *New York Herald*, May 9, 1856.

11. Mahoney affidavit, April 15, 1856, in Sen. Ex. Doc. 68, 34th Cong., 1st Sess. 128–130 (May 15, 1856).

12. Molina to Marcy, April 8, 1856, in Sen. Ex. Doc. 68, 34th Cong., 1st Sess. 131–132 (May 15, 1856).

13. Walker, *War in Nicaragua*, 196. Details of the battle at Rivas are drawn from 198–203.

14. The verdict was printed in "Court Martial of Colonel Louis Schlessinger," *New York Herald*, June 2, 1856, likely a reprint from *El Nicaraguense*.

15. "Tribute of Respect to the Late James Walker Jr.," *Nashville Republican Banner*, June 7, 1856.

16. D. Ann Herring and Alan C. Swedlund, eds., *Human Biologists in the Archives: Demography, Health, Nutrition and Genetics in Historical Populations* (Cambridge: Cambridge University Press, 2003), 24.

17. Jamison, *With Walker in Nicaragua*, 89–90.

18. Walker, *War in Nicaragua*, 214–219.

19. Franklin Pierce, "Special Message," May 15, 1856, American Presidency Project, www.presidency.ucsb.edu/ws/index.php?pid=67680. Ivor D. Spencer, *The Victor and the Spoils: A Life of William L. Marcy* (Providence, RI: Brown University Press, 1959), 371.

20. Pierce, "Special Message." Nichols, *Franklin Pierce*, 459–463.

21. Oaksmith to Walker, September 9, 1856, in Appleton Oaksmith Papers, Rubenstein Library, Duke University, accessed via Latin American Studies, www.latinamericanstudies.org/william-walker.htm. W. O. Scroggs, "Walker-Heiss

Papers: Some Diplomatic Correspondence of the Walker Regime in Nicaragua," *Tennessee Historical Magazine* 1, no. 4 (December 1915): 331–345.

22. Cong. Globe, 34th Cong., 1st Sess. 1070 (May 1, 1856).

23. *El Nicaraguense*, September 13, 1856. Jamison, *With Walker in Nicaragua*, 103–104.

24. *El Nicaraguense*, August 3, 1856, reprinted in *New York Herald*, September 1, 1856. Walker, *War in Nicaragua*, 235.

25. "The Filibustering Career of William Walker," *New York Times*, June 30, 1857.

26. Walker, *War in Nicaragua*, 252.

27. Marshall to father, August 3, 1856, in Marshall Family Papers, MSS A M367/9, Filson Historical Society, Louisville, KY.

28. *El Nicaraguense*, August 3, 1856, reprinted in *New York Herald*, September 1, 1856. Scroggs, *Filibusters and Financiers*, 206–207. Walker, *War in Nicaragua*, 252–253. "Our Granada Correspondent," *New York Herald*, October 19, 1856.

29. The quarrel between Walker and Goicouria played out in public that fall when Goicouria published in the *New York Herald* extended excerpts from their correspondence, details that then were republished by other newspapers and magazines around the country. William O. Scroggs goes into the relationship in detail in "William Walker's Designs on Cuba," *Mississippi Valley Historical Review* 1, no. 2 (September 1914): 198–211. Scroggs, *Filibusters and Financiers*, 219–220. See also Walker, *War in Nicaragua*, chap. 8.

30. Walker to Goicouria, August 12, 1856, reprinted in *New York Herald*, November 29, 1856.

13. Race, Slavery, and Walker's Empire

1. Walker, *War in Nicaragua*, 271.

2. Ibid., 261.

3. No specific evidence exists to confirm that Soulé prodded Walker to revive slavery, but the timing is significant, and Jamison, one of Walker's officers, points out in his memoir that there was no talk of slavery in Nicaragua until after Soulé's visit. Scroggs, *Filibusters and Financiers*, 209–210. J. Preston Moore, "Pierre Soule: Southern Expansionist and Promoter," *Journal of Southern History* 21, no. 2 (May 1955): 203–223.

4. Jamison, *With Walker in Nicaragua*, 99–101.

5. The muster rolls were analyzed by Alejandro Bolaños Geyer in 1972. His report and the muster rolls themselves are in the Callender I. Fayssoux Collection of William Walker Papers, folders 120 and 120A. Untallied lists of officers with dates on their commissions are in folder 121, though the records are undated and somewhat repetitive, so likely compiled at two different times by Walker's command.

6. David Deaderick, "The Experience of Samuel Absalom, Filibuster," *Atlantic Monthly*, December 1859 and January 1860. The two-part series was published under the "Absalom" pen name but later attributed to Deaderick. Walker's memoir of the war was published in April, but the *New York Times* excerpted the first chapter in January, between issues of the *Atlantic*. It seems likely Walker sent the excerpt to counter Deaderick's negative portrayal of his efforts in Nicaragua.

7. Walker, *War in Nicaragua*, 284. Jamison, *With Walker in Nicaragua*, 104.

8. "The Fight at San Jacinto," *El Nicaraguense*, September 20, 1856.

9. Unless otherwise noted, the following battle details were drawn from Walker, *War in Nicaragua*, chaps. 9 and 10; and Jamison, *With Walker in Nicaragua*, 287–299.

10. Henningsen's report on the siege to Walker was reprinted in the *Daily Alta*, February 1, 1857.

11. "The Accessory Transit Company," *New York Daily Times*, October 16, 1856.

12. "Who Is Sylvanus M. Spencer?" *New York Daily Times*, January 28, 1857. Joseph N. Scott deposition, Costa Rican Claims Convention, July 2, 1860, record group 76, 149–152, National Archives, Washington, DC.

13. Sylvanus Spencer deposition, Costa Rican Claims Convention.

14. Scott deposition, Costa Rican Claims Convention, 151. Samuel Smith Wood to his wife, December 28, 1856, Samuel Smith Wood Papers. Oliphant, *Patriots and Filibusters*, 170–190. Oliphant's work was originally published in *Blackwood's Edinburgh Magazine*, May 1857. Several first-person accounts of witnesses were printed in the January 26, 1857, issue of the *New York Times*. Unless otherwise noted, the following details are drawn from there and Walker, *War in Nicaragua*.

15. Diary entry, January 5, 1857, in A. C. Allen Papers.

16. Diary entry, January 6, 1857, in A. C. Allen Papers.

17. Doubleday, *Reminiscences*, 178–179.

18. Ibid., 176–184.

19. Walker, *War in Nicaragua*, 357–358.

20. Doubleday, *Reminiscences*, 187.

21. John M. Baldwin to Walker's father, James, in Nashville, April 28, 1857, reprinted in the Walkers' hometown newspaper: "Death of L. Norvell Walker," *Nashville Republican Banner*, May 10, 1857.

22. "The Filibusters in Nicaragua," *Dublin Review*, December 1857, 384.

23. Walker, *War in Nicaragua*, 375.

24. Deaderick, "Experience of Samuel Absalom."

25. David Anderson Deaderick Papers.

26. Stout, *Nicaragua: Past, Present, and Future*, 209–210.

27. Walker, *War in Nicaragua*, 403–405.

28. Ibid., 410.
29. Ibid., 420.

14. Walker Returns to New Orleans

1. *New Orleans Delta*, May 28, 1857.
2. Scroggs, *Filibusters and Financiers*, 304–305.
3. Ibid., 317. Carr, *World and William Walker*, 227.
4. "Welcome to General William Walker," *New York Times*, June 17, 1857, includes the observations of a reporter who traveled with Walker from Camden, New Jersey.
5. "Arrival of the Wabash," *New York Herald*, June 29, 1857. "Walker's Men," *New York Times*, June 30, 1857.
6. "General William Walker at Home," *Nashville Republican Banner*, July 9, 1857.
7. "Slavery in Central America—Manifesto of General William Walker," *New York Times*, October 18, 1857, reprinted September 2 letter from the *Mobile Mercury*.
8. Antonio Irisarri and Luis Molina to Secretary of State Lewis Cass, September 14, 1857, in House Ex. Doc. 24, 35th Cong., 1st Sess. 4. State Department circular, September 18, 1857, in House Exec. Doc. 24, 35th Cong., 1st Sess. 4–6.
9. Walker to Cass, September 29, 1857, reprinted in House Ex. Doc. 24, 35th Cong., 1st Sess. 6–7.
10. Irisarri to Cass, November 10, 1857, reprinted in House Ex. Doc. 24, 35th Cong., 1st Sess. 10–12.
11. Willard Carl Klunder, *Lewis Cass and the Politics of Moderation*, 292–293. Klein, *President James Buchanan*, 324–325.
12. See a series of letters and telegrams reprinted in House Ex. Doc. 24, 35th Cong., 1st Sess. 15–25. The detail on where the guns were hidden is from Doubleday, *Reminiscences*, 195.
13. An unsigned letter from someone traveling with Walker, published as "Movements of Walker," *Herald*, December 24, 1857.
14. Chatard's report is included in House Ex. Doc. 24, 35th Cong., 1st Sess. 58–60.
15. Walker to Paulding, November 30, 1857, in House Ex. Doc. 24, 35th Cong., 1st Sess. 60–61.
16. Ibid., 61–62.
17. Chatard to Walker, December 1, 1857, in House Ex. Doc. 24, 35th Cong., 1st Sess. 67.
18. Paulding to Walker, December 7, 1857, in House Ex. Doc. 24, 35th Cong., 1st Sess. 65.
19. Meade, *Life of Hiram Paulding*, 187–189. This biography by Paulding's daughter contains much of his communication and that of some of his underlings.

20. Paulding to his wife, Ann Marie, December 10, 1857, in Meade, *Life of Hiram Paulding*, 189–190.

21. "Message of the President of the United States," January 7, 1858, Sen. Ex. Doc. 13, 35th Cong., 1st Sess.

22. "Nicaragua: Speech of General Wm. Walker," *New York Times*, February 2, 1858.

23. "From New Orleans; From Our Correspondent," *Eagle and Enquirer* (Memphis), February 4, 1858.

24. Several histories of Walker say that a grand jury refused to indict, but in fact he and his codefendants were indicted by a grand jury, and a petit jury couldn't reach a verdict on guilt. The court file can be found in New Orleans Cases Relating to William B. Walker, record group 21, entry ELA121 NAID 251421, National Archives, Fort Worth, TX.

25. Address is in a letter from F. H. Hatch to Buchanan, September 22, 1859, in US Department of State, *Papers Relating to the Treaty in Washington*, vol. 1, *Geneva Arbitration* (Washington, DC: Government Printing Office, 1872), 676. Passenger totals are conservative estimates based on incomplete custom house records, passenger lists, and news accounts. Kemble, *Panama Route*, 77–78, 253–254. Carr, *World and William Walker*, 244–251.

26. The British diplomatic correspondence concerning the negotiations and ambitions are in Great Britain Foreign Office, *British and Foreign State Papers*, 47:698–749. "Annual Message of the President of the United States," December 6, 1858, House Ex. Doc. 2, 35th Cong., 2nd Sess., 62–64.

27. Doubleday, *Reminiscences*, 198–215. "The Filibuster Schooner Susan," *New Orleans Delta*, December 14, 1858.

28. Walker to Fayssoux, February 17, 1860, in Callendar I. Fayssoux Collection of William Walker Papers.

29. Walker, *War in Nicaragua*, preface.

30. Walker to Fayssoux, February 29, March 12, and March 26, 1860, in Callendar I. Fayssoux Collection of William Walker Papers.

31. "Sudden Descent on Honduras," *New York Herald*, September 1, 1860.

32. Walker to Fayssoux, April 28, 1860, in Callendar I. Fayssoux Collection of William Walker Papers.

15. Ruatan, Trujillo, and the End of a Dark Dream

1. "The Walker Expedition," *New York Herald*, September 1, 1860.

2. "Interesting from Ruatan," *New York Times*, June 7, 1860.

3. Salmon to Morrish, July 7, 1860, in Beeler, ed., *Milne Papers*, 2:59.

4. "Walker Expedition," *New York Herald*.

5. Details in this and the following paragraphs are drawn from an anonymous hand-written memoir of Walker's Honduras campaign, William Wyles Collection. This seems to be the basis for a first-person account attributed to Walter Stanley that is included in Jamison, *With Walker in Nicaragua*, 166–177.

6. Stanley (attributed), handwritten memoir; "Later from Walker's Expedition," *Times-Picayune*, August 25, 1860.

7. William Walker, "To the People of Honduras," reprinted in Beeler, ed., *Milne Papers*, 2:79–80. The robbery allegations are included in Walker Papers, University College London Library.

8. Details are from Stanley (attributed), handwritten memoir. Jamison, *With Walker in Nicaragua*, 166–177.

9. Unless otherwise noted, details of Salmon's actions in Honduras are from his report to Captain Samuel Morrish at Port Royal, Jamaica, the home of the British Caribbean fleet, published in Beeler, ed., *Milne Papers*, 2:88–99.

10. "Very Interesting from Honduras," *New York Herald*, October 4, 1860. Salmon's service details retrieved from Memorials & Monuments in Portsmouth, accessed May 17, 2018, www.memorialsinportsmouth.co.uk/vc/salmon.htm. The description is from *New Orleans Delta*, September 28, 1860.

11. The Code of Alfred, also called the Doom Book, was a ninth-century compilation of laws by Alfred the Great that set the stage for the foundation of English common law.

12. Reprinted in the *Sacramento Daily Union*, October 16, 1860.

13. *New Orleans Delta*, September 28, 1860.

14. Rudler's statement, dated September 11, 1860, is among trial documents in Walker Papers, University College London Library.

15. Walker's statement, dated September 10, 1860, is among trial documents in Walker Papers, University College London Library.

SELECTED BIBLIOGRAPHY

Books

Allen, Merritt Parmelee. *William Walker: Filibuster*. New York: Harper and Brothers, 1932.

Bancroft, Hubert Howe. *History of California*. Vol. 11. San Francisco: History Company, 1888.

———. *History of Central America*. Vol. 3. San Francisco: History Company, 1887.

———. *History of the North Mexican States and Texas*. Vol. 2, *1801–1889*. San Francisco: History Company, 1889.

Beeler, John, ed. *The Milne Papers: The Papers of Admiral of the Fleet Sir Alexander Milne*. Vol. 2, *The Royal Navy and the Outbreak of the American Civil War, 1860–1862*. Burlington, VT: Ashgate, 2015.

Bell, Major Horace. *Reminiscences of a Ranger, or, Early Times in Southern California*. Los Angeles: Yarnell, Caystile & Mathes, 1881.

Burns, E. Bradford. *Patriarch and Folk: The Emergence of Nicaragua, 1798–1858*. Cambridge: Harvard University Press, 1991.

Caldwell, Robert Granville. *The Lopez Expeditions to Cuba, 1848–1851*. Princeton: Princeton University Press, 1915.

Carr, Albert Z. *The World and William Walker: A Biography*. New York: Harper & Row, 1963.

Chaffin, Tom. *Fatal Glory: Narciso Lopez and the First Clandestine U.S. War Against Cuba*. Charlottesville: University Press of Virginia, 1992.

Croffut, W. A., ed. *Fifty Years in Camp and Field: Diary of Major-General Ethan Allen Hitchcock, U.S.A.* New York: G. P. Putnam's Sons, 1909.

Davis, Richard Harding. *Real Soldiers of Fortune*. Charles Scribner's Sons, 1911.

Doubleday, C. W. *Reminiscences of the "Filibuster" War in Nicaragua.* New York: G. P. Putnam's Sons, 1886.

Field, Stephen J. *Personal Reminiscences of Early Days in California with Other Sketches.* Privately published, 1893.

Folkman, David I., Jr. *The Nicaragua Route.* Salt Lake City: University of Utah Press, 1972.

Geyer, Alejandro Bolaños. *Favored of the Gods.* Masaya, Nicaragua: privately published, 2002.

——. *William Walker: The Gray-Eyed Man of Destiny.* Lake Saint Louis, MO: privately published, 1989.

Great Britain Foreign Office. *British and Foreign State Papers.* Vol. 46, *1853–56.* London: William Ridgway, 1865.

——. *British and Foreign State Papers.* Vol. 47, *1857–1858.* London: William Ridgway, 1866.

Greenberg, Amy S. *Manifest Manhood and the Antebellum American Empire.* Cambridge: Cambridge University Press, 2005.

Hardy, Richardson. *The History and Adventures of the Cuban Expedition.* Cincinnati: Lorenzo Stratton, 1850.

Horne, Gerald. *Negro Comrades of the Crown: African Americans and the British Empire Fight the U.S. Before Emancipation.* New York: New York University Press, 2012.

James, Marquis. *The Life of Andrew Jackson.* New York: Bobbs-Merrill, 1938.

Jamison, James Carson. *With Walker in Nicaragua.* Columbia, MO: E. W. Stephens, 1909.

Joyner, Hannah, *From Pity to Pride: Growing Up Deaf in the Old South.* Washington, DC: Gallaudet University Press, 2004.

Kemble, John Haskell. *The Panama Route, 1848–1869.* Columbia: University of South Carolina Press, 1990.

Klein, Philip Schriver, *President James Buchanan: A Biography.* University Park: Pennsylvania State University Press, 1962.

Klunder, Willard Carl. *Lewis Cass and the Politics of Moderation.* Kent, OH: Kent State University Press, 1996.

Lovett, Bobby L. *The African-American History of Nashville, Tennessee, 1780–1930.* Fayetteville: University of Arkansas Press, 1999.

Marryat, Frank. *Mountains and Molehills, or Recollections of a Burnt Journal.* London: Bradbury and Evans, 1854.

May, Robert E. *Manifest Destiny's Underworld: Filibustering in Antebellum America.* Chapel Hill: University of North Carolina Press, 2002.

———. *Slavery, Race, and Conquest in the Tropics: Lincoln, Douglas, and the Future of Latin America*. New York: Cambridge University Press, 2013.

———. *The Southern Dream of a Caribbean Empire, 1854–1861*. Baton Rouge: Louisiana State University Press, 1973.

Meade, Rebecca Paulding. *Life of Hiram Paulding, Rear-Admiral, U.S.N.* New York: Baker and Taylor, 1910.

Merry, Robert W. *A Country of Vast Designs: James K. Polk, the Mexican War, and the Conquest of the American Continent*. New York: Simon & Schuster, 2009.

Moore, John Bassett, ed. *The Works of James Buchanan*. Vol. 10, *1856–1860*. Philadelphia: J. B. Lippincott, 1910.

Nichols, Roy Franklin. *Franklin Pierce: Young Hickory of the Granite Hills*. Philadelphia: University of Pennsylvania Press, 1969.

Oliphant, Laurence. *Patriots and Filibusters, or, Incidents of Political and Exploratory Travel*. Edinburgh, Scotland: William Blackwood and Sons, 1860.

Owsley, Frank L., Jr., and Gene A. Smith. *Filibusters and Expansionists: Jeffersonian Manifest Destiny, 1800–1821*. Tuscaloosa: University of Alabama Press, 1997.

Pancoast, Charles Deward. *A Quaker Forty-Niner: The Adventures of Charles Edward Pancoast on the American Frontier*. Philadelphia: University of Pennsylvania Press, 1930.

Quaife, Milo Milton, ed. *The Diary of James K. Polk During His Presidency, 1845 to 1849*. Chicago: A. C. McClurg, 1910.

Quisenberry, Anderson C. *Lopez's Expeditions to Cuba, 1850–1851*. Louisville: John P. Morton, 1906.

Richardson, James D. *A Compilation of the Messages and Papers of the Presidents, 1789–1908*. Vol. 5. Washington: Bureau of National Literature and Art, 1908.

Roche, James Jeffrey. *The Story of the Filibusters*. London: T. Fisher Unwin, 1891.

Scroggs, William O. *Filibusters and Financiers: The Story of William Walker and His Associates*. New York: Macmillan, 1916.

Soule, Frank, John H. Gihon, and James Nisbet. *The Annals of San Francisco*. New York: D. Appleton, 1854.

Squire, E. G. *The States of Central America*. New York: Harper and Brothers, 1858.

Stewart, George R. *Committee of Vigilance: Revolution in San Francisco, 1851*. Boston: Houghton Mifflin, 1964.

Stiles, T. J. *The First Tycoon: The Epic Life of Cornelius Vanderbilt*. New York: Vintage, 2010.

Stirling, James. *Letters from the Slave States*. London: John W. Parker and Son, 1857.

Stout, Peter F. *Nicaragua: Past, Present, and Future*. Philadelphia: John E. Potter, 1859.

Thomas, Miss Jane H. *Old Days in Nashville, Tenn.: Reminiscences*. Nashville: Publishing House Methodist Episcopal Church, South, 1897.

Truman, Maj. Ben C. *The Field of Honor, Being a Complete and Comprehensive History of Duelling in All Countries.* New York: Fords, Howard & Hulbert, 1884.

Walker, William. *The War in Nicaragua.* Mobile, AL: S. H. Goetzel, 1860.

Wells, William V. *Explorations and Adventures in Honduras.* New York: Harper and Brothers, 1857.

———. *A History of the Central American War, and the Sonora and Kinney Expeditions.* New York: Stringer and Townsend, 1856.

———. *Walker's Expedition to Nicaragua.* New York: Stringer and Townsend, 1856.

Wheeler, John H. *Reminiscences and Memoirs.* Columbus, OH: Columbus Printing Works, 1884.

Williams, Mary Floyd. *History of the San Francisco Committee of Vigilance of 1851: A Study of Social Control on the California Frontier in the Days of the Gold Rush.* Berkeley: University of California Press, 1921.

Windrow, John Edwin. *John Berrien Lindsley: Educator, Physician, Social Philosopher.* Chapel Hill: University of North Carolina Press, 1938.

Woodward, Arthur, ed. *The Republic of Lower California, 1853–1854, in the Words of Its State Papers, Eyewitnesses, and Contemporary Reporters.* Los Angeles: Dawson's Book Shop, 1966.

Wyllys, Rufus Kay. *The French in Sonora (1850–1854): The Story of French Adventurers from California into Mexico.* Berkeley: University of California Press, 1932.

Papers and Dissertations

Allen, A. C., Papers. 1857, 1875, 1904. Dolph Briscoe Center for American History. University of Texas at Austin. Accessed via Latin American Studies, www.latinamericanstudies.org/nicaragua/Allen_Diary-1857.pdf.

Brenizer, John, Letters. Tennessee State Library and Archives, Nashville.

Deaderick, David Anderson, Papers. 1825–1873. Library of Congress Manuscript Division, Washington, DC.

Fayssoux, Callender I., Collection of William Walker Papers. 1856–1860. Latin American Library. Howard-Tilton Memorial Library, Tulane University, New Orleans.

Langerstedt, Albert. "The Political Career of William Walker." Master's dissertation, University of California, 1913.

Lawson, Royston. "William Walker: His Early Life." 1965. AC NO 1524. Manuscript Division, Tennessee State Library and Archives, Nashville.

Lindsley Family Papers. Tennessee State Library and Archives, Nashville.

Martin, Elizabeth S., Papers. Southern Historical Collection, no. 1023-z. Wilson Library, University of North Carolina at Chapel Hill.

Norvell, Caleb. Letters. Collection of John E. Norvell.

Norvell, William, Papers. Southern Historical Collection, no. 4760-z. Wilson Library, University of North Carolina at Chapel Hill.

Stanley, Walter (attributed). Handwritten memoir of Walker's Honduras campaign. William Wyles Collection, Wyles SC 221. University of California, Santa Barbara.

Walker, William, Correspondence. 1841–1855. THS I-A-5, box 3. Tennessee Historical Society. Tennessee State Library and Archives, Nashville.

Walker, William, Papers. GB 0103 MS ADD 188. University College London Library.

Wheeler, John H., Papers. Manuscript Division, Library of Congress, Washington, DC.

Williams, Isaiah Thornton, Papers. New York Public Library Manuscripts and Archives Division, New York.

Wood, Samuel Smith, Papers. MS 1083. Manuscripts and Archives, Yale University Library, New Haven, CT.

Journals and Magazines

American Historical Magazine

American Historical Review

Americas

Atlantic Monthly

California Historical Society Quarterly

Commercial Review

Harper's

Huntington Library Quarterly

Journal of Southern History

Journal of the Southwest

Middle Tennessee Journal of Genealogy and History

Mississippi Valley Historical Review

National

Pacific Historical Review

Tennessee Historical Magazine

United States Democratic Review

Newspapers

Daily Alta, San Francisco

Daily Crescent, New Orleans

Daily Delta, New Orleans

Daily National Whig

Daily Picayune and *Times-Picayune*, New Orleans

Daily Transcript, Sacramento
Eagle and Enquirer, Memphis
El Nicaraguense
Herald, San Francisco
Los Angeles Star
Nashville Republican Banner
Nashville Whig
New Orleans Delta
New Orleans True Delta
New-York Daily Tribune
New York Herald
New York Times
Sacramento Daily Union
Southern Press

INDEX

Italicized page references denote maps or illustrations